D1564393

The Erotics
of Materialism

The Erotics
of Materialism

Lucretius and Early Modern Poetics

Jessie Hock

PENN

UNIVERSITY OF PENNSYLVANIA PRESS

PHILADELPHIA

Published by
University of Pennsylvania Press
Philadelphia, Pennsylvania 19104-4112
www.upenn.edu/pennpress

Printed in the United States of America on acid-free paper
10 9 8 7 6 5 4 3 2 1

Library of Congress Cataloging-in-Publication Data

Names: Hock, Jessie, author.
Title: The erotics of materialism : Lucretius and early modern poetics /
    Jessie Hock.
Description: 1st edition. | Philadelphia : University of Pennsylvania Press,
    [2021] | Includes bibliographical references and index.
Identifiers: LCCN 2020019209 | ISBN 9780812252729 (hardcover)
Subjects: LCSH: Lucretius Carus, Titus—Influence. | Lucretius Carus,
    Titus—Criticism and interpretation. | Lucretius Carus, Titus. De rerum
    natura. Liber 4. | European poetry—Renaissance, 1450–1600—History
    and criticism. | European poetry—17th century—History and criticism. |
    Poetics—History—16th century. | Poetics—History—17th century. |
    Love poetry, Latin—History and criticism. | Erotic poetry,
    Latin—History and criticism.
Classification: LCC PN1181 .H63 2021 | DDC 187—dc23
LC record available at https://lccn.loc.gov/2020019209

CONTENTS

The Supple Snare

> Overwhelmingly in my submission to reading's supple snare, I feel love.
>
> —Lisa Robertson, *Nilling* (2012)

Seduction

In 1500, the Greek émigré Michael Marullus (b. ca. 1453/4) drowned while trying to cross the flooded Cecina River in western Italy. Marullus was a scholar and poet prominent in humanist circles in Florence and Naples, the compositor of an influential set of corrections to the text of a recently redis-covered masterpiece of classical Latin literature, Lucretius's epic poem of nature, *De rerum natura* (*On the Nature of Things*, hereafter *DRN*, composed around 50 BCE).[1] Afterward, it was widely repeated that Marullus had per-ished with a copy of *DRN* tucked into his pocket. The circumstances of his death were suggestive. The swollen river in which Marullus drowned evokes imagery from *DRN*'s most famous passage, the celebrated hymn to Venus that opens the poem, where Lucretius praises the generative power of Venu-sian desire: "denique per maria ac montis fluviosque rapaces / frondiferasque domos avium camposque virentis / omnibus incutiens blandum per pectora amorem / efficis ut cupide generatim saecla propagent" (All through the seas and mountains, torrents, leafy-roofed abodes / Of birds, and greening mead-ows, [striking seductive love / Into the] breast of every creature, and you urge all things you find / Lustily to get new generations of their kind).[2] Marullus was deeply influenced by the hymn to Venus, which he imitates in his own neo-Latin *Hymni naturales* (1497).³ Like the yearning, rushing birds and beasts of the Lucretian hymn, Marullus has been swept up by passion, though for Lucretian poetry about Venus rather than for the goddess herself. While it is plausible that Marullus did indeed die with *DRN* on his person (in the midst of preparing his commentary, he would have kept the text close), the enduring appeal of the story, repeated by Marullus's contemporaries and modern commentators alike, speaks to more than just the facts. *DRN* was a scandal in Renaissance Europe for espousing Epicurean philosophy's functional atheism and sharply reductive materialist vision of nature, in which atoms and void, and not the gods, govern nature and drive human destiny.⁴ In this context, the story of Marullus's death has a moralizing force, implying that his passionate attachment to the heretical *DRN* led to his untimely end.

Gossip also linked the death of Thomas Creech (b. 1659), one of the earliest English translators of *DRN*, to his fixation with Lucretian poetry. In the preface to his translation, Creech admits to an obsessive relationship with *DRN*, writing that he loved Lucretius "almost more than is right."⁵ In 1700, he committed suicide for unknown reasons, and rumors quickly began to fly that he had killed himself for love. As in the stories that circulated about Marullus, here life is said to follow art. The circumstances of Creech's suicide echo the influential but apocryphal tale popularized by Saint Jerome about Lucretius himself: that the Roman poet died for love, having committed suicide after being driven mad by a love potion administered by a jealous woman; *DRN* was composed in the intervals of his madness, and the poem was later revised by Cicero.⁶ Some of Creech's contemporaries, David Hopkins writes, "attributed his [suicide], admiringly or contemptuously, to an obsession with Lucretius so intense that it provoked him to emulate the Latin poet's own fabled end."⁷

The persistence of these stories—about Lucretius's love madness, Marullus's untimely death, and Creech's suicide—reveals a deep anxiety about *DRN*. They censure those who dared to tarry with *DRN*, tarring them with the brush of Lucretian heresy, and also function as cautionary tales, regulatory mechanisms for warning others of the text's dangers.⁸ Lucretius's poem was considered one of the most treacherous texts bequeathed to Christendom by pagan antiquity. While knowledge of Epicureanism had survived through the Middle Ages, this was primarily in the crude misrepresentations of its critics; most of Epicurus's vast writings were lost.⁹ *DRN*, the most complete surviving account of Epicurean philosophy, lay dormant, the handful of extant manuscripts forgotten in monastery libraries.¹⁰ When the poem began to circulate again in the latter half of the fifteenth century, after its rediscovery in 1417 by the famed bookhunter Poggio Bracciolini, it provoked fierce reactions.[11] Not only did Lucretius give thorough explanations of controversial Epicurean doctrines, but he did so in gorgeous verse explicitly designed to seduce readers to his Epicurean views. Yet although *DRN*'s hostile reception in the Renaissance and early modernity could be explained by the poem's content, both that reception's vehemence and the prominence of tropes of desire and sex in it (as in the stories that attached to *DRN*'s translators and editors) index reactions not just to Epicurean ideas but also to Lucretian poetry.[12] In *DRN*, Lucretius uses stories about sex and desire to foreground poetic issues: amorous seduction is a figure for the persuasive work of poetic language, and discussions of erotic fantasy and sex are venues for thinking through the relation between fantasy and matter, images and the things they represent. Lucretius mounts a robust defense of poetry's ability to explain mysterious natural phenomena and persuade readers of difficult philosophical doctrines. Early modern readers were attentive to Lucretius's emphasis on poetry and understood that Lucretian materialism entailed a theory of the imagination and, ultimately, a poetics, which they were quick to absorb and adapt to their own uses. Today, *DRN* is best known as a source of materialist and atheist thought in early modernity, but sixteenth- and seventeenth-century poets read *DRN* as a treatise on the poetic imagination, initiating an atomist genealogy at the heart of the lyric tradition.

Jerome's apocryphal biography of Lucretius established erotics as a flashpoint for *DRN*'s reception. The church father's accusations about the love potion had an enormous influence on Renaissance and early modern editors of Lucretius, almost all of whom approvingly repeat the story for the benefit of their readers.[13] While there is no evidence that Jerome's biography has anything to do with Lucretius's actual life—Jerome's statement that *DRN* was given its shape by Cicero is as unsubstantiated as his claims about the love philter and the poet's madness—it *does* respond to and emphasize erotic thematics within Lucretian poetry.[14] In different ways throughout *DRN*, Lucretius advertises that his poem is designed to seduce readers. In one infamous passage, Lucretius compares himself to a doctor and his verse to honey rimming a cup of salutary but bitter wormwood medicine.[15] Lucretian poetry is a "lure" that will entrap "gullible" readers to "drain the bitter cure" of Epicurean philosophy. "[D]uped but not cheated," the patients are healed, though against their will.[16] Elsewhere, Lucretius compares *DRN* to a different sort of honey. In the hymn to Venus, the poet begs the goddess to intervene with her lover, Mars, to put a stop to the Roman civil wars so that he can have peace and quiet to write his poem of nature. As the god of war lies helpless in her lap, his face upturned to catch her kisses, Venus instead lets drop words, "sweet-talk[ing] him with honeyed speech" in an effort to draw him from the fields of war and into more amorous battles.[17] The interlude foregrounds the sexual potential of linguistic seduction and the erotic power of Lucretian poetry. Having already invoked Venus as his muse, Lucretius aligns the Venus of poetic inspiration with the Venus of sexual seduction and associates his poetry with the pleasures of the flesh. Love and war are *DRN*'s overriding metaphors: atoms are said to crash together in the void like soldiers clashing in battle, and sexual desire is presented as the engine of all change and creation, as in the poem's opening lines, where it is passion for Venus that presses animals to procreate and flourish. The episode with Venus and Mars suggests that the imperative of Lucretian poetry is to shift the balance of power from war to love.

From its opening lines, and in its most gorgeous poetic set pieces, *DRN* declares itself to be a poem of seduction, one that does not shrink from using deception and the sensual manipulations of language to entice its readers. By calling attention to its seductive stratagems, *DRN* produced readers attuned to the power of poetic seduction and the potentially dangerous effects of Epicurean philosophy. Even as poetic language does crucial persuasive and explanatory work, drawing readers to Epicurean thought and illuminating the subvisible atomic basis of natural phenomena through analogy and metaphor, Lucretian protestations that Epicurean philosophy needs poetry to be understood and accepted—that the wormwood of philosophy needs poetic honey to seduce readers—potentially intensify doubt by drawing attention to the difficulty of Epicurean thought and the absence of visible proof for Epicurean teachings about nature.[18] Moreover, because Lucretius broadcasts the seductiveness of his verse, tropes of desire became prominent in *DRN*'s reception, as readers responded fiercely to what the text announces as its temptations and dangers. Such readerly anxieties manifest themselves in *DRN*'s early modern reception in narratives about Lucretius as a poet and early moderns as readers, in which *DRN*'s figures for poetic persuasion are repurposed as accounts of the poem's composition and reception. The reception of Lucretius from late antiquity onward is organized by erotic tropes that respond to the sensual presentation of poetry in *DRN*.

One of the most disturbing things about *DRN* is how forthright it is about its own powers of poetic mystification. Poetic seduction may be justifiable when the ideas a poem communicates are salutary, but poetic pleasure is equally capable of persuading readers to accept evil or harmful doctrines. This is precisely what Christian readers argued about *DRN*, maintaining that the poem's gorgeous poetry delivered a poison, not a cure, in the form of heretical Epicurean ideas about the mortality of the soul and the absence of divine providence. The love philter that Jerome says drove Lucretius mad evokes the *pharmakon* of the honey and wormwood passage; Jerome twists the image of honey rimming a wormwood draught, which Lucretius uses to justify writing philosophical poetry, to imply the opposite, that the poison of Epicurean philosophy would always triumph over the honey of Lucretian poetry. Like Lucretius himself, who complicates the presentation of his poetics by linking poetic suasion to sexual seduction, Jerome associates the poison of Epicurean philosophy with the perils of sex and desire. The love madness that Jerome says drove Lucretius to suicide is inspired by another section of *DRN*, the corruscating finale to Book 4, where Lucretius describes in agonizing detail the causes and trials of erotic obsession as well as its cures. The end of Book 4 is supposed to warn readers about the dangers of sexual desire and love—amorous obsession is a dire threat to *ataraxia*, the mental and emotional equilibrium that is central to Epicurean moral practice—so Jerome's accusation that Lucretius died for love implies that Lucretius failed to follow his own teachings. Lucretius's imputed amorous frenzy speaks to the supposed failure of Epicurean moral philosophy to produce mental equilibrium in its followers.

This book studies the legacy of Lucretian poetics in Renaissance and early modern vernacular poetry. I emphasize the seductions of Lucretian poetry because, as I demonstrate in what follows, Lucretian thinking on erotics and on poetry occupy the same theoretical terrain, so that accounts of the former—in *DRN*'s most gorgeous poetic set pieces, the hymn to Venus, the honey and wormwood passage, and the end of Book 4—illuminate Lucretian thinking on the latter.[19] The poetic implications of the honey and wormwood passage and the hymn to Venus are already well documented, and scholars have also shown how Lucretius's analogy between atoms and letters connects the verse of *DRN* to the atomist cosmos it describes.[20] This book, however, focuses on a less appreciated section of *DRN*, the end of Book 4. I show that Lucretius's description of erotic fantasy and obsession in Book 4 is central to *DRN*'s wide-ranging discussion of poetics and the imagination, as well as to the reception of those ideas in early modernity.

The end of Book 4 provocatively performs and problematizes the poetics of seduction that Lucretius lays out in Book 1. In the hymn to Venus and the

honey and wormwood passage, Lucretius establishes erotic seduction as a
figure for poetic persuasion. It is Book 4 that springs the trap set at the
beginning of the poem, what one of the most astute contemporary readers of
DRN, poet Lisa Robertson (in the line that stands as this Introduction's
epigraph), calls the "supple snare" of Lucretian poetry.[21] Robertson describes
how in Book 4, Lucretius "advise[s] the lover how to avoid unhappy love,
'for it is easier to avoid falling into love's nets, than it is to free oneself once
taken, breaking the snare Venus closes tightly around her prey.' But I fall
into the lace of the text, the vellum; caught there, I contemplate my masters.
From the point of view of the world, the site of my capture remains invisible.
Sometimes it is more like a pact than a capture."[22] While Lucretius warns his
readers against the snares of love, Robertson uses alliteration to signal the
similarity between contr*act*, p*act*, and *capt*ure, and embraces amorous entanglement as a mode of reading. To read *DRN*—to read anything, Robertson
asserts—is to be captured in an embrace so subtle, so artfully woven from the
words and stuff of the text, that many readers consent to their own seduction:
"sometimes it is more like a pact than a capture." *The Erotics of Materialism*
explores the "supple snare" of Lucretian poetry: the trap that was set with the
rediscovery of the full text of *DRN* in fifteenth-century Italy, the readers and
writers who were captured, the pacts that were made, and the poetry that
ensued. *DRN*'s theorization of the imagination, poetry, and reading had a
profound impact on early modern poetic theory and practice. Lucretius's
sixteenth- and seventeenth-century readers were absorbed by Book 4's gorgeous account of love's pleasures and pains, and they recognized that the
amorous snares Lucretius describes there illuminate the textual snares that
DRN itself deploys to seduce its readers. Book 4's account of erotic obsession
and insatiable sexual desire elucidates Lucretian ideas about poetry: the
book's reflections on the functioning of the imagination and the seductive
potential of amorous images reveal ideas about the poetic imagination and
poetic images.

Book 4 presented early moderns with sophisticated reflections on the
materiality of fantasy, which had major implications for thinking about
poetry. A thoroughgoing materialist, Lucretius maintains that images—both
mental and poetic—have actual material substance and a presence beyond
the mind or the page, which gives the figurative realm a powerful claim on
the real. Indeed, according to Lucretius it is specious to think of the imagination and "the real" as occupying different realms at all. As Amanda Jo Goldstein argues, Lucretius conceives of both matter and language in terms of

figure (*figura*), the "transient congeries of elements, composed of, and decomposing into, the myriad little bodies in motion that are nature's only permanent parts."[23] *DRN*, Goldstein concludes, is "the kind of poetry and science that results from declining to conceive of figuration exclusively as a strategy of consciousness or a linguistic effect."[24] Lucretian poetry confounds conventional divisions between words and things.

In Book 4, Lucretius delivers this theoretical payload in stunning erotic poetry that electrifies readers. In her research on annotations in early manuscripts and print copies of *DRN*, Ada Palmer finds that "the most frequently marked passage in the whole text is the section often labeled *De Rebus Veneriis*, a lengthy description of love and how to avoid its snares, which occupies the last 300 lines of Book IV. . . . So frequently is this the most heavily (or only) annotated section, that it is clear that some readers had more interest in *Rebus Veneriis* than in *Rerum Natura*."[25] It is remarkable that the end of Book 4 was so frequently and heavily annotated, given that very few Renaissance and early modern readers, according to Palmer's evidence, read much beyond the first hundred lines of *DRN* (roughly the hymn to Venus).[26] Yet although the past twenty years have seen an efflorescence of scholarship on Lucretius and Renaissance and early modern literature and culture, the role Book 4 played in Lucretius's reception in the period has gone largely unremarked.[27]

The following chapters attend to what sixteenth- and seventeenth-century poets learned from Lucretian poetics and its erotic lessons in the delicate entanglement of words and things, images and matter, poetry and nature. Critical accounts of *DRN* tend to develop arguments in relation to specific tropes or passages, the loci classici around which *DRN*'s transmission has always revolved. In part, this is because the poem was not read in its entirety for most of the Middle Ages, when it was known through the few passages that did circulate. It is also due to the structure of the poem itself, which toggles between long, technical explanations of natural phenomena and more accessible sections of gorgeous poetry—particularly the proems that open each book of *DRN*.[28] This book recovers the erotics of Lucretian materialism, and I pay particular attention to the end of Book 4 because Lucretius there uses a language of desire, whose natural home is lyric, to explore poetic issues. The lyric affinities of Book 4's theoretical language help to explain why Lucretian poetics, expounded in a didactic epic, take hold in sixteenth- and seventeenth-century lyric.[29] Another important factor, discussed in Chapters 1 and 3, is the way that poets came to associate the fragmentation of atomist matter with the fragmentations—of poet and poem—of Petrarchism, the poetic idiom that dominated Renaissance lyric. I argue that *DRN* served in the sixteenth and seventeenth centuries as a textbook of poetics, offering a stronger defense of poetry than its Neoplatonic or Horatian alternatives and leaving a complex and profound legacy in Renaissance and early modern lyric. In what follows, I analyze how Lucretian poetics came in early modernity to stand for the way that poetry—in an overused but perennially evocative play on words—*matters*, for a language whose intimacy with things gives the imagination and poetry purchase on the real, from the practice of philosophy to that of politics. In addition to Lucretius's *DRN*, I read Petrarch's *Rime sparse*; Pierre de Ronsard's sonnets and hymns; Remy Belleau's *Pierres précieuses*; John Donne's secular lyrics and sermons; Lucy Hutchinson's *Elegies, Order and Disorder*, and translation of *DRN*; and Margaret Cavendish's *Poems and Fancies*. I show how early modern French and English poets respond to Lucretius's erotic poetics: in their own poetry, in their characterization of the poetry of others, and in their accounts of how they read Lucretius. Because Lucretius expounds his poetics in a language of love and desire, the influence of Lucretius in early modernity is particularly potent in love poetry, and early moderns habitually express their negotiations with Lucretian poetry in erotically charged language derived from *DRN* itself.

Although *The Erotics of Materialism* is centrally concerned with lyric, it does not consist exclusively of readings of lyric. Indeed, the relation between lyric and nonlyric receptions of Lucretian poetics is at the heart of this book. As I have already been arguing, the sensual presentation of Lucretian poetry provoked the erotic tropes of Lucretian reception history, and the ways that readers perform their submission or resistance to Lucretian seduction index their responses to Lucretian poetics. This means that valuable evidence about the nature and circulation of Lucretian poetics in early modernity is to be found not just in, but also around, poetry: in the gossip, dedicatory epistles, autobiographies, accounts of reading and translating Lucretius, apocryphal biographies, and more that define and transmit Lucretian poetics. My readings of apocryphal Lucretian biographies (Introduction), Remy Belleau's and Marc-Antoine Muret's commentaries on Pierre de Ronsard's sonnets (Chapter 1), John Donne's sermons and letters (Chapter 3), and Lucy Hutchinson's and Margaret Cavendish's dedicatory epistles (Chapters 4 and 5, respectively) supplement and frame my readings of the verse of these poets. Their nonlyric engagements with Lucretian poetics are fascinating in their own right, but more importantly they bring into sharper focus how Lucretian ideas operate within their poetry. This interplay illuminates the way that Lucretian ideas circulated in early modernity—widely and variously, between genres and forms.

Fantasy

Lucretian atomism is uniquely invested in poetry. While Epicurus scorned poetry as frivolous, Lucretius believed Epicurean philosophy needed poetry's explanatory and persuasive power to be understood and embraced, and he justifies his choice to write in verse with a robust defense of natural philosophical poetry.[30] Epicurean philosophy, Lucretius suggests, presents significant challenges to its popularizers. Lucretius's task is to free humanity from the bonds of superstition by disclosing the mysteries of the universe, but he is hindered in this momentous undertaking by the tenacity of superstition, by the Latin language in which he writes (which has a more limited philosophical vocabulary than Epicurus's Greek), and because Epicureanism denies divine power and the immortality of the soul and encourages followers to withdraw from civic life and pursue pleasure, all of which went against conventional morality and civic practice in Lucretius's Rome.[31] These issues are matched in difficulty by the epistemological and representational issues raised by Epicurean physical theory. Because the most intimate workings of nature are invisible to the human eye—atoms are simply too small to see—atomist ideas are unprovable. The invisible atom undercuts materialism because it is difficult to establish the existence of an invisible thing, and simply asserting the existence of the invisible comes precariously close to propagating the sort of illusion Epicurus seeks to banish. What is the difference between imagining that the gods control nature and imagining that atoms do?

   That there is, in fact, very little difference is one of the major problems of Lucretian atomism. While Lucretius argues that myths about the gods should not be believed, he contends that his poem about invisible atoms should be; faith in poetry takes the place of faith in the gods. Lucretius presents poetry as particularly well equipped to tackle the epistemological aporia of the invisible atom. As a poet, he has at his disposal a whole toolbox of poetic tropes—metaphor, sound effects, wordplay, and so forth—with which to illustrate by analogy the way atoms move in space. Furthermore, in *DRN*, analogy goes beyond the illustrative comparison of like and unlike.[32]

Lucretius presents his poem as not just representative of but rather cognate with the physical universe. The alphabetical letters that make up the words of his poem are fundamentally akin to the atoms that make up things (one of the Latin words Lucretius uses for atoms, *elementa*, is also the word for alphabetical letters).[33] Lucretius formalizes the bond between the atomist cosmos and his poem with an analogy between atoms and letters, which he repeats throughout *DRN*.[34]

> quin etiam passim nostris in versibus ipsis
> multa elementa vides multis communia verbis,
> cum tamen inter se versus ac verba necessest
> confiteare et re et sonitu distare sonanti.
> tantum elementa queunt permutato ordine solo.
> at rerum quae sunt primordia, plura adhibere
> possunt unde queant variae res quaeque creari.
>
> (*DRN* 1.823–29)

[Furthermore, all through these very lines of mine, you see / Many letters that are shared by many words—and yet / You must confess that words and lines from this one alphabet / Have sundry sounds and meanings. Letters only have to change / Their order to accomplish all of this—and still the range / Of possibilities with atoms is greater. That is why / They can create the universe's rich variety.]

The way that a limited quantity of alphabetical letters variously combines into a range of different words illustrates how a limited set of atoms produces a staggering range of things. The analogy also suggests that a poem (Lucretius here refers to his own—"all through these very lines of mine") is able to figure the combinatory nature of the atomist cosmos in a particularly powerful way. The poetic text, with its dense linguistic play and bounded forms, figures the coming together of atoms into things and the bounds of the atomist cosmos (Lucretius frequently mentions the "walls of the world").[35] When he asks the reader later in Book 1 to reflect upon the fact that the words for "maple" and "flame" (*lignum* and *ignis*) contain the same letters (*DRN* 1.912), he calls attention to the way his sophisticated wordplay and soundplay make *DRN* a corollary of the nature it describes, even at the level of its smallest elements.[36]

Lucretius's understanding of poetry's relation to the natural world makes him an important participant in what Plato famously called the "ancient

quarrel between [poetry] and philosophy."[37] Plato was firmly in the philosophy camp: in the *Republic*, he ejects the poets from his ideal city for fear that
their tales of the misdeeds of gods and heroes will corrupt the youth, who are
being groomed to govern and lead. For Plato, poetry is problematic both
because of what it represents and for how representation is structured. Book
10 of the *Republic* expounds the Platonic theory of forms: things in the world
are shadows of ideal forms, and visual and linguistic representations such as
poems and paintings are shadows of things in the world. Because poets imitate things in the world rather than the ideal forms, poetry, like all representational arts, is an imitation of an imitation—ontologically, epistemologically,
and morally removed from the realm of the ideal and the good. For Plato,
poetry's corrupt content and its corrupt nature mean that it has to be tightly
controlled if it is to serve any positive purpose.

Lucretius's understanding of poetry's relation to truth is opposed to
Plato's. In powerful natural philosophical verse, Lucretius makes poetry philosophy's partner, or even a form of philosophy itself, freeing poetry from
being what it has too often been—philosophy's handmaiden.[38] While Lucretius was neither the first nor the last of the ancients to claim poetry as the
honey that sweetens philosophy—Horace was famous in early modernity
for arguing that poets seek to instruct, delight, or (better yet) do both at
once—neither Horace nor any of the other ancients thought poetry shared
in the world's primary structures.[39] Thus, although *DRN*'s famous image of
poetry as the honey rimming philosophy's bitter cup implies that poetry is a
prop for philosophy, a superficial inducement to swallow philosophical medicine, in Lucretius's presentation of Epicurean philosophy, poetry is intrinsic
rather than extrinsic to the atomist system. Poetry is an effective inducement
to natural philosophical thought not simply for its seductive beauty, but
because its beauty is as much part of the nature philosophy seeks to describe
as are trees, clouds, and birds.

The analogy between atoms and letters is one Lucretian strategy for
addressing the epistemological and representational crises produced by the
invisible atom. By asserting the fundamental likeness of letters and atoms,
words and things, Lucretius subverts what Plato presents as a fundamental
hierarchy of things over representations (and of the transcendent, inaccessible
forms over both). The fundamental sameness of rhetorical and corporeal figurality means that the complex interweavings of letters in words capably
figure forth the invisible configurations of atoms that structure all things.
Lucretius thus can ask his readers to accept the teachings of his poem even

though it is impossible to obtain ocular proof for his claims about the atomist structure of nature.

Like the analogy between atoms and letters, Book 4 of *DRN* is centrally concerned with the relation between things and representations. The book is dedicated to sense perception, which Lucretius explains is caused by the films of atoms that continuously stream off of objects.

> Dico igitur rerum effigias tenuisque figuras
> mittier ab rebus summo de corpore rerum,
> quae quasi membranae vel cortex nominitandast,
> quod speciem ac formam similem gerit eius imago
> cuiuscumque cluet de corpore fusa vagari.
>
> (*DRN* 4.46–52)

> [Now there's another crucial fact I must explain—so mark / My words—that there are images of things—a skin, or *bark* / As we can call it, shed from objects, since it bears the same / Form and likeness of whatever thing from which it came.]

These are *simulacra*, which are responsible for both reliable sense perception and errant fantasy. While *simulacra* generally transmit accurate impressions of objects to the senses, they can also be profoundly fickle. Labile and incredibly fine, *simulacra* sometimes combine midair, forming amalgam images that reflect no real object; sometimes they are generated from thin air rather than from things. Such *simulacra* infiltrate and trick the mind, sometimes producing terrifying visions of ghosts and monsters, at other times more pleasurable apparitions.[40] Lucretius lingers over the example of wet dreams, describing adolescent boys who are visited at night by visions of beauty generated from "some random body or other" (e corpore quoque; *DRN* 4.1032). Aroused by images, the boys spill their seed into the sheets.

Lucretius maps the *simulacrum*'s play of presence and absence, embodiment and disembodiment, onto the sweetness and bitterness, pleasure and pain, of sexual desire. The end of Book 4 is brimming with sex, and its disquisitions on wet dreams, the proper positions for marital coitus, and the expediency of sleeping with prostitutes contain sophisticated theories of fantasy, seduction, and desire that reveal novel ways to think about the image-making of poetry. Lucretius explains that all desire is roused by *simulacra*. However, precisely because they long for images, lovers find no relief in sex. The separation between a *simulacrum* and the body that generates it produces a category mistake that frustrates lust and makes sex a brutal affair.[41] In a startlingly vivid passage, Lucretius describes two lovers grappling with each other,

> quod petiere, premunt arte faciuntque dolorem
> corporis et dentis inlidunt saepe labellis
> osculaque adfligunt, quia non est pura voluptas
> et stimuli subsunt qui instigant laedere id ipsum
> quodcumque est, rabies unde illaec germina surgunt.
> . . . .
> sic in amore Venus simulacris ludit amantis
> nec satiare queunt spectando corpora coram
> nec manibus quicquam teneris abradere membris
> possunt errantes incerti corpore toto.
>
> (*DRN* 4.1079–83, 1101–4)

[so closely pressing / What they long for, that they hurt the flesh by their possessing, / Often sinking teeth in lips, and crushing as they kiss, / Since what lovers feel is not some pure and simple bliss— / Rather, there are stings that lurk beneath it, pains that shoot, / Goading them to hurt the thing that's made madness take root, / Whatever it may be. . . . So [in love] Venus teases [lovers] with images—[they] can't satisfy / The flesh however they devour each other with the eye, / Nor with hungry hands roving the body can they reap / Anything from the supple limbs that they can take and keep; translation modified]

Although they "devour each other with the eye," these lovers never satisfy the flesh, no matter how much they bite and crush each other's bodies in wild attempts to extract pleasure. If their desires were more reasonable—either for procreation or for brief release—they would be satisfied with mere moments of pleasure, but because they long to possess each other fully they are consumed by a ruinous and insatiable obsession. Lucretius places this perverse desire, too, under the name "Venus"—this is how Venus teases lovers with images (sic in amore Venus simulacris ludit amantis; *DRN* 4.1101).

The end of Book 4 is a poetic tour de force. Its powerful depiction of sexuality made it one of the most controversial of *DRN*'s poetic set pieces in early modernity, when it was a source of fierce disagreement and the object of intense censure.[42] Some readers and editors praised Lucretius for his practical advice on everything from sexual positions to choosing partners, while others were shocked by the passage's violence and denounced its explicit sexual content.[43] Yet while many resisted the scandals of Book 4, others succumbed. Although John Dryden acknowledged the objections of other seventeenth-century Lucretius translators, all of whom refused to render the most graphic lines into English, he gave no better explanation for his own decision to translate them than that they gave him pleasure: "Without the least Formality of an excuse . . . I own it pleas'd me."[44] Modern poets, too, have been taken with Book 4: W. B. Yeats called it "the finest description of sexual intercourse ever written."[45]

The pleasures of Book 4 are strategic. Lucretius must hold his readers' attention because he is there explicating one of Epicurean philosophy's thorniest conceptual issues, what Michel Foucault described as the "incorporeal materiality" of *simulacra*.[46] While *simulacra* are unreliable and delicate (Lucretius writes that they are like "spider webs . . . or gold to airy thinness beat" [*DRN* 4.726–27]), they are also the only bridge between bodies and the sole cause of sense perception. And although *simulacra* are made of atoms and thus firmly material, precisely because image atoms are the finest of all the atoms, *simulacra* verge away from corporeality. Poised between the corporeal and the incorporeal, *simulacra* are here-not-here, there-not-there, mutable and swift (though the *simul-* of the *simulacrum* is etymologically linked to *similis*, meaning "similar," it also evokes *simul*, "simultaneous"). Jonathan Goldberg points out that Foucault's phrase applies to atoms as well as to *simulacra*: "With 'incorporeal materiality,' [Foucault] recalls a controversy that haunts Epicureanism from the start: if atoms are themselves imperceptible, colorless, tasteless—if they lack almost every feature by which bodies can be known, virtually every characteristic that characterizes matter—in what sense are atoms material? Although we see thanks to these atomic effluxes, we do not see them."[47] What I earlier called the "category mistake" of sexual desire—the way it feeds on images but founders on bodies—also relates to the atom, to its paradoxical status as matter that cannot be comprehended by the senses. The lovers who fall in love with images but cannot sate themselves on bodies are figures for the impossibility of gaining sensory satisfaction from the atom.[48] Like the body of the beloved, mediated by the unsatisfyingly attenuated materiality of its *simulacra*, the atom is material, it is *there*, but just out of reach. The atom cannot be captured by the senses, only by images, be they *simulacra* or poetic images.

The Lucretian explanation of *simulacra* contains a commentary on poetic images and poetic pleasures. Like *simulacra*, *DRN*'s poetic images manifest the motions of atoms. By analogy, the pleasures produced by poetic images parallel the agonies and ecstasies produced by erotic *simulacra*, and *DRN*'s readers, captivated by Lucretian poetry, parallel Book 4's lovers in thrall to their fantasies. As in the honey and wormwood passage, in Book 4 Lucretius shows his hand: *DRN* is a poem designed to arouse readers, to seduce them, to entrap them. Though Lucretius advises against getting carried away in matters of love and sex, *DRN* actively endeavors to transport readers on the swells of its poetry. (To a certain extent, Lucretius proves his early modern critics right: a poem that purports to teach emotional equilibrium [*ataraxia*] relies on arousing the passions to make its points.) Just as images stoke desire for bodies, Lucretian poetry stokes desire for the atom itself, or rather, for materialist teachings about the atom.[49] Fantasy's power to provoke very real physical response thus acts as a figure for the way that poetic images of atoms can materialize convictions about the structure of nature. Wet dreams are a good example: when boys dream of beautiful bodies, their effusions of semen materialize the nebulous effluvia of the *simulacra* that invade their minds.[50] Poetic seduction is designed to impel readers to accept atomist teachings about the nature of matter. The sensual episodes of Book 4 allegorize this process while also trying to enact it.

In early modernity, the seductions of Lucretian poetry were central to the reception of Lucretian poetics.[51] In *DRN*, seduction takes strategic precedence over other aspects of Lucretian poetics—claims about the shared figurality of atoms and letters, about poetry's capacity to illuminate the invisible structures of matter—because seduction is the means by which these other claims are made. This is why *DRN* opens with the hymn to Venus, an enormously seductive passage that also thematizes seduction, rather than with, say, an extended treatment of the analogy between atoms and letters. Seduction continues to play a crucial role in the early modern reception of Lucretian poetics in part because it is the least dogmatic, and thus most portable, element of Lucretian thought. Even when illumination and conviction about materialist doctrine fails, Lucretian erotics remains a useful tool. At a time when the hegemony of Christianity rendered Epicurean ideas about the soul's mortality and the indifference of the gods particularly intolerable, it was well-nigh impossible that readers of *DRN* would accept all (or even most of) Epicurean doctrine.[52]

In spite of this—that is, even when illumination and conviction about materialist doctrine failed—Lucretian idioms of seduction remained viable and valuable for exploring theoretical issues around the materiality of fantasy and the power of poetic persuasion. Of the poets discussed in this book, only one (Margaret Cavendish) could be said to have even briefly embraced atomist materialism as a physical doctrine, yet every poet under discussion responded to and adapted Lucretian erotics in their negotiations with Lucretian poetics.

Words and Things

Foucault's conception of atomist matter as "incorporeal materiality" is a far cry from the solid state physics that is more frequently associated with Lucretian atomism.[53] Early modern mechanical philosophy, which explained all natural phenomena in terms of matter and motion, took inspiration from classical atomism, but the elegant equation of atoms, void, and swerve was not the only vision of matter Lucretius bequeathed to the period.[54] Escaping the overriding association of Lucretius with mechanical philosophy makes it much easier to grasp the ways that Lucretian atomism spoke to Renaissance and early modern poetics. If atomist matter is an incorporeal materiality, best embodied in *simulacra*, then a thinking about images and fantasy—the stuff of poetry—is at the heart of atomist materialism. *Simulacra* speak to the imaginative potential of the material world, to the dangerous powers of fantasy embedded in the stolid powers of sense. They attest to the fact that there is plenty of room in a materialist universe for the fantastic, the imaginative, the seductive—though in a much different way than the detractors of the Epicureans would have it (this fantasy is balanced between the material and immaterial, the corporeal and incorporeal, not mired in carnal gluttony). With the *simulacrum*, Lucretius illustrates the same fundamental principle he expounds in the analogy of atoms and letters: the interconnection of words and things, here images and bodies. But whereas in the analogy Lucretius emphasizes the underlying sameness of letters and atoms, here he stresses the ways in which images diverge from reality, even as they remain—however tenuously—material. Both the *simulacrum*'s effectiveness and its danger derive from its delicate position on the fault line between truth and trick, matter and illusion. As such, the *simulacrum* also speaks to the delicate balance in Lucretian materialism between matter and language, things and fantasies, objects in the world and those in the mind. The function of *simulacra* is thus dual: on the one hand, they establish the materiality of fantasy and of the imagination. On the other hand, they reveal the attenuation of matter in fantasy and demonstrate that fantasy can be dangerous and deceptive even though it is material. Though these lessons may appear divergent, they both work (though in different ways) to establish that fantasy and matter exist along the same spectrum.

The Lucretian *simulacrum* thus undermines the mode of representational thinking that has dominated Western thought since Plato, which characterizes all representation (images, words, artworks, etc.) as a falling off from truth. As I will show in Chapters 1, 2, and 3 (on Pierre de Ronsard, Remy Belleau, and John Donne, respectively), Lucretian *simulacra* appear frequently in sixteenth- and seventeenth-century lyric poetry to mark sites of contestation of the Neoplatonic poetics that dominated the age. Against Renaissance Neoplatonism, which downgraded the status of poetry and questioned its place in the social world (as when Plato kicks the poets out of his republic), Lucretius offered a way of thinking that refuted transcendence and put poetry on an equal footing with things. This fascinated poets. While Lucretian materialism was not the only materialism known to early modernity, it was certainly the strongest, and the only one to posit an equality between things and that which represented them (words, images, etc.). Augustinian semiotics, Petrarchan idolatry, and even some varieties of Platonism offered theories of language, poetry, and love that stressed the body and mortal experience. But even the most materialist wings of Platonic and Christian thought are grounded in notions of truth and meaning that place the ultimate referent of language in a transcendent realm beyond the reach of mortals (be it that of the Platonic forms or the Christian God). Margaret Ferguson explains that "Western philosophy's traditional notion of language as *mimesis*. . . . the theory of language as an imitation of something essentially *unlike* language" rests on ontological presuppositions about humanity's exile from divine truth and Presence.[55] A thinker like Augustine, whose theorizations of language laid the groundwork for all of Western semiotics, found human language "fundamentally inadequate" to expressing transcendent truths; for Augustine, "all language is a metaphorical detour in the road to God because no sequence of words, even 'proper' words, can adequately represent an atemporal and holistic significance."[56] Platonizing, Christian Renaissance love poetry presented human desire for mortal love as a stepping stone toward desire for divine love. In the *Divina commedia*, the paradigmatic example, Beatrice guides Dante in transmuting his love for her into love of God and things divine. Just as earthly desires should lead toward desire for and union with the divine, so ought earthly mediums (human language) lead toward the divine Word. In this trajectory, poetry exists as part of the striving toward an ideal, but is excluded from the site of transcendence: there is no place for human writing at the site of the Platonic idea or of the divine Word (just as, in negative theology, there is no language adequate to God).[57]

When the full text of *DRN* appeared on the scene in fifteenth-century Europe, it offered a wildly different way of understanding the relationship between words and things, and thus for conceiving of the nature of poetry. Lucretian materialism, unlike weaker Augustinian, Neoplatonic, Petrarchan, or other materialisms, denied transcendence of any kind and asserted the equality of words, images, and things. Epicureans maintained that the material world is all there is. Although the Epicurean system admits the existence of the gods, it presents them as fundamentally uninterested in human affairs: they do not meddle in human lives, and humans do not join them in an afterlife. Though mortal existence is marked by dissatisfaction and insatiability, Lucretius refuses to offer a transcendent promise of relief, either in an afterlife or in an immaterial and ideal realm of forms. The account of insatiable sexual desire in Book 4 of *DRN* represents in an amorous key a general truth about all of human life. Lucretius's advice for lovers—to moderate their desires, be practical, be reasonable—is the sort of advice that Epicurean philosophy offers about human life in general. All that can be done is to manage expectations about this life, because there is nothing after it.

The same ideas that made Lucretius a powerful new entrant into early modern semiotics and poetics also made him a strong contrarian voice in developing early modern scientific debates about the relative value of words and things. Attempts to police the imagination and poetic language were central to the construction of early modern science.[58] In his *History of the Royal Society*, published in 1667, seven years after that society's founding, Thomas Sprat praises the new scientists for eliminating linguistic flourishes from their speech and writing. Sprat's account develops ideas that had been in circulation since 1605, when Francis Bacon published *The Advancement of Learning* and advocated a new method for "restoring or cultivating a just and legitimate familiarity between the mind and things" by purifying degraded habits of thought and language.[59] Sprat mourns the language spoken directly after the creation in Eden, when Adam was able with what Sprat calls "native easiness" to give names to his fellow creatures, effortlessly assigning one word to each one thing. He hopes that his fellow scientists will be able to approximate this originary language by adopting a plain style stripped of all ornamentation. The fewer words there are, the better the odds that the two halves of the equation between words and things will add up.[60]

Although Sprat's vision for a scientific plain style relies on the (tragically lost) equivalence between words and things, the critiques of rhetoric and poetry mounted by early modern scientists made it clear that the primary object of their inquiries would always be things—not words, nor even the equivalence between words and things—and that they saw language as the natural enemy of natural inquiry. In *The Advancement of Learning*, Bacon diagnoses "the first distemper of learning" as "when men studie words, and not matter." He muses "that *Pigmalions* frenzie is a good embleme or portraiture of this vanitie: for wordes are but the Images of matter, and except they haue life of reason and inuention: to fall in loue with them, is all one, as to fall in loue with a Picture."[61] Bacon takes a Platonic (and Augustinian) line: words are not the equals of things, but rather their degenerate copies.[62] To take them for anything else is madness, a narcissistic logophilia he scornfully compares to the sculptor Pygmalion's attraction to a statue of his own making.[63] Bacon implies that representation—be it representative language or a representational art such as sculpture—regularly fails at its core mission of representing things, and instead merely represents itself. Like Pygmalion, who spurns real women but falls in love with his own creation, a statue that represents himself and his own artistry more than its ostensible subject, language all too frequently ends up representing itself rather than its objects.[64] That Bacon connects representational narcissism to sexual depravity casts light on the early modern prominence of Saint Jerome's story about Lucretius's suicide. In view of Bacon's reference to Pygmalion as an example of degenerate self-referentiality in mediums that ought to be representational, the early modern popularity of the apocryphal story of Lucretius's madness begins to look like a punishment for the Roman poet's decision to versify Epicurean philosophy, that is, for both his decision to pair natural philosophy and poetry and his robust defense of seductive, luxuriant modes of poetic expression.

In separating Lucretius the natural philosopher from Lucretius the poet, early modern scientists were following a well-trodden path. As hard as Lucretius works in *DRN* to break down the boundaries between poetry and philosophy, those very boundaries have been repeatedly reinscribed in the reception of his poetry. Fifteenth- and sixteenth-century readers of *DRN* had done the exact opposite of the British natural philosophers, denying Lucretian philosophy in order to embrace the poetry, arguing that it was possible to separate the wonders of Lucretian verse from the heretical philosophies they enclosed.[65] In his 1563 dedicatory letter to Charles IX, Denis Lambin, the greatest sixteenth-century editor of *DRN*, lays the blame for *DRN*'s heresies at the feet of Epicurus: "Albeit Lucretius attacked the immortality of the soul, denied divine providence, abolished all religions, and placed the highest good in pleasure (*voluptas*). But this fault belongs to Epicurus, whom Lucretius followed, not to Lucretius."[66] Lucretius is worthwhile for his poetry, and ought neither be blamed nor be heeded for the ridiculous notions he inherits from Epicurus. These, Lambin argues, are nothing more than the ravings of a madman: "[T]hese insane and frenzied ideas of Epicurus, those absurdities about a fortuitous conjunction of atoms, about innumerable worlds, and so on, neither is it difficult for us to refute them, nor indeed is it necessary: certainly when they are most easily disproved by the voice of truth itself or by everyone remaining silent about them."[67] This view was widespread: Ada Palmer argues that partitioning Lucretian poetry off from Epicurean philosophy likely kept *DRN* out of the censors' lists. In 1557, in the midst of preparing revisions for the Inquisition's *Index*, Michele Ghislieri—the future Pope Pius V—"wrote to the Inquisitor General of his concern that, in aiming to stifle truly dangerous works, they might draft language that would also target such authors as Lucian and Lucretius, whose works, like *Orlando Furioso* and the *Decameron*, were not dangerous because everyone knew to read them as fables, not seriously."[68] Ghislieri conceives of poems as inconsequential—fables, toys, the stuff of children and madmen—incapable of corrupting a strong mind.[69] Moreover, it was not only poets and inquisitors who approached Lucretian philosophy this way: even natural philosophical poets were prone to read the content of Lucretius's poem as a fable. Maurice Scève, the sixteenth-century French poet whose long cosmographical poem, *Microcosme* (1562), was deeply indebted to Lucretius, rejected atomism wholesale, indicating that absorbing Lucretian lessons about didactic style need not lead to an acceptance of Epicurean philosophy.[70]

Modern criticism has followed suit. From the Romantics onward, the strong tendency to separate *DRN*'s proems from the poem's expository passages, the purple passages from the long technical explanations, has manifested itself in several ways. In the nineteenth century, scholars saw Lucretius as a poet divided against himself, one who betrays his own doubts about the doctrines he espouses. In the words of M. Patin, this is "L'Antilucrèce chez Lucrèce."[71] Patin finds it particularly telling that Lucretius uses religious imagery (particularly in the hymn to Venus) even as he argues against myth and religious superstition.[72] Like Blake, who in "The Marriage of Heaven and Hell" accused Milton of being "of the Devils party without knowing it," Patin argues that the gloriousness of Lucretius's poetry in passages like these betrays the poet's passion for the gods, for myth, for vain pleasures, even as he argues against them.[73] Lucretius (perhaps unconsciously) rebelled against Epicurean thought even as he struggled to elucidate and defend it.[74] The notion that Lucretius endured a psychic dislocation between the parts of himself that supported and those that denied Epicureanism feeds into Jerome's tale about the love philter and Lucretius's madness. This story reinforced the sense that Epicurean philosophy was so distant from standard orthodoxy that it could simply be ignored as madness.

Methodology and Chapters

This book studies how five poets—Pierre de Ronsard (1524–1585), Remy Belleau (1528–1577), John Donne (1572–1631), Lucy Hutchinson (1620–1681), and Margaret Cavendish (1623–1673)—adapted Lucretian poetics to their own sixteenth- and seventeenth-century purposes. These poets offer declensions on a shared set of Lucretian ideas and images related to poetry and the imagination. *DRN*'s accounts of seduction and erotic fanatsy work through a set of issues with enormous poetic resonance: the relation between images and things, words and matter, poetry and nature, fantasy and reality. The poetry of Ronsard, Belleau, Donne, Hutchinson, and Cavendish responds to Lucretian erotics and to the poetics conveyed in that erotics. These poets evince a consistent interest both in what Lucretius posits as the materiality of the phantasmatic and in how he posits it: in a language of love, desire, and sex whose natural home is lyric.

Despite this consistent core of interest, the very different cultural contexts in which these poets wrote leads to significant diversity in their adaptations of Lucretius. Beginning in France around the middle of the sixteenth century and coming to a close after the restoration of the monarchy in England, in the final decades of the seventeenth, this book covers substantial ground. The poets under discussion come from different countries, write in different languages, are of different genders, and have different intellectual backgrounds, politics, and poetic goals. They all treat *DRN* as a conceptual workbook for poetic problems, but the experiments they undertake in relation to Lucretius are carried out under very different conditions. *The Erotics of Materialism* tracks the accretion of Lucretian experiments across centuries, languages, and nations, analyzing both the diversities and the continuities of these poets' moves in relation to an erotic Lucretian poetics.

The diversity of these authors allows me to make a claim for a lyric tradition of Lucretian poetics—a cumulative, adaptive, flexible tradition that is coherent but not restricted. Because these poets are responding not only to Lucretius, but also to other vernacular writers whose work they read as being in conversation with Lucretius, there is continuity even in diversity. For example, in his first book of sonnets, published in 1552, Pierre de Ronsard recasts Petrarchism in Lucretian terms, reimagining the amorous tears and sighs that constituted Petrarch's *Rime sparse* as atoms that collide in the void of his own body and produce his *amours*, or love poems. Ronsard pits Lucretian materialism against the idealizing Neoplatonism that dominated the Petrarchan poetics of his time in order to test the efficacy of lyric language within natural philosophical and political discourse. Meanwhile, writing in England around the turn of the seventeenth century, John Donne also links the fragmented matter of atomist physics to the fragments—of bodies, emotions, and verses—of Petrarchan lyric. In his praise poems, Donne declines to play the Petrarchan lover because he doesn't want to "fall apart," to act out, in amorous fashion, the same jarring fragmentation of matter that he associates with both the new world picture of the seventeenth century and Petrarchan love poetry. In the context of the revival of interest in atomist physics that was taking place in Donne's time, the association between atomism and Petrarchism takes on new—and fraught—force. While pairing atomism and Petrarchism was a way for Ronsard to contest the idealist, Platonizing, currents that dominated lyric practice in his day, when Donne, writing in the waning of Petrarchism, links the fragmentations of atomist matter to those of Petrarchan verse he does so to critique and renovate a Petrarchan style that he finds tired and ineffectual. Though context proves decisive for the value Ronsard and Donne each attach to Lucretius, the pattern of their thought is remarkably consistent. Both poets associate atoms with the fragmentary poetics of Petrarchism, and do so with allusion to the Lucretian analogy between atoms and letters. Ultimately, differences between Ronsard's and Donne's Lucretianizing poetry bespeak not the incoherence of the lyric tradition indebted to Lucretius, but rather its tenacity and flexibility.

Early modern poets looked not just to *DRN*, but also to their recent predecessors and peers, for their sense of Lucretian poetry and its contemporary affordances; these poets learned Lucretian poetics both from *DRN* and from later poets whose work they read through a Lucretian lens. Donne, for example, admired Ronsard's poetry. It is possible that his characterization of the sympathy between Petrarchism and atomist cosmology was born from his reading of Ronsard's atomist sonnets. Ronsard had already interpreted Petrarchan poetry as Lucretian. Though we cannot know how well Petrarch knew *DRN* (he certainly knew short sections of the poem and some Epicurean ideas indirectly), Ronsard draws connections between the scattered atoms of Lucretian cosmology and Petrarch's scattered rhymes, using atomist cosmology to intensify the way Petrarchan poetry stages poetic creation through bodily fragmentation. Ronsard and Belleau may have developed this way of thinking together. They were close friends who dedicated poems to each other and who wrote on similar Lucretian themes. Belleau edited and commented one of Ronsard's volumes of love poems; in his commentary, he points out Ronsard's debts to *DRN*. Meanwhile, Hutchinson and Cavendish were contemporaries and neighbors who came from opposite ends of the political spectrum: Hutchinson was a stout parliamentarian, and Cavendish a proud royalist. A sense of competition may have spurred them on in their Lucretian undertakings (Cavendish's atomist poetry and Hutchinson's translation of *DRN*). The way that these poets read and respond to each other's work demonstrates that a recognizable Lucretian influence on poetry developed in sixteenth- and seventeenth-century France and England not just because poets were reading *DRN*, but because poets read each other's work as Lucretian (whether it was or not, as in the case of Ronsard's interpretation of Petrarch). Early modern dialogues around Lucretian ideas developed not just in reference to *DRN* itself, but among contemporaries, constituting a vibrant tradition of intertextual reading. This approach illuminates the broad diffusion of Lucretian ideas in a time when *DRN* itself was feared and mocked for its heretical ideas.

While no single set of poems or poets can give a complete picture of the reception of Lucretian poetics in early modernity, the selected poets allow me to sketch the historical arc of a distinctive moment in the history of Lucretian reception. Both before the midpoint of the sixteenth century and after the first three-quarters of the seventeenth, poets extracted very different poetic questions, and answers, from *DRN* than did the poets described in this book. By the mid-sixteenth century, the text of *DRN* was well established, and new and authoritative editions of the poem were widely available. Belleau and Ronsard probably first read *DRN* in the 1514 Paris Navagero edition or the 1515 Venice Aldine edition. Later they would have enjoyed Denis Lambin's magisterial editions of Lucretius, the first of which was published in 1563 in Paris and Lyon, and then reprinted in 1564, 1565, and 1570 (Lambin dedicated Book 2 of his magnificent 1563 edition of *DRN* to Ronsard).[75] Poets like Ronsard and Belleau began to adapt Lucretius in vernacular as well as neo-Latin poetry, in lyric as well as didactic or epic forms. These vernacular adaptations of Lucretian poetry were freer and more adventurous than the neo-Latin Lucretian poetry that had come before. Charlotte Polly Goddard writes that "with the rise of the vernacular and the gradual decline of Latin, Lucretian imitation moved into a new stage. It was no longer based on the borrowing and manipulation of specific words or phrases in poems of the same language, genre, and metre."[76] This is where my story begins.

French poets in the second half of the sixteenth century felt a twofold pressure to defend and enrich their vernacular literary tradition. They strove to match the French language and French literature to Latin and Greek, but also Italian, models by translating old forms and inventing new ones, while also struggling against the sense that the Wars of Religion (1562–1598) could destroy any progress they had already made. Chapter 1 discusses Pierre de Ronsard's Lucretianizing of Petrarchism, mentioned above. Chapter 2 argues that both Ronsard and Remy Belleau found resources for defending and enriching French lyric in Lucretius's discussion of erotic fantasy, which crowns Book 4 of *DRN*. They apply Lucretius's language of love to the political crises of their time, adapting Lucretian theories about sexual reproduction to illustrate new ways of thinking about the reproduction of France's social, political, and creative economies.

Chapter 3 turns from sixteenth-century France to seventeenth-century England to demonstrate the continuing importance of Lucretian poetics in a period more commonly associated with the birth of modern scientific atomism. While John Donne's lament in *The First Anniversary* (1611) has drawn critical attention to what he there presents as the devastating epistemological, moral, and social impacts of early modern science, particularly atomism, I argue that Donne's engagement with Lucretius stands between a scientific understanding of the structure of the universe and a description of human or erotic relation. Through readings of Donne's diverse uses of Lucretian imagery and concepts in the *Songs and Sonnets* and the praise poems, I show that Donne draws on Lucretius to contest Petrarchan influence and seek a new lexicon for erotic love. Linking the fragmentation of Petrarchan lyric to the fragmentation of a dying world, Donne characterizes Petrarchizing verse as exhausted and incapable of establishing relations, whether between poet and patron or poet and beloved.

However, even as Donne's critique of Petrarchism unfolds through Lucretian images, he develops his new erotic lexicon in conversation with different Lucretian concepts and images. That is, even as Lucretius helps Donne to deconstruct Petrarchism, he also helps him to construct alternative ways of thinking about the workings of love and the writing of love poetry.

Like Pierre de Ronsard and Remy Belleau, the sixteenth-century French poets I discuss in the book's first two chapters, Donne connects Lucretianism and Petrarchism. Unlike these earlier poets, however, Donne was witness to the rise of modern scientific atomism, and his poetry looks forward to the epistemological, social, and religious crises that would come to a head in England in the civil war and the scientific revolution (circumstances decisive for Lucy Hutchinson and Margaret Cavendish, discussed in this book's final two chapters). The chapter on Donne therefore functions as what Cavendish, in her book of atomist poems, calls a "claspe," a bridge between two sections of a book. In addition to marking temporal and spatial transitions—between the sixteenth and seventeenth centuries, between France and England—Chapter 3 is also the site of a migration in my methodology. While the first two chapters of book are primarily interested in the microworkings of Ronsard's and Belleau's poetry, and while I continue to close read poetry in the final three chapters of the book, the chapter on Donne opens out onto the chapters on Hutchinson and Cavendish, writers who, like Donne, were invested in theorizing as well as in practicing Lucretian poetics. All of the book's chapters tend to offer frameworks for interpretation rather than definitive readings of particular texts, and that tendency is especially evident here, where I move between the *Songs and Sonnets*, *The First Anniversary*, verse epistles, elegies, letters, and sermons. This is intentional: I aim to do justice to the diversity and complexity of Donne's Lucretian thinking and the way this thought breaks the boundaries of genre. The book's focus broadens in this chapter as I move outward into the social, theoretical, and literary critical contexts of Lucretian poetics. These contexts illuminate the work that Lucretius is made to do in Donne's (and Hutchinson's and Cavendish's) poetry, and is necessary because the contexts of Lucretian reception themselves broaden in this period. The growing popularity of atomist physics is one important context, and it is essential for understanding how Donne and Cavendish put Lucretius to work in their poetry. A second is the appearance in the mid-seventeenth century of the first vernacular translations of *DRN*, which made the poem available to new readers. Translations were widely assumed to target women readers, who were less likely to have Latin.

Chapters 4 and 5 both address the appeal *DRN* held for early modern women. Chapter 4 takes as its starting point Lucy Hutchinson's delayed dedication (1675) of her verse translation of *DRN* (carried out in the 1650s, Hutchinson's was likely the poem's first complete English translation), which denounces her early labor in harsh and overtly sexualized terms. Reprising themes from this Introduction, I show that Hutchinson's repentance for her "wanton dalliance with impious books" responds to the many different ways in which *DRN* was eroticized in early modernity: the long history of erotic responses to Lucretian poetry instantiated by *DRN*'s own poetics of seduction; the libertine climate around Lucretius during the Restoration period; and the sexual discourse around early modern women's writing, particularly intense for a woman translating a text as scandalous as *DRN*.[77] Yet although her dedication vociferously rejects the wayward poetics and morality Hutchinson associates with the pagan Lucretius, Lucretian desire plays an important part in her elegies and her biblical epic, *Order and Disorder* (1679), as a figure for painful, yet unavoidable, human desire. Hutchinson's late poetry thus attests once more to the importance of desire and seduction in Hutchinson's response to *DRN*, reinforcing the book's broader argument about the importance of erotics in the early modern reception of Lucretius.

Like Donne's, Hutchinson's reaction to Lucretius is violent. *DRN* was a particularly contentious text from antiquity onward because its claims about physics as well as ethics contravened first Roman, and later Christian, civic and religious practices and doctrines. Because Lucretius was so controversial, every sixteenth- and seventeenth-century poet who drew on Lucretius reformed Lucretian thought with Platonic, Aristotelian, Stoic, Skeptical, but above all Christian ideas. Each of the poets discussed in this book go a certain distance with Lucretius, then adapt or repudiate him. These efforts to tame and disavow Lucretius do not constitute unequivocal refusals of all Lucretius had to offer; rather they are indices of engagement, however fraught. The subject of Chapter 5, Margaret Cavendish, goes further with Lucretius than perhaps any other early modern poet. Cavendish's 1653 *Poems and Fancies*, a collection of atomist poems, cultivates a Lucretian poetics and epistemology that stay with Cavendish throughout her entire career. Although the unhappy critical fate of *Poems and Fancies* has downgraded the status of atomism and poetry alike in Cavendish's corpus, Cavendish does not reject atomism in her later works (as is often argued), because her atomism is focused less on materialist dogma than on Lucretian poetics.[78] Like Lucretius, Cavendish espouses a skepticism of truth claims while endorsing the capacity of imaginative literature to educate and convince where "facts" cannot. Cavendish adapts these Lucretian ideas to her own seventeenth-century moment, responding to both the situation of women and the burgeoning scientific establishment by rejecting experimental values in favor of a vision of nature and human reason in which fancy and the imagination, not experiment, are the proper tools for natural inquiry. If natural philosophy is better conducted in the freewheeling imagination than in the laboratory, seventeenth-century women were as—if not more!—qualified to be natural philosophers as men. Lucretian poetic natural philosophy offered a model for a new science that was not predicated on a (masculine) domination of nature, but rather attempted to think with it, in a feminine register.[79]

The book ends with a brief epilogue on libertine poetry, which takes "The Imperfect Enjoyment" by John Wilmot, Earl of Rochester (1647–1680), as a case study in the course taken by Lucretian erotics after the age of experimentation with Lucretian poetics that is the focus of this book. If my story begins with the adventurous vernacular adaptations of *DRN* that began to appear around the middle of the sixteenth century, it ends with the rise of libertinism near the end of the seventeenth, when poets in both France and England launched Lucretian erotics and Epicurean philosophy on a new trajectory. Libertine poets like Rochester wrote sexually explicit poetry praising promiscuous erotic experience. At the end of Book 4 of *DRN*, Lucretius explains that love's pains can be avoided through promiscuity. Homing in on Lucretius's apparent endorsement of infidelity, libertines characterized Lucretius as a libertine avant la lettre and transformed Lucretian erotics into a physical and philosophical program. By fixing the erotics of Lucretian materialism within a specific contemporary philosophical system, libertinism marks a decisive shift in the possibilities available to Lucretian poetics. For Rochester, Lucretius is a philosopher of the body and a poet of uninhibited sex. For the poets that are the focus of this study, Lucretian erotics spoke neither to unbridled hedonism nor to Epicurean dogma, but rather to poetic questions: the delicate balance between fantasy and bodies, images and things, poetry and nature.

Materializing the Lyric Tradition: Lucretius and the Poetry of Pierre de Ronsard

Les petitz corps

In its first four lines, "Les petitz corps," the thirty-seventh poem in Pierre de Ronsard's first collection of sonnets, the *Premier livre des Amours* (1552), sketches a Lucretian universe:

> Les petitz corps, culbutans de travers,
> Parmi leur cheute en byaiz vagabonde
> Hurtez ensemble, ont composé le monde,
> S'entracrochans d'acrochementz divers.[1]

> [The tiny bodies, tumbling askew / In their vagabond plunge / Crashing together, composed the world, / Crisscrossing in countless couplings.][2]

Ronsard gives the essentials of the atomist cosmology Lucretius versifies in *DRN*. Particles of matter, *petitz corps*, fall through space. Crashing into one another—they *[h]urtez ensemble*—their collisions make the world. The word *composé* near the end of the third line links cosmic creation to poetic composition, a comparison reinforced in the fourth, which plays on the Lucretian analogy between atoms and alphabetical letters: the letters of the interlocking word pair *s'entracrochans d'acrochementz* mimic atoms crossing each other in space. The self-consciously balanced wordplay gestures toward the poem's careful composition, in tension with the declared randomness of the chance swerve of atoms in the void (the Lucretian *clinamen*), which Ronsard renders as a *byaiz vagabonde*.

These lines, however, refer not to the atomist cosmos writ large, but rather to the internal dynamics of the poet's body. Under the influence of a beautiful woman, Ronsard's overwrought emotions swerve inside him like atoms in the void, crashing together fortuitously to form the amorous universe of his love poems, the *amours*:

> L'ennuy, le soing, & les pensers ouvers,
> Chocquans le vain de mon amour profonde,
> Ont façonné d'une attache féconde,
> Dedans mon cuœur l'amoureux univers.
>
> (lines 5–8)[3]

> [Weariness, worry, and vague thoughts, / Striking the void of my deep love / Of fruitful unions have fashioned, / An amorous universe in my heart.]

Over the course of the poem's first and second stanzas, the set of elements changes: in the first stanza, it is atoms that *[h]urtez ensemble* to *compos[er] le monde*, while in the second, a lover's emotions and cares collide in a void of amorous feeling (*[c]hocquans le vain de mon amour profonde*). If atoms are the building blocks of the atomist cosmos (what Lucretius frequently called *minima*, never once using the Greek term "atom"), these new particles— *[l]'ennuy, le soing, & les pensers ouvers*—are the *minima* of Renaissance lyric poetry, and have been from the moment Petrarch declared his verses to be made "di quei sospiri ond' io nudriva 'l core" (of those sighs with which I nourished my heart) in the opening sonnet of his *Rime sparse*.[4]

Ronsard's sonnet transforms the sighs and tears of the Petrarchan tradition into atoms, the poet's deep love (*amour profonde*) into the depths of his amorous body. The ancient atomists had argued that there is only body and void, but Ronsard playfully describes a void within the body. Under the sign of Venus—the Lucretian muse—Ronsard conflates the constitutive elements of two different poetic vocabularies, Lucretian and Petrarchan. "Les petitz corps" reads the Lucretian analogy between atoms and alphabetical letters, between the cosmos and the poem describing it, back into the Petrarchan lyric tradition of which Ronsard was an heir. Though we cannot know whether Petrarch himself read *DRN* (he certainly knew short sections of the poem and some Epicurean ideas indirectly), Ronsard draws connections between the scattered atoms of Lucretian cosmology and Petrarch's scattered rhymes. "Les petitz corps" materializes Petrarchism, using atomist cosmology to intensify the way Petrarchan poetry stages poetic creation through bodily fragmentation.

Over the course of this chapter (on Ronsard) and the next (on Ronsard and his friend and fellow Pléiade poet, Remy Belleau), I show that Lucretius was an organizing theme in poetic problems in sixteenth-century France, and that Lucretian influence in the period extends beyond the basics of atomist physics or the well-known poetic set pieces from *DRN* that circulated widely among poets.[5] *DRN*'s materialist theory of the imagination, account of erotic obsession, and treatment of the relation between poetry and politics made Lucretius a powerful voice around poetics. Ronsard was no orthodox Lucretian—nobody in the sixteenth century was; they all reformed Lucretian thought with Platonic, Aristotelian, Stoic, Skeptical, and above all Christian ideas—but the confrontations he stages at the site of the poet's body in poems like "Les petitz corps," where he materializes the tears and sighs of the Petrarchan tradition, draw on Lucretius to rethink poetry's power to act within and upon the material world. Ronsard pits Lucretian materialism against the idealizing currents that dominated the lyric poetics of his time in order to test the efficacy of lyric language.

Ronsard explores the poetic affordances of Lucretian materialism by staging collisions between newly rediscovered Lucretian ideas and long-established poetic and philosophical traditions. In Ronsard's poetry, well-worn tropes of medieval and Renaissance love poetry, such as the lover's abundant tears and sighs or the obsession with the image of the beloved, are revised in pointedly Lucretian ways, often by emphasizing the materiality of those very tropes (the lover's tears, sighs, and glances) and the senses responsible for processing those materials (the lover's sight, hearing, and amorous touch). Although it is tempting to characterize atomism as anchoring one pole of a binary between materialism and idealism, corporeality and incorporeality, Lucretius is in fact a theorist of all manner of materialities. *DRN* explores the gradations of matter, things that are robustly material (cobblestones, bones) as well as those (dreams, erotic fantasies) made of atoms so delicate that they flirt with incorporeality. These are *simulacra*, the films of atoms that stream from bodies and stimulate the senses. As I explain in the Introduction, *simulacra* are material, and their forms mimic those of the objects from which they flow. But while most *simulacra* are reliable representatives of the things that generate them, some errant *simulacra* combine to form new images that reflect no real object; others self-generate out of thin air.

Lucretius illustrates the deceptive potential of images with an example that, like images themselves, is suspended between reality and the imagination: sexual desire.

> tum quibus aetatis freta primitus insinuatur
> semen, ubi ipsa dies membris matura creavit,
> conveniunt simulacra foris e corpore quoque
> nuntia praeclari vultus pulchrique coloris,
> qui ciet irritans loca turgida semine multo,
> ut quasi transactis saepe omnibu' rebu' profundant
> fluminis ingentis fluctus vestemque cruentent.
>
> (*DRN* 4.1030–36)

[For those in adolescence's riptide, [into whom / Seed is penetrating] for the first time—then images invade, / Images of some random body or other—bringing news / Of a lovely face and radiant complexion's rosy hues. / This irritates and goads the organs, swollen hard with seed— / Such that frequently, as if he'd really done the deed, / A youth floods forth a gush of semen so he stains the sheet; translation modified]

These lines emphasize how detached from bodies *simulacra* are. It is not just that such fantasies are born from image-films, but that an unidentified, even imaginary body generated them. Nevertheless, or perhaps because of this, *simulacra* are able to stir the sleeper's body with desire. As the passage so provocatively describes, fantasized images produce a very real physical response.

Waking desire functions the same way: lovers become enamored of *simulacra* and seek to sate their lust on the bodies that generated those seductive images. However, precisely because they long for images, lovers find no relief in sex. Lucretius presents desire as a category mistake, falling in love with images but making love to bodies, which frustrates lust and makes sex a brutal affair.

> quod petiere, premunt arte faciuntque dolorem
> corporis et dentis inlidunt saepe labellis
> osculaque adfligunt, quia non est pura voluptas
> et stimuli subsunt qui instigant laedere id ipsum
> quodcumque est, rabies unde illaec germina surgunt.
> . . . .
> sic in amore Venus simulacris ludit amantis
> nec satiare queunt spectando corpora coram,
> nec manibus quicquam teneris abradere membris
> possunt errantes incerti corpore toto.
>
> > (*DRN* 4.1079–83, 1101–4)

[so closely pressing / What they long for, that they hurt the flesh by their possessing, / Often sinking teeth in lips, and crushing as they kiss, / Since what lovers feel is not pure and simple bliss— / Rather, there are stings beneath it, pains that shoot, / Goading them to hurt the thing that's made madness take root, / Whatever it may be. . . . / So [in love] Venus teases [lovers] with images—[they] can't satisfy / The flesh however they devour each other with the eye, / Nor with hungry hands roving the body can they reap / Anything from the supple limbs that they can take and keep; translation modified]

Although they "devour each other with the eye," these lovers can never satisfy the flesh, no matter how much they bite and crush each other's bodies in wild attempts to extract pleasure. Were their desires more moderate—for procreation or momentary release—they might be satisfied with mere moments of pleasure, but because they long to possess each other fully they are consumed by a ruinous and insatiable obsession.

Because they are generated by the objects from which they flow, image atoms are secondary and not as massy as those that constitute bones or flesh. They exist at the border of materiality and immateriality, reality and illusion. Ronsard's poetry is attentive to the ambiguities of Lucretian materialism, particularly of the erotic *simulacrum*. In the thirtieth sonnet of the *Premier livre des Amours*, the speaker repeatedly entreats the *simulacrum* of his beloved—which he variously calls an *idole*, *vain portrait*, and *songe*—to stay with him through the night as a substitute for the actual body of his lady:

"Las, où fuis tu? Atten encor un peu, / . . . seuffre au moins que par songe / Toute une nuict je les puisse embrasser" (Wait, where are you going? Wait just a little longer / . . . at least let me embrace those limbs / In dreams all night long; lines 9, 13–14). Ronsard imagines that he might extract some sexual satisfaction from the lady's image, but if anything, his fantasy dramatizes two Lucretian truisms: that all love is a love of images, and that no sexual desire can ever be satisfied. That Ronsard can get neither lady nor her image to stay with him through the night does not make him the exception to a rule of amorous satisfaction, but rather proof that erotic satisfaction is always impossible. As Philip Hardie writes of the desperate lover in *DRN* Book 4, "The lover is at the mercy of *simulacra*, atomic film-images coming from the object of his desire; his sexual appetite has no other object than these flimsy phantoms, and hence there is no possibility of ever satisfying the appetite, unlike the appetites of hunger and thirst which can easily be assuaged by the ingestion of quantities of food and drink."[6]

There is a long tradition of the amorous image, informed by Aristotelian and Neoplatonic theories of the imagination, which nourished medieval and Renaissance poetry and which predates the rediscovery of the full text of *DRN* in the fifteenth century.[7] Lucretius is distinct from this tradition not just in genealogy but because he emphasizes the materiality of the amorous image: *simulacra* may be made of the finest atoms, but they are still made of atoms.[8] The nocturnal fantasies populating Ronsard's *Amours* draw from both traditions, sometimes within the same poem. The sixty-ninth sonnet of the *Premier livre des Amours*, for example, steps back from the specific Lucretian narrative of nighttime fantasy to reflect more generally on the phenomenon of the amorous image. Editors and critics have long recognized the Lucretian influence here because Ronsard uses the Lucretian term *simulacrum*. Whereas Plato, like most of the ancients, believed that sight worked through extromission, with the eye projecting a beam outward to capture and transmit the forms of things to the mind, Lucretius defended an intromission theory.[9] Ronsard's poem opens with a Lucretian account of how vision works. Things cast off *simulacra*, which hit the eyes:

> Si seulement l'image de la chose
> Fait à nos yeulx la chose concevoir,
> Et si mon œil n'a puissance de veoir,
> Si quelqu'idole au devant ne s'oppose.

> (lines 1–4)

[If the image alone of a thing / Causes our eye to see that thing, /
And if my eye is powerless to see / Unless some image stands before
it.]

This explanation quickly gives way to ironic complaint: only a jealous God
would give a lover eyes so small that they hold barely any images of the lady:

> Que ne m'a faict celuy, qui tout compose,
> Les yeulx plus grandz, affin de mieux pouvoir
> En leur grandeur la grandeur recevoir
> Du simulachre, où ma vie est enclose?
>
> (lines 5–8)

[Why didn't he who made everything give me / Bigger eyes, whose
great size / Would allow them to better receive / The simulacrum,
in which my life is enclosed?]

Ronsard asserts the materiality of amorous images, using Lucretian theory to
facilitate his lover's complaint.

Lucretian materialism was wildly contentious in sixteenth-century
France, and Ronsard's use of Lucretian ideas in an utterly conventional
poem comes off as pointedly silly. This humor authorizes the cascading
syncretisms that close the poem. Lucretian *simulacra*, the image-films that
carry the lady's figure from her body to the lover's eyes, become a Platonic
"idea" of divine beauty, while the Epicurean gods, deities whose only know-
able attribute is that they care nothing for human affairs, are transformed
into the jealous, interventionist God of the Bible.

> Certes le ciel trop ingrat de son bien,
> Qui seul la fit, & qui seul veit combien
> De sa beaulté divine estoit l'idée,
>
> Comme jaloux du tresor de son mieux,
> Silla le Monde, & m'aveugla les yeulx,
> Pour de luy seul seule estre regardée.
>
> (lines 9–14)

[Indeed, Heaven (which alone created her, and which alone knew /
How divine the Idea of her beauty was), ungenerous with its

goodness, / As though jealous of such precious goods / Blinkered the world, and blinded my eyes, / So that by heaven alone she could be seen.]

A poem that is overtly Lucretian at its opening is firmly Neoplatonic and Christian by its end. This sort of slippage is frequent in the *Amours*. "Les petitz corps" has a similar movement: although the first two stanzas are obviously materialist, the final stanzas pivot firmly toward an emphasis on the incorporeal.

> Mais s'il advient, que ces tresses orines,
> Ces doigtz roisins, & ces mains ivoyrines
> Froyssent ma vie, en quoy retournera
>
> Ce petit tout? En eau, air, terre, ou flamme?
> Non, mais en voix qui tousjours de ma dame
> Par le grand Tout les honneurs sonnera.

(lines 9–14)

[But should these golden curls, / These rosy fingers, and these ivory hands / End my life, how will this little world / Return? As water, air, earth, or fire? / No, rather as a voice that will eternally fill / The great World with my lady's honors.]

The rejection of an elemental logic—*eau, air, terre, ou flamme*—and the emphasis on an eternally perduring voice push these lines away from a materialist conception of both cosmology and poetry. While Lucretius says that atoms themselves never perish, he also emphasizes the inevitable decay of any composite body and flatly denies the existence or immortality of an incorporeal soul. Ronsard rejects the material elements of the body for an eternal voice that is necessarily incorporeal insofar as only incorporeal things can last forever. On this, at least, Lucretius, Plato, and the Christian theologians could agree.

In both poems, an ideological slippage leads to a resolution that emphasizes perdurance and eternity, be it of divine beauty or poetic voice. In "Si seulement l'image," the lady's beauty is revealed to be of divine origin. In "Les petitz corps," the threatened dissolution of the poet's body is recuperated by the promise that even after *[c]e petit tout* dissolves back to its primordial elements the poem will praise the lady for eternity. Ronsard's irreverent

yoking together of incompatible belief systems, with incompatible visions of
the natural world, reinforces the coherence and stability of his poetic world.
As many of Ronsard's critics have noted, his sonnets are far from philosophically consistent, and readers would do well not to look to them for a clear
exposition of Ronsard's views. As Philip Ford argues, "Lucretian science . . .
may be the starting point for some of Ronsard's love poetry, but it is put to
purely poetic purposes in these poems and does not imply any intellectual
commitment to it on the part of the poet."[10] Whether Ronsard believes in
one or another philosophy is beside the point, because his valorization of
poetry by means of atomism, or against Platonism, operates despite or even
in tandem with his ironizing of those very systems. This is demonstrated by
his promiscuous use of philosophical sources; in his sonnets he draws from
(to name only a few) Hesiod's *Theogony*, Thales, Genesis, and Plato's
Timaeus, as well as later reworkings of those classic texts, such as Ficino's
interpretations of Plato, to describe the creation of the universe and the form
of the natural world.[11] Ronsard's abundant philosophical sources are always
subordinate to his poetic project: he does not use atomism or Platonism to
make truth claims about the universe or engage in philosophical debate, but
musters their rich implications to evoke poetic worlds.

Ronsard's pointed syncretism reinforces the coherence of his poetic
world, which demonstrates itself to be powerful enough to subordinate a
wide variety of natural philosophical systems to its own logic—that of love.
Over and over again, Ronsard sets up contests between the natural universe
and his amorous universe in which the latter emerges triumphant and love is
shown to govern both. In "Plus tost le bal," the twenty-sixth sonnet in the
1552 *Amours*, amorous infidelity threatens to destroy not only the possibility
of a poem, but the harmony of the universe. Repeating the refrain "plus tost,"
Ronsard denies that he will ever love another woman than the one he loves
now:

> Plus tost les cieulx des mers seront couverts,
> Plus tost sans forme ira confus le monde:
> Que je soys serf d'une maitresse blonde,
> Ou que j'adore une femme aux yeulx verds.
>
> (lines 5–8)

[Rather the walls of the universe crumble / Rather the world lose its
form, / Than that I dedicate myself to a blonde mistress / Or love a
woman with green eyes.]

The interdependence of the love-world and the natural world is so strong that should Ronsard's heart stray, the very bounds of the heavens will crack, and the world soul will be released into the void. Love and fidelity are linked with form, both poetic and cosmic.

If Ronsard is invested in shoring up poetic worlds, Lucretius is a counterintuitive interlocutor. Lucretian materialism denies that all save the most basic elements of matter—atoms—will inevitably perish, and the Lucretian analogy between atoms and letters implies that no literary works will perdure either, only the alphabetical letters that make up their lines.[12] The Lucretian refusal of poetic monumentality stands in stark contrast to the craving for eternal literary fame that inspired classical and Renaissance poetry alike. At the end of the *Metamorphoses*, Ovid claims immortality for his poem: "Iamque opus exegi, quod nec Iouis ira nec ignis / nec poterit ferrum nec edax abolere uetustas" (And now my work is done: no wrath of Jove / nor fire nor sword nor time, which would erode / all things, has power to blot out this poem).[13] Ovid's body will age and eventually perish, but his name will live on immortal, carried on the wings of his poem.[14] Like many other Renaissance poets, Shakespeare claims the same immortalizing power for poetry, writing that his sonnets will preserve the beauty that wretched Time degrades. Sonnet 15—a pointed reference to Ovid's monumentalizing at the end of Book 15 of the *Metamorphoses*—boasts that:

Where wasteful time debateth with decay,
To change your day of youth to sullied night;
And all in war with time for love of you,
As he takes from you, I engraft you new.[15]

Although Lucretius refuses literary monumentality, he offers poetry a different prize: value in the here and now. While both "Les petitz corps" and "Si seulement l'image" have Lucretian openings and Platonizing finales, and while many poems in the *Amours* espouse a thoroughgoing Platonism, other sonnets from both Ronsard's early and later sonnet collections move in the opposite direction, from a Platonic emphasis on idealized and incorporealized "love" toward a Lucretian focus on the body, often overtly sexualized.[16] The fiftieth sonnet in the *Premier livre des Sonnets pour Helene* (1578) chastises Helene for falling prey to Platonic doctrines that overprize the spiritual and ignore the body:[17]

Bien que l'esprit humain s'enfle par la doctrine
De Platon, qui le vante influxion des cieux,
Si est-ce sans le corps qu'il seroit ocieux,
Et auroit beau louer sa celeste origine.

(lines 1–4)

[Though the human spirit is vaunted by / Plato, who praises the
sky's influence over it, / Without the body, the spirit would have a
hard time / Boasting of its celestial origins.]

Helene should not forget what the soul and the *esprit* owe the body: "La
matiere le rend plus parfait et plus digne" (Matter perfects and dignifies the
soul; line 8).

Or' vous aimez l'esprit, et sans discretion
Vous dites que des corps les amours sont pollues.
Tel dire n'est sinon qu'imagination

Qui embrasse le faux pour les choses cognues:
Est c'est renouveller la fable d'Ixion,
Qui se paissoit de vent et n'amoit que des nues.

(lines 9–12)

[Now, you love the soul, and indiscreetly / You say that bodies pol-
lute love. / Such claims are pure fancy, / which confuse falsehoods
with well-known facts: / You revive that old story about Ixion / Who
satisfied himself with wind and only loved clouds.]

Although the poem is framed as a philosophical critique, it becomes clear in
its final lines that what is at stake is sexual experience. Ronsard chastises his
beloved for maintaining a Platonic fondness for spirit: she would have him
be another Ixion, embracing clouds rather than her own lovely body.

The same sentiment is presented even more bluntly in a sonnet published in 1578 in the *Premier livre des Sonnets pour Helene* but suppressed in
the 1584 edition of Ronsard's *Œuvres*, perhaps for its impishly frank sexuality:

En choisissant l'esprit vous estes mal-apprise,
Qui refusez le corps, à mon gré le meilleur:

De l'un en l'esprouvant on cognoist la valeur,
L'autre n'est rien que vent, que songe et que feintise.

(lines 1–4)

[You are wrong to choose the spirit / And reject the body (which I
hold superior): / We know the body's value through experience, /
While the other is nothing but air, dream, and illusion.]

Ronsard concludes the poem by declaring: "Je n'aime point le faux, j'aime la
verité" (I love falsity not one bit, but I love truth; line 14). The poem makes
an easy joke about the renowned chastity of his addressee, Hélène de Surgères, and the poet's complaint about his lady's sexual reticence also serves to
defend her reputation. Though it is playful, Ronsard's commentary on the
relative merits of body and soul packs a theoretical punch: while the Platonic
theory of forms presents the body as a weak reflection of an immortal soul,
Ronsard asserts precisely the opposite. The body, in its obvious materiality,
is the original (*la verité*), while the soul—*rien que vent, que songe et que
feintise*—is the body's false copy (*le faux*). Employing the same resonant
vocabulary of image and dream used in the earlier *Amours* to describe the
tantalizing and sexually available *simulacrum* of his lady, Ronsard applies
Lucretian concepts to subvert Platonic truisms and imply that the soul is the
simulacrum of the body.

The stakes of the playful philosophical contests in poems like "Les petitz
corps" and "En choisissant l'esprit" become clearer in sonnet 60 of the *Premier livre des Amours* ("Pardonne moy, Platon"). Here, Ronsard accuses Plato
of marginalizing poetry: he is less concerned with the expulsion of the poets
from Plato's ideal republic than with his sense that Platonic idealism denies
the material realities of both physical love and love poetry. Making the Lucretian argument that language, like all things, is material, Ronsard calls into
question Plato's schema of the natural world and, in so doing, forcefully
introjects poetry into natural philosophical discourse. Ronsard begins his sonnet by accusing Plato of having been wrong about the impossibility of the
void:

Pardonne moy, Platon, si je ne cuide
Que soubz la vouste & grande arche des dieux,
Soit hors du monde, ou au centre des lieux,
En terre, en l'eau, il n'y ayt quelque vuide.

Si l'air est plein en sa courbure humide,
Qui reçoyt donq tant de pleurs de mes yeulx,
Tant de souspirs, que je sanglote aux cieulx,
Lors qu'à mon dueil Amour lasche la bride?

(lines 1–8)

[Pardon me, Plato, if I don't believe / That under the dome and
great vault of the gods, / Or beyond the earth, or at the center of
everything, / In the earth, in the waters, there isn't a void of some
sort. / If I don't believe that the air—which absorbs so many tears
from my eyes, / So many sighs, which I cry to the heavens / When
Love gives rein to my sorrow— / Is full in its damp curve?]

While Plato denies the existence of a void, Lucretius defends it. Engaging
this debate, Ronsard dramatizes the implications Lucretian atomism has for
poetry's relationship to the world in general, and for the discourse of philosophy in particular. Were there no void, where would his tears and sighs go?
He disputes Plato's philosophical system on poetry's terms: the poetic trope
of the poet's abundant tears and sighs, reconceived under the sign of Lucretius as having a material presence, proves the impossibility of the voidless
universe. The poem imagines the world forced to adapt to poetry's terms,
which here are Lucretian: particle and void, tears and *vuide*. As in "Les petitz
corps," here Ronsard seems to identify poetic cosmology with Lucretius. Platonic philosophy, Ronsard implies, doesn't make space for poetry, but Lucretian atomism does. In the second stanza of the poem Ronsard compares the
materiality of his *souspirs* to the lines of his poetry: the heavens need a void
to hold both his tears and their corollary and double, his verses.[18] Atomism
gives Ronsard's lyrics a material presence that challenges Platonic philosophy's disavowal of poetry's real-world value and significance.

Reading Ronsard Reading Lucretius

When the full text of *DRN* began to circulate in the final quarter of the
fifteenth century, Renaissance poets set about reconstructing the poem's place
in literary history. Prior to its rediscovery and recirculation, *DRN* had been

available only in brief snippets quoted in other texts, but readers in mid-sixteenth-century France had access to important new editions of the poem.[19] Medieval readers knew that Lucretius had been a powerful influence on Augustan literature, but Renaissance readers could trace those connections themselves, marking resonances between *DRN* and beloved classical texts like Virgil's *Aeneid* and *Georgics,* Ovid's *Metamorphoses,* and Horace's *Odes.*[20] Michel de Montaigne (1533–1592) tattooed his copy of *DRN* with these familiar names.[21] Like Montaigne, Ronsard would have read *DRN* looking for connections between Lucretius and other classical authors; he would have reconstructed *DRN*'s influence, reading familiar classical, medieval, and contemporary literature through a new Lucretian lens and identifying traces of Lucretius in those texts. And yet, accompanying the thrills of rediscovery and recognition and the humanist labor of textual rehabilitation, there may have been another feeling and another labor: regret that earlier centuries had not known this difficult, scandalous, but undeniably beautiful and important poem, and the imaginative labor of envisioning what Renaissance poetry would have become had *DRN* not been lost. Lyrics like "Les petitz corps" insert Lucretius back into the literary traditions that flourished while *DRN* languished, unread, in monastery libraries. Behind these poems lie probing questions: How would Petrarchism have been different if it had been nourished by Lucretius? What if, alongside Plato, Ovid, and Horace, Lucretius had been a wellspring for Renaissance lyric poetics?

Unfortunately, while Montaigne's heavily annotated copy of Lambin's groundbreaking 1563 edition of *DRN* was recovered in 1989 (and subsequently edited by Michael Screech), only one of Ronsard's copies of *DRN* has been found: a presentation copy of Lambin's 1570 edition of *DRN* that postdates by many years Ronsard's first and formative readings of *DRN,* which must have taken place in the late 1540s and early 1550s.[22] Montaigne was an extraordinary reader of *DRN*: his is one of the most, if not *the* most, vigorously annotated extant sixteenth-century copies of *DRN,* and his *Essais* attest to a profound engagement with Lucretian ideas.[23] As Ada Palmer has shown, readers in the first century of *DRN*'s Renaissance dissemination were primarily interested in reconstruction—"of the author, of the ancient world . . . and of the more perfect Latin and Greek written and spoken by the ancients."[24] Guided by a humanist educational agenda that emphasized reading as a moral experience that would "steep the reader in classical virtue," fifteenth-century readers annotated Lucretian passages pertinent to questions of Epicurean moral philosophy, vocabulary, poetry, and notabilia far more than they did those explaining the heretical atomist philosophy.[25]

Palmer's study seeks to explain what she calls the "strange conjunction of [*DRN*'s] fast dissemination and slow intellectual reception."[26] When *DRN* spread so quickly and was read by so many, why were there no full-throated "Epicureans" until Pierre Gassendi (1592–1655) in the middle of the seventeenth century? Her answer: "If by the seventeenth century Lucretian atomism and mechanical models of nature penetrated more seriously into scientific discourse, this increased interest in heterodox science was enabled by a radical transformation of the common reading agenda, which can be traced over the course of the sixteenth century."[27] By the seventeenth century, the "moral filter" of humanist reading was finally collapsing, and it was possible to read Lucretius for his radical ideas. Blessed with relatively stable and readable editions of the text, late sixteenth- and seventeenth-century readers of *DRN* were able to move beyond philological and reconstructive readings to explore Lucretius's controversial ideas. But even in the late sixteenth and seventeenth centuries, humanist modes of reading persisted alongside these new and radical interpretations, often in the same reader. Montaigne is an instructive example: like a good humanist, he kept lists of uncommon words in his copy of *DRN* and marked errors in the text, but unlike all but a very few of his humanist predecessors and contemporaries, he also grappled with the poem's difficult and contentious philosophical and poetic ideas. Whereas most readers leave Lucretian heresies unremarked, Montaigne is quick to point them out them in his bold scrawl—*contre la religion*—but his lively awareness of the danger of Lucretian ideas did not keep him from *DRN*. Montaigne's "Que philosopher c'est apprendre à mourir" (I.20) and the magisterial "Apologie de Raimond Sebond" (II.12) both contend with Lucretian arguments about death.[28]

Like Montaigne, Ronsard was an extraordinary reader of Lucretius. While no heavily annotated copy testifies to how Ronsard read his *DRN*, his love poetry shows that he attended to the poem's deep structure, extracting the lyric implications of Lucretius's didactic epic and evaluating Lucretian ideas with an eye to how they might redirect classical and Renaissance poetic traditions.[29] It has become common in the scholarship of recent years to reflect upon *DRN*'s "modernity," but this sort of thinking makes any Renaissance and early modern engagement with *DRN* that is not carried out on modernity's terms—of radical religion and science—look stale or backwards.[30] Ronsard does not read *DRN* like a seventeenth-century protoradical, anticipating the atheism and science of the Enlightenment, but he also does not only read like a humanist, reconstructing *DRN*, Lucretius, or the Latin of the ancients. Ronsard uses Lucretius to reimagine his literary inheritance and thus redirect the future of French poetry.

In life, Montaigne and Ronsard did not run in the same circles, but intellectually they were part of the same group of innovative readers and adapters of Lucretius.[31] Denis Lambin imagines one such grouping in the dedications to his editions of *DRN*. Lambin dedicated his 1563 edition of *DRN* to Charles IX, but also separately dedicated each of the books: Book 2 to Ronsard, whom he hails as first among French poets,[32] and Book 4 to Marc-Antoine Muret (1526–1585), Ronsard's compatriot in the Pléiade, discussed below.[33] Groupings of French Lucretians, however, predate the release of Lambin's *DRN* editions. The "brigade" of upstart young poets dubbed the "Pléiade" by Ronsard were clearly reading Lucretius together in the years before Ronsard released his *Amours* in 1552.[34] Modeled on Marsilio Ficino's Neoplatonic Academy, the Pléiade were a group of like-minded poets on a mission to defend and glorify vernacular language and literature. While the poetry of the Pléiade is deeply influenced by Ficinian Neoplatonism, Pléiade poets also contested the dominance of Neoplatonic Petrarchan poetics in important ways (Joachim du Bellay's 1549 *Défense et illustration de la langue française*, the manifesto of Pléiade poetics, is stoutly anti-Petrarchan). It is tempting to see their Lucretian engagements as a way of differentiating their poetics from the Neoplatonic poetics associated with Ficino and his followers, but the fact that the Pléiade poets read Lucretius together does not mean that they were "Lucretian" in any straightforward sense. Ronsard and his compatriots were Christians, and they were also magpies and syncretists, drawing upon myriad classical sources to achieve their poetic goals. What it does mean is that they were apt to recognize and respond to Lucretian elements in each other's poetry. Their Lucretian engagements took shape not only through their readings of *DRN* itself, but in conversation among themselves, with their friends and fellow poets.

The commentaries on the first and second books of Ronsard's *Amours* by his fellow Pléiade poets Marc-Antoine Muret and Remy Belleau illuminate the shared study Pléiade members made of *DRN*. In 1553, the second edition of the first volume of *Amours* (to Cassandre) was released, accompanied by a commentary by Muret; Belleau's commentary on the second volume of the *Amours* (to Marie) was added to the first edition of Ronsard's *Œuvres* in 1560.[35] Both commentaries discuss the Lucretian influence on the *Amours* at length. Ronsard himself may have been the puppet master behind the commentaries, and it is possible that the interpretations of the poems are largely his own.[36] If this is true, the commentaries speak directly to Ronsard's interpretations of and engagements with *DRN*. If it is in fact Muret and Belleau commenting, we learn something equally valuable: how interpretations of *DRN*, and communal interest in specific Lucretian ideas and tropes, emerged among groupings of contemporaries in sixteenth-century France.

Marc-Antoine Muret was a poet, humanist, philologist, and editor, a sometime member of the Pléiade and an intimate of the great *DRN* editor Denis Lambin.[37] His commentary on Ronsard's first volume of *Amours* demonstrates a deep knowledge of *DRN* and identifies—though fails to fully appreciate—the novel uses to which Ronsard puts Lucretius in poems like "Les petitz corps." His remarks on that sonnet explain the atomist creed that atoms swerving together in the void produce all things: "The Poet says that tiny bodies of feelings come together within him in this way."[38] Muret's commentary on another extraordinary poem, sonnet 42 of the *Premier livre des Amours*, returns to the "petitz corps" of these materialized affections. In this sonnet, Ronsard once again compares his body to the cosmos, invoking the trope (found in different forms in Hesiod, Empedocles, and Ovid) of a primordial Chaos brought to order by Love. Like that chaos, Ronsard's body was "Sans art, sans forme, & sans figure entiere, / Alors qu'Amour le perça de ses yeulx" (Entirely without art, form, or figure / Until love pierced it through the eyes; lines 7–8). In the penultimate tercet, Ronsard pushes the conceit into Lucretian territory. Love gives Ronsard's entrails a specific form, rolling them into the same little bodies that populate "Les petitz corps": "Il arondit de mes affections / Les petitz corps en leurs perfections" (From my affections he smoothed / Little bodies in their perfections; lines 9–10). Muret comments that "he speaks of his affections as if they were corporeal. And in fact, some of the ancients thought that our souls were made of tiny round bodies. The discussion is in Book Three of Lucretius."[39]

While Muret knows that Ronsard's materialization of amorous emotions is Lucretian, he does not consider the poetic implications of Ronsard's move. In general, Muret's commentary is preoccupied with mediating between classical authorities. His goal is to elucidate the poems and enlighten the reader: now Ronsard is referring to Plato, now Aristotle; this is Lucretius, that Ficino, and so on.[40] While Muret respects the ancients, he applauds Ronsard's syncretism, asserting the right of poets to alter (*fausser*) whatever they want to fit their poetic fancy. Explaining sonnet 60, "Pardonne moy, Platon" (discussed at length above), in which Ronsard disputes Plato's denial of the void, Muret enumerates ancient sources on the question, beginning with the atomists: "The ancients disagreed whether or not there was a void. Leucippus, Democritus, and Epicurus said there was, because if everything was full, there would be no movement. Their arguments are explained in Lucretius in the first book."[41] Against both the atomists and the Stoics, Muret affirms the opinion of Plato and Aristotle, who deny the void. According to Muret, Ronsard's choice to side with Lucretius is a question of poetic privilege: "Nevertheless, the author asserts the privilege of Poets, who are always free to affirm the false and dispute the true as they see fit, to better fit their conceptions."[42] In Muret's reading, Ronsard knows that Lucretius is philosophically wrong, but wields poetic privilege to make him *poetically* right. Muret's subordination of philosophy to poetry prevents him from seeing clearly the poetic influence of Lucretius on Ronsard. For Muret, *DRN* is a source for the best-known and most contentious principles of atomist physics—the mortality of the soul and the godless universe of atoms, void, and swerve—but when atomist concepts appear in the *Amours* to Muret it says everything about Ronsard's poetic privilege and nothing about the poetic potential of materialism.

Unlike Muret, Belleau is acutely attuned to Lucretian poetry and poetics. While Muret's commentary generally paraphrases, then cites Lucretius for explanations of Epicurean principles (the commentary on sonnet 51—"The argument is in the third book of Lucretius"—is typical), Belleau quotes extensively from *DRN*, plunging the reader into the poem itself.[43] Belleau treats Lucretius as a poet as well as a philosopher, and he is just as likely to group Lucretius with other Latin poets as with the Greek atomist philosophers Leucippus, Democritus, and Epicurus. Above all, Belleau's commentary links Lucretius and Ovid as experts on love, and Book 4 of *DRN* with Ovid's *Remedia amoris* as texts diagnosing and curing the pains of love. One of Ovid's major avenues of influence from the medieval period into the Renaissance was as an authority on love, its pursuit, its pains, and its cures. Lucretius had long been associated with Ovid—before the rediscovery of *DRN* in the fifteenth century, readers would have been most likely to encounter his name in either Ovid's *Amores* 1.15 or one of the medieval grammarians—but Belleau makes a more specific connection.[44] In his remarks on Ronsard's chanson 35, "Je ne veulx plus que chanter," which describes how when his lady is gone a *faulce imagination* (false imagination; line 18) keeps her image before his eyes, Belleau cites Lucretius on the *simulacrum*: "[N]am si abest quod ames, praesto simulacra tamen sunt / illius et nomen dulce obversatur ad auris" (For though your love be absent, still the images remain, / The darling name of the beloved ringing in your ear; *DRN* 4.1061–62).[45] As Ronsard remarks tartly, "Amour vrayement est une maladie" (Love truly is a disease; line 73).

That love is a disease was a commonplace in the Renaissance. Ronsard's poem states it explicitly, invoking doctors who call love a *fureur de fantaisie* (a disease of the imagination) in which the mind is tormented by amorous images. Ronsard despairs of his fantastical plague, writing: "J'aymerois mieux la fiebvre dans mes venes, / Ou quelque peste, ou quelqu'autre douleur, / Que de souffrir tant d'amoureuses peines" (I would rather have fever in my veins / Or some plague, or some other pain, / Than to suffer so much from amorous pains; lines 77–79). Lucretius was a recognized theorist of disease—*DRN* ends with a justly famous account of the plague of Athens—and *DRN* was freely cited in medical texts into the seventeenth century.[46] The end of Book 4 of *DRN*, which describes the snares of love and how to avoid them, treats love as a disease. In the lines following those quoted in Belleau's commentary on Ronsard's chanson, Lucretius advises how to avoid being ensnared by images.

> sed fugitare decet simulacra et pabula amoris
> absterrere sibi atque alio convertere mentem
> et iacere umorem collectum in corpora quaeque
> nec retinere, semel conversum unius amore,
> et servare sibi curam certumque dolorem.
>
> (*DRN* 4.1063–67)

> [It's best to flee away from images, and to steer clear / From the fodder that love feeds upon—it's better to direct / Your attention somewhere else, and spend the fluids that collect / On any body— rather than retain them and remain / Fixed ever on one love, laying up stores of pain.]

The recommended cure for passion is promiscuity: the afflicted must ensure that his stores of seed do not build up.[47] Ovid's advice in the *Remedia amoris*, a companion piece to the *Ars amatoria* (2 CE), is remarkably similar:

> Hortor et, ut pariter binas habeatis amicas
> (Fortior est, plures siquis habere potest):

Secta bipertito cum mens discurrit utroque,
Alterius vires subtrahit alter amor.[48]

[I advise you to have two mistresses at once (a tough man is he who can take on more); when the attention, parted in twain, shifts from this one to that, one passion saps the other's force.]

Commenting on Ronsard's "Elegie a son livre," Belleau again presents Lucretius as an authority on love and its cures: "The author, after having been long punished by his Cassandra, and seeing that his service was rewarded only with trials and cruelty, deliberated, and following the cures of Lucretius and of Ovid, took the correct medicine to purge himself of this evil, which was to abandon the beloved person."[49]

The Ovidian tradition of *remedia amoris* provided Renaissance readers with a valuable context in which to situate and understand *DRN*. Ovid's poetic persona as a lover and an authority on love was well known to readers, and operated as a model for how to understand Lucretius and his poem. Like Ovid, Lucretius presented himself as an authority on love, and he was also notorious for his love life. As I explain in the Introduction, Renaissance biographies of Lucretius foregrounded Jerome's apocryphal story that Lucretius committed suicide after being driven mad by a love potion administered to him by either his wife or his mistress. Belleau was not alone in grouping Lucretius with Ovid as teachers of *remedia amoris*. George Sandys, the English translator of Ovid's *Metamorphoses*, pairs the two explicitly in the commented edition of his *Ovid's Metamorphoses Englished* (1632, following the partial 1621 edition and the complete 1626 edition). In his commentary on the Salmacis and Hermaphroditus story from Book 4 of the *Metamorphoses*, he glosses the text first with Ovid's *Remedia amoris* (1.135–50), then with Book 4 of *DRN* (4.1076–1113).[50] Sandys introduces the Ovid of the *Remedia* as a "*Physition*" of love whose advice to the afflicted is to avoid sloth ("First practise this: An idle life forsake").[51] The lines from *DRN* reinforce the Ovidian warning by showing in devastating psychological detail the impossibility of finding satisfaction in love. Describing Salmacis's fervor, Sandys writes: "The reason why louers so strictly imbrace; is to incorporate with the beloued, which sith they cannot, can neuer be satisfied. Thus with the vanity and vexation thereof to the life expressed by *Lucretius*."[52]

Renaissance readers were right to group Lucretius and Ovid, and not just because of the *remedia amoris* tradition. As Philip Hardie has argued, parts of the *Metamorphoses* narrativize Lucretian teachings, particularly those contained in Book 4. Hardie emphasizes the importance of "ocular illusion" in *DRN*'s explanation of sensual love, and locates the same accent in Ovid's myths, arguing that Narcissus is a purposeful representation of Lucretian lessons: "Lucretius' powerful analysis and evocation of the illusions of sense perception and desire in *DRN* 4 are nowhere put to more effective use than in Ovid's fable of the credulous boy Narcissus, duped both by aural and ocular illusions, and unable to cure himself of a desire incapable of satisfaction because it is aroused by sense perceptions that do not emanate from a substantial other."[53] In *DRN* Book 4, Lucretius evocatively describes sexual desire as being like trying to quench thirst in a dream.

> ut bibere in somnis sitiens cum quaerit et umor
> non datur, ardorem qui membris stinguere possit,
> sed laticum simulacra petit frustraque laborat
> in medioque sitit torrenti flumine potans,
> sic in amore Venus simulacris ludit amantis.
>
> (*DRN* 4.1097–1101)

[As in a dream, when a man drinks, trying to allay / His thirst, but gets no real liquid to douse his body's fire, / And struggles pointlessly after mere images of water, / And though he gulps and gulps from a gushing stream, his throat is dry, / So [in love] Venus teases [lovers] with images; translation modified]

Like Lucretius's ardent adolescent, Narcissus also "struggles pointlessly after mere images of water." He is the lover—the dreamer—par excellence, who would drink from the fountain of love but cannot catch up its waters in his hands, because his desire is fueled by images and therefore insatiable.[54] The beautiful boy, tired from the chase, lies down by a fountain to quench his thirst: "dumque sitim sedare cupit, sitis altera creuit, / dumque bibit, uisae correptus imagine formae / spem sine corpore amat, corpus putat esse quod [umbra] est" (But while he tries / to quench one thirst, he feels another rise: / he drinks, but he is stricken by the sight / he sees—the image in the pool. He dreams / upon a love that's bodiless: now he / believes that what is but a shade must be a body).[55] Catching sight of himself in the pool, Narcissus falls in love with the watery figure. He mistakes his own reflection (which

Ovid calls *simulacra*, "mere images") for the real body of another person and so is inflamed with love.

> quid uideat nescit, sed quod uidet uritur illo
> atque oculos idem qui decipit incitat error.
> credule, quid frustra simulacra fugacia captas?
> quod petis est nusquam; quod amas, auertere, perdes.
> ista repercussae quam cernis imaginis umbra est.
> nil habet ista sui; tecum uenitque manetque,
> tecum discedet—si tu discedere possis.[56]

[He knows not what he sees, but what he sees / invites him. Even as the pool deceives / his eyes, it tempts them with delights. But why, / o foolish boy, do you persist? Why try / to grip an image? He does not exist—/ the one you love and long for. If you turn / away, he'll fade; the face that you discern / is but a shadow, your reflected form. / That shape has nothing of its own: it comes / with you, with you it stays; it will retreat / when you have gone—if you can ever leave!]

As in Lucretius, Narcissus mistakes an image (his reflection, or *umbra*) for the body from which it springs. His solipsism—that he falls in love with his own image—serves to emphasize the cruel separation of bodies from their alluring images. Ovid's tale reads as a warning about Lucretian love, the love fueled, but also thwarted by, images.

Ovid was one of the most imitated and influential classical authors in the Renaissance. His poetic persona was defined by two characteristics: he was an exile, and he was a lover. The latter provided a frame within which readers encountering *DRN* in full for the first time could understand the poem. *DRN* came to be associated with Ovid's *Remedia amoris*, and Lucretius to be linked with Ovid as a lover and a physician of love. It is possible that astute readers would also have associated *DRN* with Ovid's *Metamorphoses*, given that some of the most famous tales in the *Metamorphoses* contain echoes of *DRN* or even narrativize Lucretian lessons on love and ocular illusion. The Ovidian retellings of the myths of Narcissus, Pygmalion, and Actaeon—all of which draw on *DRN*—became in Petrarch's hands founding myths of Renaissance poetics. Ronsard's poetry draws on Lucretius to revise the lyric poetics to which these myths gave rise. Ironically, he uses Lucretian atomism to challenge a Petrarchan tradition that was already, at second hand, subtly Lucretian.

Ronsard's Hymns

The passages on love at the end of *DRN* Book 4 provided a significant frame for the Renaissance reception of *DRN* and were an important influence on Ronsard's love poetry. However, vernacular love lyrics are not the first place scholars have looked for the mark of Lucretius in Renaissance poetry. A far more logical site is neo-Latin poetry, particularly didactic or natural philosophical verse. The *Hymni naturales* (1497) of the Greek-born Michael Marullus, for example, were deeply indebted to Lucretian poetry. Marullus was one of the important early imitators and editors of *DRN*. Though his untimely death in 1500 prevented him from ever publishing his own edition of *DRN*, his notes and emendations exerted a major influence on later editors. Marullus's hymns, overtly Neoplatonic but with strong Lucretian strains, were important to later poets, such as Ronsard, who plundered them for material.[57] Marullus considered Lucretius a great poet of Nature, writing in his epigram 1.16 that "Natura magni versibus Lucretii / *Lepore* Musaeo illitis" (Nature is indebted to the verses, daubed by the *charm* of the Muses, of great Lucretius).[58] Marullus chooses an important Lucretian term—*lepos*—to praise the master, revealing precisely which Lucretian vision of nature so appealed to him: the springtime glory of the hymn to Venus that opens *DRN*. There, Lucretius praises Venus as "Aeneadum genetrix, hominum divumque voluptas, / alma Venus" (Life-stirring Venus, Mother of Aeneas and of Rome, / Pleasure of men and gods; *DRN* 1.1–2), she who gives life to all of nature and maintains it in its flourishing by stoking desire in all things. Fueled by a desire for Venus, "ferae pecudes persultant pabula laeta / et rapidos tranant amnis: ita capta *lepore* / te sequitur cupide quo quamque inducere pergis" (beasts, the wild and tame alike, go romping over the lush / Pastureland and swim across the rivers' headlong rush, / So eagerly does each pant after you, so do they heed, / Caught in the chains of *love*, and follow you wherever you lead; *DRN* 1.14–16, emphasis mine). Lucretius begs the goddess to inspire him as she does the teeming earth: "aeternum da dictis, diva, *leporem*" (endow my words with *grace* that never fades; *DRN* 1.28, emphasis mine). *Lepos* (charm, grace, love) is the Lucretian word for the passion for Venus that captures the hearts of the animals and the power he hopes the goddess will give his verse. The striking opening lines of *DRN* governed by Venusian charm (*lepos*) are Marullus's favorites; his hymns are shot through with images and turns of phrase from across *DRN*, but particularly from the hymn to Venus.[59]

Simone Fraisse has documented the major strands of Lucretian influence on sixteenth-century French poets: they drew primarily upon *DRN*'s great poetic set pieces, the hymn to Venus and praise of Epicurus from the proem to Book 1, and the infamous proem to Book 2, which illustrates the negative pleasure of *ataraxia* with the image of a bystander watching shipwrecked sailors.[60] The hymn to Venus is a constant touchstone in Ronsard's seasonal hymns, first published in 1563 as *Les quatre saisons de l'an* (dedicated to four secretaries of state),[61] as is the famous tribute to Epicurus.[62] In finely drawn mythological detail, Ronsard's hymns recount the origin and attributes of the seasons—hemaphroditic Spring, progenitor of them all; robust, masculine Summer and Winter; and darkly feminine Autumn.[63] The last is the outcast of the family, who is entrusted to the care of a nurse and grows up unaware of her divine origins. On the brink of adolescence, Autumn is sent to seek out her parents, Nature and Soleil. Autumn's journey takes her through the homes of two of her siblings, first the palace of Printemps, where she steals a crown of flowers, and then the seat of her brother Esté, where she takes several brilliant rays "[p]our en parer son chef" (with which to adorn her head; line 326). From there she arrives at the palace of Mother Nature, where she is met with a mind-boggling cornucopia: "Là sont dedans des pots sur des tables, encloses / Avec leurs escriteaux les semences des choses, / Que ces jeunes garçons gardent, à celle fin, / Que ce grand Univers ne prenne jamais fin" (There, held in labeled containers / On tables are the seeds of things, / Which the young men guard, so that / This great Universe never ends; lines 349–52).[64]

Like Lucretius's Venus, Ronsard's Nature cultivates the seeds of things (*les semences des choses*) to ensure the earth's cycles of fertility and reproduction. Though Autumn is also a goddess of earthly cycles and a daughter to Nature, she presents a challenge to Nature's cyclical fertility. When Autumn appears at her home, Nature drives her away, saying:

Tu perdras tout cela que la bonne froidure
De l'Hyver germera: tout ce que la verdure
Du Printemps produira, et tout ce qui croistra
De meur et de parfait quand l'Esté paroistra:

Tu feras ecouler les cheveux des bocages,
Chauves seront les bois, sans herbes les rivages,
Par ta main Phthinopore, et dessus les humains
Maligne respandras mille maux de tes mains.

(lines 361–68)

[You will destroy everything that the good chill of Winter will put
forth, everything that the greenery of Spring will produce, and
everything ripe and perfect when Summer comes; you will make the
hair of the groves fall, the woods will be bald, the riverbanks will
lack plants through your destructive hand, and you will evilly spread
with your own hands over mankind countless aches and pains.][65]

All of Nature's other children take part in her fecund cycle: Winter germi-
nates (*germera*) the seeds that Spring brings forth (*produira*), and which Summer matures (*paroistra*). Autumn, however, threatens to destroy what her
siblings have wrought with her cold and plaguey hand. Under her watch,
leaves fall from the trees and diseases flourish.[66]

Autumn is the season of disease, and Ronsard associates her above all
with the disease of love. While her mother, like Lucretius's Venus, is associated with desires that are naturalized through reproduction, Autumn is linked
to the seductive arts and the unnatural passions they produce. Autumn's
erotic appeal is one of her hymn's major themes. All four of the seasonal
hymns have romantic plotlines, but the "Hynne de l'Autonne" dwells upon
the young season's amorous education and goes behind the scenes to expose
the tricks women and goddesses use to seduce men and gods. As Autumn
nears adolescence, her nurse tells her that it is time to learn the arts of seduction—how to dance, curl her hair, appraise her appearance, and speak and
play delicately, in short, "À pratiquer d'amour l'amertume et le doux, / Et
par telle finesse acquerir un espoux" (To practice the sweet and the bitter of
love / And in this way to win a husband; lines 159–60). Lucretius warns
against this sort of feminine dissembling in *DRN* Book 4, reminding the
reader in a striking bit of potty humor that even pretty women shit, and that
it smells just as foul from a lovely as from an ugly behind. "nec Veneres
nostras hoc fallit; quo magis ipsae / omnia summo opere hos vitae poscaenia
celant / quos retinere volunt adstrictosque esse in amore" (Our Venuses are
on to this—that's why they take great pains / To hide the backstage business
of life, keeping unaware / Those whom they wish to hold bound fast, caught

in desire's snare; *DRN* 4.1185–87). This "backstage business" (*poscaenia*) is precisely what's kept out of view in the other hymns, such as "L'Hynne de l'Esté," where the reader only catches the play's final act: Esté, inflamed by a sudden passion for Ceres, taking her as his wife: "tout soudain / De sa vive chaleur luy eschaufa le sein, / La prist pour son espouse" (all at once / Her lively heat inflamed his breast, / And he took her to wife; lines 211–13). In Autumn's hymn, however, the machinery behind the curtains is revealed when Autumn's nurse explains the hard work that goes into so inflaming a man's passions and tutors her in how "[à] faire d'un sou-ris tout un peuple malade" (to make an entire people sick with one smile; line 154).[67]

As Lucretius makes quite clear in *DRN*, there is more than one sort of love, more than one Venus. There is the fecund springtime goddess of Book 1, *alma Venus* (*DRN* 1.2), who drives all things under the sun to flourish and reproduce. Then there is the dangerous seductress of Book 4, who drives lovers to madness. This is also our Venus (Haec Venus est nobis; *DRN* 4.1058)—Lucretius writes, having just described how deeply the weapons of Venus (Veneris . . . telis; *DRN* 4.1052) can wound. The Venus of Book 4 tricks lovers with fantasies (sic in amore Venus simulacris ludit amantis; *DRN* 4.1101), capturing them in love's snares (Veneris . . . nodos; *DRN* 4.1148). To the first Venus we owe everything; the second must be avoided and contained. It is the Venus of Book 4, she of erotic fantasy, lust, and obsession, who dominates in Ronsard's sonnets. Even in the hymns, written under the aegis of *alma Venus*, she persists, particularly in the "Hynne de l'Autonne." While Ronsard's Nature is aligned with the Lucretian Venus of *DRN* Book 1, that springtime goddess of natural fertility, Autumn evokes the dangerous Venus of *DRN* Book 4, the siren who carries the amorous plague of erotic obsession. Both are goddesses of love, but different loves: Nature promises birth and regeneration, Autumn disease.

As in *DRN*, where the lustful obsession of Book 4 is presented as a threat to the healthy reproduction of Book 1, in the "Hynne de l'Autonne," Autumn's type of love threatens to pervert and destroy Nature's.[68] The *peste* that Autumn sends through her future husband Bacchus's bones is one of the many *maladies* at her disposal, for hers is the season of illness and wildfire plagues. Ronsard highlights this attribute in his account of Autumn's journey to find her parents. When she goes to seek Auton, the south wind associated with her season, to ask him for passage to the Heavens, she encounters the den of "vieille Maladie," depicted as an old wolf giving teat to her swarming litter of diseases.

Elle avoit un grand rang de tetaces tirées
Longues comme boyaux, par le bout deschirées,
Que d'un muffle affamé une engence de maux
Luy suçoyent tout ainsi que petits animaux,
Qu'elle (qui doucement sur sa race se veautre)
De son col retourné lechoit l'un apres l'autre,
Pour leur former le corps en autant de façons
Qu'on voit dedans la mer de sortes de poissons,
De sablons sur la rade, et de fleurs au rivage
Quand le jeune Printemps descouvre son visage.
        Là comme petits loups les caterres couvoit,
Et là la fiévre quarte et tierce se trouvoit,
Enflures flux de sang langueurs hydropisies,
La toux ronge-poumon, jaunisse pleuresies,
Lenteurs pestes charbons tournoyement de cerveau,
Et rongnes dont l'ardeur fait allumer la peau.

                                        (lines 193–208)

[she had a long row of elongated teats, as long as entrails, frayed at
the ends, and they were being sucked ravenously by a mob of aches
and pains, just like little animals, which she, gently sprawling over
her offspring, licked in turn with upraised neck, in order to fashion
their bodies in as many shapes as we can see monstrous fish in the
sea, grains of sand on the road, and flowers on the riverbank when
early Spring reveals his face. There she kept warm, just like wolf
cubs, Catarrhs, and there could be found quartan and tertian Fevers,
Swellings, flows of blood, Langors, Dropsies, lung-gnawing Coughs,
Jaundices, Pleuresies, Clamminess, Plagues, Carbuncles, dizziness,
and the mange, whose heat burns the skin.][69]

Vieille Maladie presents a perverted vision of fertility: whereas Nature cultivates the seeds of things to ensure that the world never ends, vieille Maladie
nurtures disease-pups that will kill those very seeds. Lucretius's springtime
Venus, whom Ronsard's Nature so much resembles, causes all things to
flourish. It is she "quae mare navigerum, quae terras frugiferentis / concelebras" (throng[s] the fruited earth / And the ship-freighted sea; *DRN* 1.3–4).
For her, "inde ferae pecudes persultant pabula laeta / et rapidos tranant
amnis . . ." (beasts, the wild and tame alike, go romping over the lush /

Pastureland; *DRN* 1.14–15). Ronsard uses the same language for the offspring of vieille Maladie, comparing them to fish in the sea, the sands, and the flowers that rise up to greet spring, yet this is no springtime fertility, but rather a perversion and destruction of it.

Conclusion

Simone Fraisse, the great scholar of antique and French literature who in 1962 authored what is to this day the only book-length monograph on the sixteenth-century French reception of Lucretius, was frustrated by what she saw as the Pléiade poets' lack of responsiveness to the resources Lucretius made available to love poetry: "The modern reader is rather disappointed to see how little love poets drew from *De rerum natura*."[70] Fraisse argues that in terms of Lucretian borrowings there was little or no development from the early sixteenth century to the full bloom of the French Renaissance in the second half of the century.[71] Like their predecessors, the Pléiade poets failed to feel and reproduce the full force of Lucretius's voluptuous tribute to Venus in Book 1 of *DRN*, and reduced the "magnificent hymn to the eternal powers of fecund nature" to a few elegant images and even more tired clichés.[72]

Though the analysis of her book focuses on borrowings from the hymn to Venus, Fraisse recognized that Lucretius has more than one Venus, *DRN* more than one resource for love poets. She is even more scathing about the perceived failure of the Pléiade poets to attend to Book 4 of *DRN*: "There is more: in book four, Lucretius wrote great, daring, and sometimes painful pages on love. They left not a single trace in the poetry of the Pléiade. Were they feared for their honesty and their cruelty? It seems, quite simply, that nobody read them."[73] In the preceding pages, I have focused on this Venus, and this Lucretius, and have tried to show that this Venus, this *DRN*, *was* an organizing theme in both Ronsard's love poetry and his seasonal hymns. Though Ronsard obviously knew and appreciated the hymn to Venus, he turns more often to the Lucretius—and Venus—of *DRN* Book 4. Ronsard's Lucretius is above all a theorist of the imagination and of love, as well as a practitioner of the *remedia amoris*. Ronsard found that this Lucretius spoke to key themes in Renaissance lyric, and used him to contest and revise the lyric traditions of his age.

Poetry in a Time of War: Lucretius and Poetic Patrimony in Pierre de Ronsard's *Sonnets pour Helene* and Remy Belleau's *Pierres précieuses*

Pierre de Ronsard remained engaged with Lucretius throughout his career as a sonneteer.[1] His final sonnet collections, the first and second books of the *Sonnets pour Helene* (1578), reprise favored Lucretian leitmotifs from the early sonnets but endow them with new, politicized, meanings. Written in the midst of the French Wars of Religion (1562–1598) about a woman who shares a name with Helen of Troy (whose story famously combines love and conflict), the *Sonnets pour Helene* is deeply invested in questions of war and French history in a way that the 1552 *Amours*, written before the outbreak of the conflict, are not. In the later collection, the political context in France and the mythical echoes of Hélène de Surgères's richly evocative name place an enormous pressure on issues of specificity and iterability. Playing on the lady's name, Ronsard reflects on what it means to write French poetry as the inheritor of a long classical and continental poetic tradition. This is bound up with another, related, question, of what it means to love and write about women, like Hélène de Surgères, or earlier, Cassandra Salviati, whose names recall the women (Helen of Troy; Cassandra, the thwarted Trojan prophetess and daughter of Priam and Hecuba) who inspired so much classical poetry. Ronsard's sonnets purport to praise specific women, but they also court repetition. The question, as Ronsard puts it in the first line of the twenty-second sonnet of the first book of *Amours*, is how to "[c]ent et cent foys penser un penser mesme" (to think the same thought hundreds of times). In the context of the 1552 *Amours*, the issue is likely one of how to write hundreds of sonnets about the same woman, but in the *Sonnets pour Helene* such a question takes on historical, and literary historical, dimensions: In what sense is the sixteenth-century Frenchwoman an echo, or a copy, of Helen of Troy? How do Ronsard's poems echo, or repeat, ancient models?

It is in the midst of such questions that the Lucretian *simulacrum*, a concept fundamentally concerned with originality, imitation, and iterability, comes to play a role in Ronsard's politically and historically minded later sonnets. The *Sonnets pour Helene* draw on the conceptual affordances of the *simulacrum* to answer difficult questions about the place of French poetry in both European literary history and in the context of the Wars of Religion. Ronsard was not alone in applying Lucretius's erotic tropes to the political crises of his time. His friend and fellow Pléiade poet Remy Belleau also pushes Lucretius's thinking on the *simulacrum* into the realm of politics, using it to think about how the wars endanger the development of French letters as well as France's place in literary history. While *DRN* is deeply concerned with questions of war and state, Lucretius does not link the *simulacrum* explicitly to these issues. Ronsard and Belleau do, innovating on Lucretius's own treatment of the relation between love, war, and poetry. In Chapter 1, I argued that Ronsard's sonnets use Lucretius to mediate Renaissance lyric traditions and rethink poetry's power to act within and upon the material world. While that chapter focused on epistemological questions, this chapter turns to politics to explore how Ronsard and Belleau exploit the *simulacrum* to think about the stakes of poetic production in a time of war.

Ronsard and Belleau may have felt a kinship with Lucretius as poets of civil war. Although the date of *DRN*'s composition is contested, the poem was undoubtedly written sometime before or during Rome's civil war between Pompey and Caesar (49–45 BCE), and many features of the poem refer to civil unrest.[2] The poem's opening hymn to Venus is explicit on this point. The first line of *DRN* reminds readers that Venus is the mother of Aeneas (*Aeneadum genetrix*), and thus the mother of Rome as well.[3] Positioning Venus as a protector of his city, Lucretius asks her to bring peace to Romans by intervening with her lover, the war-god Mars, to "effice ut interea fera moenera militiai . . . omnis sopita quiescant" ([m]ake the mad machinery of war drift off to sleep; *DRN* 1.29–30).[4] Her power of love offsets and subdues his bellicosity. Europe in the sixteenth and seventeenth centuries was riven by conflicts both civil and international, and Lucretius's experience and explicit thematization of writing as a poet during wartime resonated with early modern poets who were also negotiating the relationship between poetry and conflict. French poets like Ronsard and Belleau used Lucretius to think about the experience of the French Wars of Religion and the role of poets in France during the wars. Later English poets, including Lucy Hutchinson and Margaret Cavendish, discussed in Chapters 4 and 5, respectively, also negotiated *DRN*'s political resonances during the English Civil War and Protectorate.

Myth and Image in Ronsard's *Sonnets pour Helene*

In the *Sonnets pour Helene*, Ronsard repeatedly reflects upon the relationship between love and war, particularly the appropriateness or usefulness of writing love poetry in a time of armed conflict. In a sonnet originally published as part of the *Amours diverses* (1578), but later included as the twenty-sixth sonnet of the *Second livre des Sonnets pour Helene*, he asks: "Au milieu de la guerre, en un siecle sans foy, / Entre mille procez, est-ce pas grand' folie / D'escrire de l'Amour?" (In a time of war, in a faithless century, / Amidst a thousand trials, is it not madness / To write of Love? lines 1–3). In sonnet 51 of the *Premier livre des Sonnets pour Helene*, however, he anticipates his own question with an answer that evokes Lucretius's hymn to Venus. Love itself can bring war to an end.

> Si les François avoient les ames allumees
> D'amour ainsi que moy, nous serions en repos:
> Les champs de Montcontour n'eussent pourry nos os,
> Ny Dreuz ny Jazeneuf n'eussent veu nos armees.
>
> Venus, va mignarder les moustaches de Mars:
> Conjure ton guerrier de tes benins regars,
> Qu'il nous donne la paix, et de tes bras l'enserre.
>
> (lines 5–11)

[If the souls of the French were inflamed / With love, like mine, we would rest easy: / Our bones would not rot on the fields of Montcontour, / Nor would Dreuz and Jazeneuf have seen our armies. / Venus, go toy with Mars's mustache: / Entice your warrior with gentle glances / Into giving us peace, and encircle him in your arms.]

Ronsard paraphrases Lucretius's hopeful scenario of Venus seducing Mars away from battle: "Effice ut . . . ," pleads Lucretius. "Conjure . . . ," begs Ronsard. Inflamed with love, preoccupied by poetry, Ronsard himself offers a positive example to his countrymen: if all Frenchmen were in love, they would wield pens instead of arms, write sonnets instead of going into battle.

Ronsard also offers a second (and contradictory) argument for the power of love poetry: that love itself is a kind of war. Sonnet 63 of the *Premier livre des Sonnets pour Helene*, the penultimate poem in the collection, opens with the stark contrast between Ronsard's sonnet-writing and the battles raging around him in France.

> Je faisois ces Sonnets en l'antre Pieride,
> Quand on vit les François sous les armes suer,
> Quand on vit tout le peuple en fureur se ruer,
> Quand Bellone sanglante alloit devant pour guide.
>
> (lines 1–4)

[I wrote these sonnets in the Pierian cave / When Frenchmen could be seen sweating in their armour / When everyone could be seen rushing around in a fury, / When bloody Bellona went before them as a guide.]

Though Ronsard draws a sharp distinction here between his poetic retreat and the crowded battlefield, his repeated calls to observe the costs of war— *Quand on vit . . . Quand on vit . . .* —also recall the insistent invitations in the first sonnet of the first book of his *Amours* to bear witness to his struggle with love.

> Qui voudra voyr comme un Dieu me surmonte,
> Comme il m'assault, comme il se fait vainqueur
> . . . .
> Qui voudra voir une jeunesse prompte
> A suyvre en vain l'object de son malheur,
> Me vienne voir.
>
> (lines 1–2, 5–7)

[Whoever wants see how Love has mastered me, / How he assails and conquers me . . . Whoever wants to see youth / Ready to vainly follow the object of its pain / Look to me.]

The echo between the two sonnets, the first composed at the very beginning of Ronsard's career as a sonneteer, the second at the very end, frames the trajectory of Ronsard's lyric career as one of extended amorous battle. Moreover, it emphatically connects the anguish of love with that of war. Thus, though the later sonnet frames the writing of love poetry as both a withdrawal from war and a relief from war (Ronsard writes in the ninth line of the sonnet that poetry can "tromper les soucis d'un temps si vicieux" [assuage the cares of such a vicious time]), the sonnet as a whole reveals love, and love poetry, to have more in common with war than it may at first appear. The final tercet of the sonnet ends on an almost heroic note, with Ronsard, champion of love, declaring: "L'autre guerre est cruelle, et la mienne est gentille: / La mienne finiroit par un combat de deux, / Et l'autre ne pourroit par un camp de cent mille" (That other war is cruel, but mine is pleasant: / Mine will end in one-to-one combat / While a hundred thousand in battle could not end the other war; lines 12–14).

When the *Sonnets pour Helene* came out in 1578, Ronsard was already in his midfifties, and the lady to whom the collection was dedicated, Hélène de Surgères, was no longer young herself. Ronsard brilliantly exploits the idea of the older man as Petrarchist and the older woman as his beloved by using her *âge*, or "age," as a clever way to discuss the problems of contemporary France—the historical *âge* in which they both live. Thus, when Ronsard declares midway through sonnet 12 of the *Premier livre des Sonnets pour Helene*, "Je me sens bien-heureux d'estre nay de son âge" (I am happy to have been born of her age; line 9), it could mean either at her age, or in the same historical period as her.

Lucretius provides Ronsard with the pivot between old age, *âge*, and the problems of the historical age, also *âge*. The Lucretian theory of *simulacra* organizes the historical dynamic of the *Sonnets*, which muster what has always been at the core of myth—a temporality that transcends historical specificity through iterability—by eschewing the primacy and superiority of the original and embracing the *simulacrum*. One reason the *simulacrum* is such a potent idea in the *Sonnets pour Helene* is because the myth of Helen of Troy contains its own story about images. Herodotus, Stesichorus, and Euripides (and, in a different way, Homer) all explore the idea that the Helen who was the cause of the Trojan War was not the real woman, but rather her *eidōlon*, image or likeness, created by Hera after the judgment of Paris. As Euripides tells it in his play *Helen*, the real Helen was never actually present in Troy at all, and waited out the entire war in Egypt.

The duality of the *simulacrum*, which occupies a place in a material hierarchy but also admits and sometimes encourages confusion between the real and the phantasmatic, offers Ronsard an array of theoretical affordances for thinking about hierarchy and multiplicity, which he uses to subvert the historical and literary primacy of Helen of Troy over Hélène de Surgères. By upending the relationship between model and copy, body and image, Ronsard can prioritize the Frenchwoman over Helen of Troy, even while admitting the temporal priority of the Greek original. Or, at other times, the *simulacrum* enables the effacement of the real woman—Hélène de Surgères —and establishes in her place the possibility of Helen, a *simulacrum* disassociated from the corporeal and thus temporally mobile, a string of Helens across time and across myth. In sonnet 12 of the *Premier livre des Sonnets pour Helene*, the priority between original and copy is reversed when Ronsard compares his beloved to Venus: "Deux Venus en Avril (puissante Deité) / Nasquirent, l'une en Cypre, et l'autre en la Saintogne" (In April, two Venuses [powerful Goddess] / Were born, the one in Cyprus, and the other in Saintonge; lines 1–2). Ronsard takes up the ideas of *eidōlon* and *simulacrum*, related concepts from two different traditions, to claim that his beloved is not a copy of Helen of Troy, or in any way derivative. Rather, she is the original: "La Venus Cyprienne est des Grecs la mensonge, / La chaste Saintongeoise est une verité" (The Cypriot Venus is a Greek lie, / The chaste Santongeoise is true; lines 3–4).

The upshot of this comparison, which could seem like base flattery, is that Ronsard construes a literary object—Hélène de Surgères—equal to Helen of Troy, even to Venus. Through the doubleness of the *simulacrum*, he effects a *translatio imperii et studii*, transferring political legitimacy along with poetic content and valorizing France as an empire and French as a literary language in complex comparison with Troy and the depictions in both Latin and Greek of the Trojan War and of Venus. We can think back to the line with which I began my discussion of the *Sonnets*: when midway through sonnet 12 of the *Premier livre des Sonnets pour Helene* Ronsard declares, "Je me sens bien-heureux d'estre nay de son âge" (I am happy to have been born of her age; line 9), just as he declared in the fourth sonnet, "Bien-heureux qui l'adore, et qui vit de son temps!" (Happy is he who worships her, and who lives in her time! line 14). Ronsard seems to be emphasizing the lady's now-ness, her glorious contemporaneity. Nevertheless, as vehemently as Ronsard claims to fix the lady in his present, his real goal is to locate her in ancient Greece as well as in sixteenth-century France. Her moment can be infused with both not because these times and places are the same, but because their radical difference is newly mediated by the *simulacrum*. What starts as a rethinking of a stock trope of love poetry—falling in love with images—in Ronsard's adroit hands becomes a question of myth, literary and imperial power, and how to stabilize an unstable political present with the status and heft of a historico-mythical imperium. In using the tropes of love poetry to accomplish this, Ronsard also spells out the ways that even the lightest of genres, the sonnet, might build history, and even a poet might perform politics. The *Sonnets*, in short, valorize their own genre as well as France.

Art and State in Remy Belleau's Prometheus and Ixion Poems

Although Remy Belleau is today far less well-known than Ronsard, he was acknowledged by his contemporaries as one of the most innovative members members of the Pléiade, and the most erudite.[5] He wrote across traditions and took special pleasure in new and uncommon genres, producing among other things a translation of the Anacreontic odes, a pastoral compilation, a commentary on Ronsard's second book of *Amours*, sacred eclogues translated from the Song of Songs, poems about assorted small objects, and a collection of poems about precious stones.[6] Belleau's poetry provides an excellent case study in how painstakingly sixteenth-century French poets responded to and expanded upon Lucretius's demanding vision of poetry's political role. Belleau appreciated the implications that *DRN*'s forays into the language of pleasure and the genres of love have for politics as well as for poetry. For Belleau, working through the text, language, and themes of *DRN* was a way to propose how poetry could participate in the stabilization and perpetuation of the turbulent French nation, wracked by the Wars of Religion. In *Les amours et nouveaux eschanges des pierres précieuses* (1576, hereafter *Pierres*), Belleau, a careful reader of Lucretius, uses desire as a master metaphor for

both politics and art, drawing inspiration from *DRN*'s persistent thematization of erotics; like Ronsard, Belleau uses Lucretian erotics as a way of thinking sixteenth-century French politics. He combines what at first glance
appear to be sharply opposed Lucretian treatments of desire in order to articulate a particular vision of French patrimony. The *Pierres* is an important site
for this thinking because the stones operate as emblems of a French land
being despoiled of its literary heritage (and possible literary futures) by war,
but also because through his discussions of gems and their craftsmen Belleau
can broach broader questions about artistic production and image-making in
general.

Expounding Epicurean philosophy in verse, Lucretius adapts Greek and
Latin love lyric traditions to express the central Epicurean concept of *ataraxia*
(mental calm), as well as its opposite, mental torment, through the tropes
and vocabulary of love poetry. In *DRN*, the frenzies of lust provide a vocabulary for everything from the cycles of nature (Book 1) to the vagaries of sense
perception (Book 4). Moreover, Lucretius's appeals to Venus to serve as his
muse and guide his project to fruition amid the disruptions of the Roman
civil wars brings war and peace, too, into the orbit of pleasure: the goddess is
beseeched to seduce warlike Mars to bring peace to Romans. Thus—in a
departure from Epicurus, who believed that one must remove oneself from
the world to achieve *ataraxia*, an ideal accomplished in his secluded garden
school—Lucretius politicizes *ataraxia* as much as he eroticizes it.[7] In *DRN*,
ataraxia gains political currency as a concept that can describe national unrest
as well as individual turmoil.

In its early modern reception, *DRN*'s simultaneously erotic and political
treatment of *ataraxia* yields two "plots" that map *ataraxia* and the peaceful
state, or conversely, mental disturbance and the state of war, onto romantic
scenarios. The first plot takes the form of a conventional courtship, where
moderate affection and mutual compatibility yield stability and a healthy
family. The second showcases the melancholic lover of Petrarchan verse, the
youth whose burning passion typically goes unfulfilled, threatening to destroy
him. The key features of these plots are also drawn from *DRN*, specifically
from the hymn to Venus that opens Book 1, and from the end of Book 4, with
its mutually reinforcing accounts of sense perception and lust. The critical
reception of *DRN* from the classical to the contemporary has tended to divide
"good" from "bad" desire and align them with these two sections of the poem.
With its idyllic springtime setting and capering young animals, the hymn has
been understood as a positive vision of desire as natural profusion and healthy

procreation. As such, it appears to be directly opposed to the ravishing description of lust that overshadows Book 4, which in comparison to Book 1 reads as a scathing denunciation of desire, sex, and even love. In such a reading, the hymn's vision of nature—roused by Venus to an unbroken cycle of desire and procreation—is that of the Epicurean garden writ large, a naturalist vision of *ataraxia*. Although desire drives animals to procreate, Nature as a whole maintains her equilibrium because of their coupling. Book 4, on the other hand, offers a perverse and unsettling vision of lust. Here, the human lovers are plagued by amorous fantasies and ravaging desires. Unlike the naturalized desire of Book 1, Book 4's lust is revealed to be onanistic and sterile.

For Belleau, nature's vigorous but balanced procreative cycles in Lucretius's hymn to Venus evoke a pastoral vision of natural abundance and a well-governed state, whereas Book 4's raging but impotent lust suggests a fever dream of war and civil unrest. The commonsense link between sexual desire and the state was no less compelling for being so simple—procreation. In Belleau's time, the religious wars made issues of family and offspring all the more pressing: with Catholics and Protestants violently opposed to one another, royal marriages could determine the faith of a whole country and force mass conversions (and executions). The generation of healthy heirs (hopefully within the legal bonds of marriage) is the foundation of monarchy, and it is in the context of this basic dynastic imperative that several of Belleau's poems call upon the dichotomized plots of Lucretian desire to symbolically consolidate hierarchy and the means of producing and preserving civil power.

It is ironic that Lucretius, who worked so zealously to dismantle the power the gods held over men's minds, should serve to articulate divine and monarchical hierarchies, yet this is precisely his function in Belleau's retellings of certain pagan and Old Testament stories, where the sexual peccadilloes of rulers and rebels illustrate the success and failure of human governments. Both Belleau's pastoral compilation, the *Bergerie*, and his *Pierres* include poems about Ixion and Prometheus that use *DRN* Book 4's account of lust for erotic images to dramatize the destruction of the hierarchies that stabilize human life—the family and the state—while also proposing a stability grounded in artistic as well as sexual (re)production. These poems intensify Lucretius's attention to the role poetry might play in political stability. The poem about Ixion ("L'amour ambitieux d'Ixion," from the *Seconde journée de la Bergerie*, published in 1572) and the two poems about Prometheus (the

"Complainte de Promethee" from the *Seconde journée de la Bergerie* and "Pro-méthée premier inventeur des anneaux et de l'enchasseure des pierres," from the *Pierres*) magnify the prominence Lucretius gives poetry by adapting *DRN* Book 4's description of erotic images into a commentary on image-making in general, not just the production of children, but also artistic production. By combining the image-making that is procreation with the image-making that is artistic creation, the Prometheus poems in particular depict stable society as the pairing of procreative and creative acts. While Belleau's use of Lucretius is socially conservative (against the antireligious orientation of *DRN* itself), his use of Lucretian poetics is radical, pushing beyond even his source's construction of poetry's practical and political uses.

While Belleau's Prometheus poems tend toward social stability, "L'amour ambitieux d'Ixion" describes the consequences of disrupting social and religious hierarchies. Like the classical myth from which it is drawn, the poem describes a man whose lust for both blood and sex endangers not only the structures that support the institution of the family but also the boundaries between gods and men.[8] The poem opens with a gleeful account of Ixion's pride and the devastating ingenuity of Jupiter, the god who puts him in his place: "Je chante d'Ixion l'emprise audacieuse: / L'impudence, l'orgeuil, et l'idole venteuse" (I sing of Ixion's audacious endeavour: / Of his impudence, his pride, and his airy idol).[9] Jupiter has forgiven Ixion for the sin of murdering his father-in-law, and as a token of mercy invites the mortal to dine with the gods. Puffed up with pride and poisoned by ingratitude, Ixion has the gall to fall in love with Juno, his host's wife. Outraged, the goddess tells her husband about the human's advances, and Jupiter concocts a punishment for the impudent Ixion, creating a fake Juno, an avatar of clouds, which he sends to the human (this is the "idole venteuse" of the first lines). Unaware that she is a mere replica of the real Juno, Ixion attacks and impregnates this "fille de la nuë" (daughter of clouds; line 237), who later gives birth to the Centaurs. Ixion's punishment is in keeping with his crime: having put on airs and grown intoxicated on the vapors of ambition, he falls for a creature of clouds and air.

Both Belleau and Lucretius rely on the theme of lust to explore the frontiers between humans and gods, bodies and images. The first two lines of *DRN*, where Lucretius invokes Venus as "Aeneadum genetrix, hominum divumque voluptas, / alma Venus" (Life-stirring Venus, Mother of Aeneas and of Rome, / Pleasure of men and gods), make clear the poem's interest in what can be a dangerously porous boundary between humans and gods, one most often breached because of lust. Goddess, mother to one of the greatest mortals ever to live, lover to both mortals and deities and equally beloved by both, Venus with her charms charts the dangerous path between gods and men.

If the Lucretian hymn to Venus presents a naturalist portrait of earthly stability as vigorous procreation, Belleau's poem about Ixion offers a horrific counterpoint of wasteful lust and bastard genealogies. The poem paraphrases its account of lust directly from Book 4 of *DRN*, using it to signal the dangers of ambition and breaking hierarchy. The power of Belleau's verse here owes much to Lucretius: the description of Ixion's lust for the cloud-Juno reworks the Roman poet's breathtaking description of sexual fantasy and thwarted desire in Book 4. Lucretius there explains that sexual desire is produced by images—*simulacra*—constituted by the effluvia of atoms emanating from bodies. Longing for images, but loving with bodies, lovers tear at each other trying to grasp the *simulacra* that enchanted them: "faciuntque dolorem / corporis et dentis inlidunt saepe labellis / osculaque adfligunt" (they hurt the flesh by their possessing, / Often sinking teeth in lips, and crushing as they kiss; *DRN* 4.1079–81). They do so because "Venus simulacris ludit amantis / nec satiare queunt spectando corpora coram" (Venus teases [lovers] with images—lovers can't satisfy / The flesh however they devour each other with the eye; *DRN* 4.1101–2, translation modified). From *DRN* Book 4's sadistic spectacle of infinitely thwarted satisfaction, Belleau identifies two crucial elements: that love feeds on empty images rather than the meat of real bodies, and the compelling description of desperate lovers teased by amorous *simulacra*. Belleau's rendition of the passage follows Lucretius closely. When Ixion sees the "idole" of Juno he mistakes her for the real goddess, substituting image for body as Lucretius's lovers do.

> Il l'embrasse, et la baise, et comme furieux,
> Luy presse l'estomach, mord la bouche et les yeux,
> Les levres, et le col de la feinte menteuse,
> Appaisant les fureurs de sa flamme amoureuse
> D'embrassemens legers, et d'un baiser pipeur
> Sous le vif contrefait de l'image trompeur:
> Sucçotant, mordillant, à petites secousses
> Le coural imité de ses deux levres douces.

> (lines 183–90)[10]

[He embraces it, kisses it, and maddened / Grabs its belly, bites the mouth and eyes, / The lips and the neck of the lying illusion, / Quenching the fury of his amorous flame / In sweet entanglements and with a trickster kiss / On the lively counterfeit of the fraudulent image: / Sucking, nibbling, with little tugs / The imitated coral of its two sweet lips.]

Jupiter's weapon, the "amoureux nuage" (amorous cloud; line 138) that stands in for Juno, is a Lucretian *simulacrum*, a love-image substituting for the real body that drives its admirer to frenzies of passion and violence. Like the lover in Lucretius, Ixion is damned to paw and bite at an image.

Belleau is a particularly interesting instance in Lucretian reception history because he links two tropes that are unrelated in *DRN* in order to develop Lucretius's already notable emphasis on poetry into a more robust argument for how poetry interacts with politics. "L'amour ambitieux d'Ixion" broadens the implications of the Lucretian *simulacrum*, which in Belleau's hands discloses not just a theory of sight or lust (as in Lucretius), but also of the (re)production of art and political and social stability. In *DRN*, the *simulacrum* as amorous fantasy expresses the torments of a mind that has lost *ataraxia*. Belleau goes beyond Lucretius, yoking the concepts of *simulacrum* and *ataraxia* together in order to express artistic potential. The *simulacrum*'s implications for art already come into play in Belleau's description of the airy image of Juno that Jupiter painstakingly crafts (in line 4 it is called an "[o]uvrage industrieux") to fool Ixion. Transforming the *simulacrum* into an artistic image, Belleau comes full circle to the question that so interested Lucretius himself: how art, particularly poetry, participates in stabilizing states.

By interpreting the *simulacrum* as an artistic, and not just a sensory, image, Belleau transcends the unsophisticated love plots that have been mapped onto *DRN* in order to allegorize political stability without ever mentioning sex. Instead, he foregrounds artistic production. Belleau's two poems about Prometheus, the "Complainte de Promethee," from the *Seconde journée de la Bergerie*, and "Prométhée premier inventeur des anneaux et de l'enchasseure des pierres," from the *Pierres*, trace a narrative similar to that of the Ixion poem—an upstart tries to steal for man what belongs rightfully to the gods—but have the opposite outcome. Like "L'amour ambitieux d'Ixion," they pivot on Lucretius's explanation of amorous *simulacra*, but instead of

the plot allegorizing mental and social unreset as lust, the story of Prometheus
is framed as a new narrative about how art produces social stability.

In Belleau's "Complainte de Promethee," Prometheus offers a positive
model of image-making as human creativity and creation. His original creative act is the shaping of man with the fire he stole from the gods. It is
Prometheus "[q]ui premiere entreprit d'une main larronnesse, / Mesme
dedans le sein, et sous la main maistresse / De ce grand Jupiter, de desrober
le feu / Pur, celeste, et divin" (who first undertook, with thieving hands, / In
the very bosom, and under the guiding hand / Of great Jupiter, to steal fire /
Pure, celestial, and divine; lines 45–48). Before Prometheus's theft of fire,
men were like clay effigies, thick with earth but brittle and fragile, prone to
breakage and dissolution, like things that a potter would make at his wheel
(lines 49–56). Men were dead, "sans aër, sans feu, sans esprit, et sans ame"
(without breath, without fire, without spirit, without soul; line 57), but Prometheus fires these dead forms (again, like a potter), injecting breath and
spirit into brute matter. The resolute materiality of Prometheus's creation
stands in opposition to Ixion's airy lover and his offspring's vacuous ambition. The materiality of Prometheus's men, even after they are imbued with
fire, bespeaks exactly the sort of animal vitality that both Jupiter's Juno-
simulacrum and Ixion's "children" lack. Unlike Ixion, head in the clouds, this
earthly man is humble. Though brought to life with divine fire, he does not
aspire beyond his station. Instead, it is he

> Qui a fait et basti des temples et des villes,
> Rengé les citoyens dessous les lois civiles,
> Et les peuples errans tous ralié en un,
> Fait fumer les autels, d'encens et de parfun.

> (lines 201–4)

> [Who shaped and built temples and cities, / Organized citizens
> under civil laws, / And gathered the wandering people into one, /
> And made the altars smoke with incense and perfume.]

Prometheus's man creates a civil society that praises rather than threatens the
gods: instead of breaking the heavens and rupturing hierarchy, these people
live under peaceful laws, tilling the land and keeping their altars lit.

Prometheus's first creation, man, motivates his second, rings. Belleau's
second Promethus poem, "Prométhée premier inventeur des anneaux et de

l'enchasseure des pierres" (appropriately included in his collection of poems about gemstones, the *Pierres*) describes the birth of fine gem work. After Hercules frees Prometheus from his chains, Destiny decides that Prometheus's theft of the eternal flame ought to be immortalized in some way so that it would be remembered forever. For this reason, Prometheus "[q]u'à jamais dans le doigt porteroit, attachée / Dans un anneau de fer, une pierre arrachée / Au sommet bruineux du roc Caucasien" (always wore on his finger, set / In an iron ring, a stone taken from / The foggy summit of the Caucasian rock).[11] The earlier "Complainte de Promethee" had already positioned Prometheus as not just the maker of men, but also as the first artisan and father of all the arts, a man "qui pour enrichir les premieres beautez / Du monde malpoli a les arts inventez" (who invented the arts / to enrich the first beauties of the brute earth; lines 215–16). In "Prométhé, premier inventeur des Anneaux et de l'enchasseure des Pierres" he focuses his point on gem work, writing that Prometheus is the first to "mist la pierre en œuvre/ Dans un anneau de fer, industrieux manœuvre" (set a stone / In an iron ring, a clever move; lines 67–68). The *œuvre / manœuvre* rhyme stresses the connection between the crime—an undercover raid—and the creation.

Like all fine art forms, the fancy work of gems and rings participates in the glorification of the state, perpetuating power by ennobling it with beauty and riches. Prometheus's ring thus marks and upholds his political achievement: the making of a ring commemorates the creation of man and the foundation of civil society, but also supports that society. That first ring of Caucasian stone generates a long and increasingly illustrious tradition reinforcing the glory and might of kings.

> Du fer on vint au cuivre, et à l'estain encor,
> De l'estain à l'argent, et de l'argent à l'or,
> Des pierres d'un rocher aux pierres plus eslites,
> Emeraudes, Rubis, Diamans, Chrysolithes.
> Et cela qui restoit pour marque d'un malheur,
> Des Princes et des Rois fust la gloire et l'honneur.
>
> (lines 69–74)

[From iron we came to copper, and then to pewter, / From pewter to silver, and from silver to gold, / From stones out of rocks to more rareified stones, / Emeralds, Rubies, Diamonds, Chrysoliths, / And

that which was the emblem of some misfortune, / Became the glory
of Princes and of Kings.]

Belleau nimbly reminds his readers that precious stones, no matter how
murky their origins or occult their uses (these he explores in the *Pierres*), are
always reminders of courtly economies of economic and symbolic power and
the grandeur and nobility of kings. Procreative genealogies and artistic economies stabilize the state by re-producing it. Using *DRN*, which makes desire a
master metaphor for both nature and poetry, Belleau presents not just nature
but also poetry as cyclical. Like genealogy, artistic traditions cycle, regenerate,
and perpetuate when, as with Prometheus, a single act of creativity becomes
an artisanal tradition, and what was elsewhere figured as sexual desire
becomes creative force.

Poets, Kings, and the Pleasures of Narrative

Belleau's final collection of poetry proposes a vision of artistic productivity
similar to the one developed in the Prometheus poems as a vision of French
patrimony. Like the *Bergerie*, with its idyllic vision of pastoral economies, the
Pierres present a coherent vision of French poetry's social and political utility.
The collection, which was published in the same volume as two collections
of Belleau's religious poetry, the *Discours de la vanité* and the *Églogues sacrées*,
was dedicated to the French king, Henry III. The collection, display, and
exchange of gemstones was particularly popular at Henry's court: the king
himself collected gems, as did Belleau, whose will includes a list of his treasures.[12] The *Pierres* graft an interest in political power onto a minor vein of
natural history writing (the lapidary). Tapping into long traditions of natural
philosophical writings on stones, Belleau draws comparisons between political leadership and the control of nature. King David is the central figure in
this constellation of political and natural power. In David, the famous biblical poet-king, royal and natural philosophical powers are wedded. In chapter
1 of Belleau's *Discours de la vanité*, David ruefully remembers his now-lost
dominion over Israel and nature alike.

> J'ay porté d'Israel le sceptre dans la main,
> J'ay pressé sous le joug les ondes du Jourdain,
> J'ay fouillé, j'ay cherché pour sçavoir et connestre

Toute ame qui soupire, et qui vivant prend estre
Sous la voûte du Ciel, pour sçavoir les raisons,
Le tour et le retour des temps et des saisons,
Ouvrant le sein fecond de la mere Nature,
Qui donne le tetin à toute creature:
Et croy que ce grand Dieu transmist ce vain desir
Dans le cueur des humains, non pas pour le plaisir,
Mais pour les travailler, et les tenir en crainte,
Alterez de sçavoir sous honneste contrainte.[13]

[I governed Israel with sceptre in hand, / I subdued the waves of the
Jordan, / I ransacked, I searched, to learn and know the reasons, /
Each soul that breathes, and living takes its being / Under the vault
of the Heavens, to know the causes, / The revolution and return of
time and the seasons, / Opening the fecund bosom of mother
Nature, / Who suckles every creature: / And best believe that great
God places this vain desire / In the heart of humans not to give
them pleasure / But to test them, to keep them fearful, / To make
them thirst after knowledge under honest constraint.]

The parallel structure ("J'ay porté . . . J'ay pressé . . . J'ay fouillé . . .") stresses
that political leadership—"J'ay porté d'Israel le sceptre dans la main"—
couples seamlessly with the control of nature—"J'ay pressé sous le joug les
ondes du Jourdain." David seeks out the mysteries of nature, and his engagement with the elements—fire, earth, water, air—and the frontiers between
earth and sky are related to his human dominion and the establishment of
his state. Although his power over the river Jordan might be more miracle
than "science," the next lines clearly describe human curiosity and research
into nature rather than divinely inspired power. Moreover, unlike *DRN*,
where inquiry into the nature of things frees people from fear of the gods,
Belleau's *Discours de la vanité* show how curiosity, mother of natural philosophy, subjugates people to fear and divine constraint.

Adopting the ancient idea of the poet as expert in all human knowledge,
Belleau affiliates philosophy with poetry, philosopher-poets with kings.[14] In
a poem dedicated to J. Helvis, another royal tutor (Belleau himself served as
tutor to Charles d'Elbeuf, son of the Marquis d'Elbeuf), author of a "Miroüer
du Prince Chrêtien," Belleau writes that a good prince

Nous apprend une autre science
Plus seure, et dont l'experience
Est vraïe, et proufitable à tous,
Non pas la cause de l'humide,
L'infini, le plain, ou le vuide.[15]

[Teaches us a different and more certain / Knowledge, the experience
of which / Is true, and useful for everyone, / Not the cause of the
sea, / The infinite, the plenum, or the void.]

Statecraft and the poetic craft are both "science"; though the king's craft is
grounded in practical application rather than esoteric investigation, both have
nature as their ground and field of expertise. Kingship is construed along the
same channels as artistic production: kings and poets are alike in their knowledge and mastery, poets of the earth, and kings as founders of social order.
As the tutor to Charles d'Elbeuf and poet to the Guise family, Belleau was
ideally situated to appreciate (and to benefit from) the similar interests of
poetry and statecraft.[16] Nature, as Belleau writes in the opening of the poem
to Helvis, is the realm of the poet, "Celui qui cherche la matiere, / L'esprit,
et la cause premiere / Des semences de l'univers" (He who seeks after
matter, / The spirit, and the primary cause / Of the seeds of the universe)
in verse, but also of the king, who organizes nature—men, animals, land,
plants—with his laws.[17]

Belleau draws out the link between poets and kings beyond natural philosophy by linking it to the pleasures of narrative. In a dedicatory epistle to
the *Pierres*, "Au Tres-Chrestien Roy de France et de Pologne Henry III,"
Belleau praises the French sovereign as a prince "qui prend plus de plaisir à
discourir des secrets de la Philosophie et choses naturelles et qui plus honore
ceux qui font exercise en ce mestier" (who takes most pleasure in discovering
the secrets of Philosophy and of natural things, and who most honors those
who practice this profession; lines 11–13). The king will glean a double pleasure from Belleau's book: readerly pleasure from the narratives of the poems,
and an additional pleasure from discovering the world of stones. Hoping to
convince the king to accept his dedication of the stone-poems, Belleau
reminds Henry that he is fond of these riches from "l'Inde Orientale" that
circulate freely at court (line 28). Precious stones, with their "vertus et
beautez" (virtues and beauties; line 6), are "rare" and "digne" (rare and noble;
lines 1, 2) enough to be gifts for a king. Moreover, Belleau's poems, culled

from the "riche et sacré cabinet des Muses" (Muses' rich and sacred collection; line 3), actually surpass the gems they describe because they are indestructible and eternal: "[L]a violence des ans ne sçauroit offenser, comme les vulgaires qui tirent leur naissance de la terre, subjettes à corruption" (The violence of time cannot harm them, unlike those vulgar things that are born of earth and thus subject to corruption; lines 7–8). Even the diamond is a child of the earth.

What excites Belleau most, however, is not the old cliché of immortal verse, but rather the conviction that the stone-poems will give the king a particular pleasure thanks to what Belleau describes as "ceste mienne et nouvelle invention d'escrire des Pierres" (my new invention of writing stones; lines 17–18). Belleau will not drily enumerate the properties of stones like the lapidary writers of yore; instead, he makes them come alive, "tantost les déguisant sous une feinte métamorphose, tantost les faisant parler, et quelquefois les animant de passions amoureuses et autres affections secrètes, sans toutesfois oublier leur force, ny leur propriété particulière" (sometimes disguising them in an invented metamorphosis, sometimes making them speak, and sometimes animating them with amorous passions and other secret affections, without ever forgetting their force or their particular properties; lines 18–22). Like people, Belleau's stones have stories—they speak and they love. Animation describes the stones, but also Belleau's poetic process, which he describes as animating stones by writing them. The remains of the lapidary tradition—stones themselves—are tugged from the earth and live again at the touch of Belleau's new style.

Belleau takes care to preserve the integrity of the lapidary tradition even while striving to "animate" it with his new poetic style. The animated stones retain their old characteristics—the medicinal and spiritual properties that filled the columns of lapidaries for millennia. Belleau takes pains not to forget this lore, "[c]e que j'ay songneusement recueilly de la fertile moisson des autheurs anciens qui en ont parsemé la memoire jusques à nostre temps" (that which I have carefully collected from the fertile harvest of ancient authors, in which is preserved—even today—their memory; lines 22–25). It is a lovely image, a poet collecting memory's harvest, the flowers and fruits of ancient authors. There was much to gather: the lapidary tradition that came down to Belleau was remarkably rich, spanning classical sources from Pliny to Galen down to the Christian lapidary of Marbode of Rennes.[18]

Belleau's innovation is one of style, not content, introducing the tropes and transformations of Ovidian poetry, first and foremost, but also the idylls and trials of the Petrarchan lyric, into the lapidary tradition. Whereas Belleau's closest predecessor and contemporary in the lapidary tradition—Jean de La Taille and Jean Lemaire de Belges, respectively—would write semiallegorical, seminatural philosophical stone-poems, Belleau's are mythological love poems.[19] And although in the first stone-poem, "L'améthyste, ou Les amours de Bacchus et d'Améthyste," Belleau declares—in a stock poetic boast that preeningly claims "newness" while borrowing language from Hesiod—that he will ascend to heretofore-unbreached heights with his new writing, he instead delves into the ground, hewing newness in Solomon's mines and Orpheus's hell. Using the Ovidian and Petrarchan traditions to put pressure on the lapidary, Belleau will revive Lucretius as an object lesson for his new style.

Belleau's new style produces the readerly pleasure that he describes in his dedication. After the dedication and liminary poems, the book of *Pierres* opens with a "Discours des pierres précieuses." It appears in prose in 1576 but is replaced in the 1578 *Œuvres* by a longer verse version that Belleau's friends must have found in his papers after he died. In the 1576 version of the "Discours," Belleau writes that in his *Pierres* readers "prendront plus de plaisir que si je les eusse simplement descriptes, sans autre grâce et sans autre enrichissement de quelque nouvelle invention" (will take greater pleasure than if I had simply described them, without gracing them with some new invention or enhancement; lines 123–26). Because they appeal directly to the reader, the stones' forces are a shortcut around problematic pagan sources even as they draw from them, and reinforce Christian mores even while reworking the Christian cosmos. Readerly pleasure marks the success of Belleau's poems, indicating that he has successfully revivified ancient texts, transformed the occult properties of minerals into the narrative efficacity, and circumvented any application of stone lore that could promote the purposes of false religion.

Both the prose and the verse versions of Belleau's introductory "Discours" go into detail about adapting material from the ancients. In 1576, Belleau writes that "[e]scrivant ce petit discours des Pierres précieuses, j'ay bien voulu suyvre, avec toute religion, l'opinion des anciens autheurs qui nous ont laissé, par leurs doctes et divins escrits, les vertus et propriétez particulières d'icelles, comme provenantes des Planètes et de l'influs céleste des Estoiles" (writing this little discourse of Precious Stones, I very much wanted to follow—religiously—the opinion of ancient authors who bequeathed to us in their wise and divine writings the virtues and particular properties of those stones, as deriving from the Planets and the celestial influence of the Stars; lines 1–6). A relatively straightforward homage to ancient sources is quickly complicated, however, when Belleau expands upon his religious reservations about the ancients ("avec toute religion"). Apparently, certain ancient philosophers claimed that stone lore was a "vanité . . . à la superstitieuse religion, loix et ordonnances des Prestres Caldées, qui nous ont pu entretenir de telle folle et légère créance" (vanity . . . of the superstitious religions, laws, and orders of the Chaldean Priests, which were able to maintain us in such a foolish and superficial belief; lines 9–12). The 1578 version is even more provocative:

Qui [prestres de Caldée] ont ceste caballe en l'Egypte fondée,
A fin d'entretenir les peuples ignorans
Sous telles vanitez et signes apparans,
Pour les espouvanter et les tenir en crainte
De quelque opinion, fust–elle vray ou feinte.

(lines 10–14)

[Who began that cabal in Egypt / In order to keep the people ignorant / With such vanities and signs / To horrify them and keep them afraid / Of whatever opinion, whether it was true or false.]

The Chaldean priests use the mystery of natural phenomena ("signes apparans") to terrify their subjects and subjugate them to religion. As far as Belleau is concerned, it is this subtle manipulation of natural signs that falsifies Chaldean religion. The opinions themselves—in terms of natural science—could be true or false ("vray ou feinte"), or mere opinion. Truth is not an essential quality, but the product of its use, and here it is the use of the ideas that is at stake: insights into nature are true or false by virtue of their relationship to religion. The truth status of ancient knowledge is destabilized because it is organized under the banner of "superstitieuse religion." Used in the service of paganism, centuries of knowledge about stones and stars are mere opinion. Revived by Christian writers, the same "facts" are true. In this light, Belleau's dedication to the king takes on new dimensions: the new writing of stones is a Christian preservative against ancient error, but it is also more generally about the control of natural science and the errors and manipulations of religion—in short, about power. Of course the king would be interested.

With his ancient sources, Belleau confronts the troubled relationship between religion, knowledge, and politics, precisely the challenge faced by sixteenth-century France during the Wars of Religion. According to Lucretius's rousing tirade against religious superstition in Book 1 of *DRN*, it was from such religious oppression (and its partner, political oppression) that Epicurus saved the Greeks.

> Humana ante oculos foede cum vita iaceret
> in terris oppressa gravi sub religione
> quae caput a caeli regionibus ostendebat
> horribili super aspectu mortalibus instans,
> primum Graius homo mortalis tollere contra
> est oculos ausus primusque obsistere contra,
> . . . .
> quare religio pedibus subiecta vicissim
> obteritur, nos exaequat victoria caelo.
>
> (*DRN* 1.62–67, 78–79)

[When human life lay on the ground obscenely, in full view, / Prostrate, crushed beneath the weight of Superstition, who / Stretched down her head from heaven's realms and with her ghastly gaze / Loomed over mortal men, the first among them who dared raise / His human eyes to her was Greek, the first man to withstand her. . . . Therefore it is the turn of Superstition to lie prone / Trod underfoot, while by his victory we reach the heavens.]

Mortals live in fear because they do not understand the operations of the heavens and earth, and, attributing them to obscure whims and powers of the divine, fall captive to religious beliefs.[20] Belleau, too, sees how the wondrous properties of stars and stones could be used to hold a people in thrall to a false religion, and, like Lucretius, proposes to escape the terror of these signs from the sky through a new and different study of nature. In the "Epitaphe de François de Lorraine, Duc de Guyse" from the first day of the *Bergerie*, Belleau describes God's majesty and humanity's fear at great length.

> C'est luy seul qui retien, qui conduit, & qui guide,
> Ce que dessus la terre, & dedans l'air liquide,
> Et ce qu'au fond des eaux, vit, souspire, & se meut,

Puis le tranche, & l'alonge, & le rompt quant il veut:
Et ne sert d'avoir peur des pestes de l'Autonne,
Des fievres de l'esté, puis que sa faux moissonne
En tout tems nostre vie, & qu'on ne peut charmer
Les tourbillons rouans de l'écumeuse mer,
Le foudre ny l'éclair, les vents, ny les orages,
Rien ne sert de savoir augures, ou presages,
Voir trembler le poulmon des boucs, ou des aigneaux,
Ny le vol gauche ou droit des profetes oiseaux,
Puis que nos jours, nos ans, nostre mort, nostre vie,
Est de la main de Dieu ou conduitt ou ravie,
Puis que les feux du Ciel, le sort, & le destin,
Menteurs, ne peuvent estre auteurs de nostre fin.[21]

[He alone holds, drives, and guides / That which breathes and
moves underground and in the liquid air / And lives in the depths
of the waters, / Then divides, extends, and breaks it when he so
desires. / And it is pointless to fear Autumn's plagues / Or the fevers
of summer, since their deceit culls us / Throughout our lives, and
since nobody can charm / The beating whirlwinds of the foamy
Sea, / The thunder and the lightening, the winds and the storms. /
It is pointless to seek out auguries or predictions, / To watch the
lung of the bulls or of the lambs tremble, / Or the veering flight of
the prophet-birds, / Since our days, our years, our death, our life /
Are in the hand of God who leads, or ravishes / And since the fires
of the Sky, strength, and destiny, / Are liars that can be only the
authors of our doom.]

The list of fears is extremely Lucretian, but whereas the Roman poet locates
the antidote to fear in the comprehensive explanatory power of atomist physics, Belleau finds relief from fear in God. Men are indeed "prisonniers de
la mort" (death's prisoners), subject to God's whim, but it is precisely his
absolute control that should reassure them.[22] The inadequacy of human speculation, which finds its support in God's absolute control, is Belleau's
consolation.

Although Belleau will take inspiration for his Christian lapidary poetics
from the pagan Lucretius, in tackling the same quandrary as Lucretius,
Belleau emerges with different tactics grounded in Christian faith. In the

1576 version of the "Discours" introducing the *Pierres*, Belleau explains the relationship of natural knowledge and religion. Even if ancient priests used an appearance of truth (the vast knowledge of philosophers and poets about stones and stars) to hide falsity (the errors of pagan religion), Belleau holds the writings of the ancients in the highest esteem and pledges to honor their memory. The ancient wisdom will be redeemed through a Christian revivification that transforms human understanding of precious stones. Despite his critique of pagan religion, Belleau's deep admiration of—and debt to—the ancients touchingly manifests itself as a pressing sense of duty. His text, he says, is "pris de la meilleure part de ceux qui en ont escrit, tant pour honorer leur mémoire que pour vous faire participans de mon petit labeur" (taken from the best of those who have written about it, both to honor their memory and to draw you into my little work; lines 117–20). Whereas Lucretius argues that only clear and penetrating insight into the causes of things will allay fear for those held in thrall to the mysterious manifestations of a cruel nature, Belleau suggests that combining the empirical wisdom of the ancients with a reverential comportment toward these signs—a Christian gaze and narrative practice—will uncover the authentic wonders of nature.[23] "Toutefois ne voulant faire tort aux cendres et précieux restes de la vénérable antiquité, comme d'Orphée et autres, je me suis proposé les ensuyvre, non pour vous déguiser le faux sous une apparence de vérité, mais pour tousjours admirer les œuvres de ce grand Dieu, qui a divinement renclos tant de beautez et de perfections en ces petites créatures: remettant le tout à l'expérience de la force et vertu d'icelles, et discrétion du lecteur" (Nevertheless, not wanting to wrong the ashes and the precious remains of venerable antiquity, such as Orpheus and others, I undertook to follow them, not to disguise falsehood as truth, but so as to always admire the works of this great God, who divinely enclosed so many beauties and perfections in these tiny creatures. Thus I place everything at the discretion of the reader and in the experience of the force of these stones; lines 12–21). Orpheus, who made the rocks sing with his lyre, is an important touchstone for Belleau, who will not, however, use his beautiful music in the service of false religion. Belleau's music is not the pagan lyre's: he writes poems that marvel at the glory of God's works and purport to put the reader in contact with the unadulterated majesty of creation.

In short, Belleau keeps the natural wonders of the ancient lapidarists, but does away with their knowledge claims. He does not attempt to derive natural laws from the earth, but presents its gemstones to provoke wonder.

In this, he echoes centuries of theological writings about the distinction between the Old and New Testaments, the subjection to Jewish law and the clarity of Christ's new rhetoric, though he displaces onto paganism the characteristics usually associated with the Old Testament. The true religion has nothing to hide, and nature's wonders unfurl themselves as quickly before the simple and admiring gaze of a Christian as they hid from the flawed erudition of pagan investigations.[24] Jean Braybrook sees this emphasis on wonder as an espousal of the role of ancient divine poets who revealed truths mythically rather than empirically, appealing to the imagination rather than reason "in order to make readers receptive to ideas and possibilities they would otherwise have excluded."[25] Although Belleau certainly abandons reason for a different sort of engagement with nature, his is less a reprise of the ancient theological poets than a repositioning of poetry in relation to Nature.

By focusing on wonder rather than knowledge, Belleau opens a field for what he calls in the 1576 *Discours* "la force et vertu" (force and virtue; line 20) of stones. The term "force" combines two categories: the traditional properties and magic of gemstones (provoking valor, curing the flu, enforcing chastity, etc., properties which Belleau himself lists at great length in his poems) and Belleau's animative narrative style. "Force" is an idea broad enough to encompass the dynamics of natural wonder as well as literary style, by appealing to the direct effect of stones upon the human mind and imagination—their force, which is to say, their medicinal and magical properties. Given that this "force et vertu" consists of precisely the properties that the ancients catalogued in such detail, how does Belleau imagine his poems to be presenting stones any differently? What makes his treatment singular and allows him to display the stones' forces?

The answer lies in the literary corollary of force, animation, which is announced in the title of the collection: the "nouveaux eschanges." Unlike the ancients or his Christian contemporaries, Belleau writes stones under the guise of change, animating them and giving them stories to live out; the *Pierres* describe these metamorphoses of stones (their "eschanges"). Over the course of these transformations, the stones metamorphose from myth to rock, narrative to "force." The most inanimate things, stones, become through the magic of poetry the elements of metamorphic narrative. In the process, real stones become stone-poems, and their natural powers narrative force. Language replaces stone, and stone is made word. This is perhaps Belleau's rendition of Paul's use in 2 Corinthians 3 of the metaphor of stone and heart to describe the difference between Jewish law and the law of the Gospels: "You are a letter of Christ, prepared by us, written not with ink but in the Spirit of the living God, not on tablets of stone but on tablets of human hearts."[26]

The first *Pierre*, "L'améthyste, ou Les amours de Bacchus et d'Améthyste," best renders the transfer between narrative and natural force. The poem describes the genesis of amethysts from the solidified tears of the eponymous nymph, turned to stone after she supplicates Diana to save her from Bacchus's lust. As her body stiffens, her tears fall like hail and land on the Indian sand, where they turn to rocks.[27] Bacchus, distraught and enraged, plucks one of the grapes from his crown and squeezes its juices onto the stone,

> Qui depuis en vertu de ce germe divin
> N'eut le visage teint que de couleur de vin,
> Violette, pourprine en mémoire éternelle
> Du Dieu qui pressura de la grappe nouvelle
> Le moust qui luy donna la couleur et le teint
> Dont l'Améthyste encor a le visage peint.

> (lines 299–304)

[Who, because of this divine seed, afterwards / In eternal memory, always had a face / The color of wine, violet, purple, / Of that God who squeezed from the new grape / The juice that gave it color and tint, / With which the Amethyst's face is still painted.]

The amethyst gemstone is a distillation of the emotions and narrative of the Amethyst myth, because the forces that the stone bears are drawn from the mythical scenario: Belleau explains that the bearer of an amethyst will never become inebriated from wine, and if someone finds an ametheyst on Indian gravel, he will turn into a stone, losing life and voice, just like the nymph.

Construing the powers of stones as derived from their origin myths sets Belleau's stone-poems apart from other lapidary lore, which standardly held that stones derived their miraculous powers from their relationship with the stars. The idea that magnets might draw their force not from stars but from the earth itself didn't gain much of a foothold until William Gilbert's *De magnete* (1600). Stones were thought to be linked to the heavens, and to share the qualities of their celestial counterparts, yet in Belleau's amethyst poem, the miraculous properties of stones spring from the solidified saps of myth, and the amethyst stone's force thus derives from narrative development rather than astral synchronicity. This is true of all Belleau's *Pierres*, in which stones have occult properties not because they are influenced by the stars but because of narrative accretion, because they have stories. Stones are less stone-stars than objects that come to be through a mythical transformation. Narrative force supplants the astral, often appearing in the poems (as in the amethyst poem) condensed in the figure of hardened juices—saps, ambers. This difference is notable because instead of static unities of earth and cosmos, Belleau produces mobile meanings through flexible mythical narrative. Thus, although Belleau's new style serves a Christian worldview, his method relies on pagan underpinnings whose implications destabilize the ties between heavens and earth that underlie Christian as well as pagan cosmology.

Magnetic Desires in Belleau's *Pierres*

Belleau's contemporaries recognized the *Pierres* as the poet's most important collection.[28] Belleau died in 1577, and his friends quickly brought out his *Œuvres poétiques* (1578) in two pocket-sized volumes, placing the *Pierres* at the head of the first.[29] This arrangement, along with Ronsard's famous epitaph for Belleau, which makes the *Pierres* his head*stone*, demonstrates the priority Belleau's friends and colleagues gave the *Pierres* in his body of work.[30] It is not only a particularly good collection of poetry—combining as it does the styles Belleau perfected throughout his career—but a crystallization of the themes that traverse his poetry. A life's work converges in the *Pierres*, which give Belleau's vision of how poetry can effect a *translatio imperii et studii* in war-torn France. Lucretius plays a central role in the *Pierres*. The animation that is the crucial element of Belleau's new Christian style of writing stones is laid out most clearly in the poem on the magnet, long stretches of which imitate Lucretius's description of magnets from the end of *DRN*. Belleau Christianizes Lucretian thematics, while remaining deeply reliant on the pagan poet's articulation of magnetic attraction.

What Belleau calls his "nouvelle invention d'escrire des Pierres" was part of a widespread effort on the part of French poets to renovate French literature both by translating and adapting ancient works and by developing specifically French modes of writing. They expressed this work in terms of newness: reintroducing ancient forms, tropes, and styles into French both revived Latin antiquity and created a new French language and literature. The project of reviving classical literary forms and using them to invigorate French language and literature motivated most of Belleau's poetic works. His translation of the Anacreontic odes, for example, provided an opportunity for Belleau and the other members of the Pléiade to think about the revival of antique literature and the way that historical circumstances can help or hinder the flourishing of literary traditions. In the dedicatory epistle "Au Seigneur Ivlles Gassot secretaire du Roy," Belleau blames war for relegating Rome's texts to obscurity in the first place.

> C'est chose tres-certaine, que les changemens d'Empires, diversité de Republiques, de langues, de meurs, guerres, et seditions populaires, ont esté premiere occasion, qu'un nombre infini de livres memorables ne sont venus jusques à nous, qui presque les derniers entre tous, avons receu la cognoissance des bonnes lettres, et sciences liberales: Plainte ordinaire des Romains mesmes, qui apres avoir trié et tiré des thresors de la Grece, et des cendres de la venerable Antiquité, ce qui restoit de plus rare, et de plus precieux, ont enrichi presque tout le monde de leur larcin.[31]

> [It is quite clear that shifting Empires and the multitude of Republics, languages, customs, wars, and popular seditions have been the primary reason that so many memorable books have not come down to us, we who have only lately learned belles lettres and the liberal sciences. The same grievance was shared by the Romans themselves, who selected and drew whatever remained that was rare and precious from the treasures of Greece and the ashes of venerable antiquity, and enriched the entire world with their theft.]

Books are lost in the rage of war and sedition that destroys empires. Belleau, whose translation rescues Anacreon from the ruins of ancient Greece, is a mirror image of the Romans themselves, who had recovered, translated, and disseminated the works of the Greeks, themselves earlier lost to upheaval and decline.

With civil unrest over religious difference building in France, Belleau and the other Pléiade poets worried over this interlinked cycle of war and literary decline. Rome's books were cut down in their maturity, buried in their country's battlefields, and France's were now in danger of being aborted, relegated to the tomb before even seeing the light of day.[32] As Belleau writes in the same dedicatory epistle to the volume of Anacreontic odes, "Et pour venir à cest heur, ou malheur, combien depuis vingt ans, avez vous veu des livres avortez en naissant, '*Plustost ensevelis sous les flancs de la terre, / Que jouïr bienheureux des beaux rayons du jour?* '" (And to speak of today's troubles, how often in the last twenty years have you seen books aborted even as they are born: "*Buried in the earth / instead of happily enjoying the rays of the sun?*").[33] The gemstones of Belleau's *Pierres* bring together the metaphorics of dead earth and buried books that came to dominate the Pléiade's presagings of national doom, provoked by growing civil unrest that eventually erupted into the civil wars. The stone-poems have a metaphorical coherence that suits them to the ambitious poetic project of saving France's literature from decline and obscurity. Like Rome's fallen soldiers and forgotten books, the stones that populate Belleau's collection are buried in the earth. Reviving the lapidary genre for French literature, Belleau will bring the buried ghosts of ancient glory to life in contemporary France. Styling himself a new Orpheus, Belleau writes poems that animate the dead, bringing life from the soil. Symbolically, the stones represent the flowering of the French land, the regeneration of literary tradition, the enrichment of French language and literature, even the promise of material riches and French success abroad, in the lands of precious stones.

Poetic innovation, the revitalization of literary traditions, fights France's slow decline into sterility. If Belleau's texts construe stones as repositories of lost knowledge, here they are also seeds, "semences," simultaneously evoking primordial natural elements and the fertility of the earth, precious particles that could seed France's fertile plain and ward off her looming sterility. The animation that vivifies the subjects of Belleau's stone-poems renders hard, immobile stones living things, life forces. Rather than dead matter, they are emblems of vitality and of the transmission of life—the communication of their properties into the bodies of their bearers. The stone-poems are themselves the seeds of France's literary tradition, examples of the richness of French culture as much as they are the flowers of Greece and Rome, blooming again from the tomb. In the *Bergerie*, Belleau's shepherds Charlot and Francin use a language of stones, seeds, and fecundity to discuss France's woes. In the first poem included in the first day of the *Bergerie*, which begins "C'est de long tems Charlot," Francin argues that in this age of sedition and bloody ambition, France has become infertile.

> depuis que la France
> Couve dedans son sein, le meurtre, & la vengeance,
> La France ensorcelee, & surprise d'erreur,

De guerre, de famine, & de peste, & de peur,
France le petit œil, & la perle du monde,
Est maintenant sterile, au lieu d'estre feconde?[34]

[Since now France / Fosters murder and vengeance in her bosom, /
France, tricked and surprised by error, / By War, famine, plague,
and fear. / Is France, the little eye and pearl of the world / Now
sterile instead of fertile?]

The vocabulary of fertility and birth, burial and the tomb, links the horizons
of natural and literary possibility, such that newness functions as a category
for thinking the rise and fall of nations. Belleau takes the metaphorics of war
and imperial decline seriously and not only reinvests them with positive force
(living stones instead of dead books), but extends the metaphor to conceive
of French poetry as part of French patrimony, France's natural resources.

The destruction of the religious wars is natural and agricultural, but also
mythical. Charlot responds to Francin saying: "Ny voy tu des forests le plus
épais feuillage, / Qui ne porte sinon à regret son ombrage? / Les Faunes, les
Sylvains, de tous cotez espars, / Se mussant, ont quitté leurs forests aux soud-
ars" (Can you not see the thinned foliage of the forests / Which no longer
bear shade? / The Fauns, the Forest-folk, all dispersed, / Hide themselves and
have abandoned their forests to troops).[35] The forest is depicted as the spiritual home of poetry, and the destruction of France is embodied in the
destruction of her lands, forests, and myths. When the forests die, so does the
source of poetry. When Belleau presents his *Pierres* he is pointedly revitalizing
France's withering mythical resources, attempting to reenergize ancient literary modes (the mythical, Ovidian metamorphoses) and avenues of knowledge
(the lapidary), to enable a new French poetry. He shares this project with all
of the poets of the Pléiade, particularly Ronsard, who echoes the same themes
in his "Elegie de P. de Ronsard, à Chretophle de Choiseul, Abbé de Mureaux," one of the liminary verses that introduces Belleau's volume of Anacreontic odes. Ronsard imagines the Pléiade poets themselves as examples of
France's great literary fertility. First, he describes poetic talent as a miraculous
gift from God, like the seeds that lie dormant only to spring up when the
warm season arrives. In a similar way, poets are the seeds and fruit of Mother
France:

Ainsi la France mere a produit pour un tems,
Comme une terre grasse, une moisson d' enfans

Gentilz, doctes, bien–nez, puis ell' s' est reposée,
Lasse, ne se trouvant à porter disposée

. . . .

Meintenant à son tour, fertile, elle commence
A s' enfler tout le sein d' une belle semence.[36]

[Thus for a time Mother France, / Like rich land, produced a flurry
of children / That were gentle and well-born, then she rested, /
Weary and indisposed. . . . Now, once more, fertile, she begins / To
grow heavy with a lovely seed.]

This "belle semence" is Belleau himself, conceived to "accomplir la setieme
Pliade" (make the seventh Pléiade) Ronsard then launches into an encomium
of Belleau's poetic innovations.[37]

For Belleau, stones are emblems of his cultural project of renovating
classical poetic models so as to vivify and preserve French poetry, even in the
face of war. As becomes evident in "La pierre d'aymant ou calamite," one of
the key classical texts that Belleau intends to revive is Lucretius's *DRN*, which
serves as the major source for the poem. The poem on the magnet is the
centerpiece of Belleau's lapidary collection: singular for its force rather than
its beauty, "La pierre d'aymant ou calamite" is unlike Belleau's other gems,
representing the very power of animation that defines Belleau's poetic project.
As Evelien Chayes has noted, it is the only stone in the collection that does
not require (or admit) any artistic working. It is not ornamental but a plain
metaphor of inner power.[38] Like Lucretius's Venus—who in *DRN*'s opening
hymn is at once the muse of poetry, the object that spurs the lust and procreation of nature, and the broker of peace—Belleau's magnet is an emblem of
force operating at all levels of France's vast material and mythical economies,
combining amorous attraction, the drive toward peace, literary style, natural
fertility, human curiosity, and Christian love. Indeed, although it is his last
work, the *Pierres* is Belleau's first and only collection of love poetry. As Jean
Braybrook writes, "Prior to 1576, Belleau had not produced an individual
collection of love poems, although he had written Petrarchist sonnets and
baisers in the manner of Secundus. At last, at the age of 48, he brings out his
Amours—and writes, not of a woman, but of gems."[39]

Rather than love poetry for stones, however, the collection is a love poem
to France, with a stone, the magnet, as its romantic hero. The magnet might
seem an unlikely protagonist for a love poem, but in Belleau's hands the

magnet is the very picture of heated desire. Belleau describes the magnet's action in terms taken directly from Petrarchan poetry. Aren't there enough wonders of nature, he marvels,

> Sans les avoir armez et de mains et d'accroches,
> De petits hameçons, de secrettes approches,
> Des traits mesme d'amour, pour attirer à soy
> Le fer opiniastre et luy donner la loy?
> . . . .
> La Calamite errante, et de soif altérée,
> De ne sçay quelle ardeur cruellement outrée,
> Evente ce métal, halletant et soufflant
> D'un désir importun, qui chaud la va bruslant:
> Puis l'ayant découvert, le chérist et l'embrasse,
> Le caresse, le baise et le suit à la trace.
>
> (lines 17–20, 33–38)

[Without having armed them with hands and clasps / With tiny hooks, with secret passages, / With the very arrows of love, how could they draw to themselves / The stubborn iron, and rule it? . . . The wandering Magnet, parched with thirst, / Cruelly roused by who knows what ardor / Fixes upon that metal, huffing and puffing / With importunate desire, which burns it with its heat: / Then having found it, treasures and embraces it / Caresses it, kisses it, and follows in its tracks.]

The magnet is an impassioned lover, panting and chasing like a dog on the hunt.[40] From here, Belleau's text moves back to *DRN* to explain the magnet's mysterious force. Lucretius's description of the magnet crowns the section of Book 6 that gives explanations for a wide range of natural phenomena—thunder, lightning, thunderbolts, waterspouts and whirlwinds, clouds, rainbows, earthquakes—and precedes the final passage of *DRN*, with its harrowing account of the causes of disease and the great plague of Athens. Its pride of place indicates that Lucretius, like Belleau, recognizes the magnet's attractive force as a potent symbol for desire and the important role it plays in his vision of the world. As Belleau will do, Lucretius first impresses the reader with the astonishing qualities of the magnet: it can hold together chains of rings with its pervasive force. Before explaining how the magnet works, Lucretius repeats his explanation of vision from Book 4: "Principio omnibus ab rebus, quascumque videmus, / perpetuo fluere ac mitti spargique necessest / corpora quae feriant oculos visumque lacessant" (First of all, from every object visible and showing, / A stream of particles must be perpetually flowing, / Particles that strike the eyes and trigger sight; *DRN* 6.921–23). The emission of atoms from bodies is also the cause of sounds, smells, and tastes. Belleau paraphrases all of these points closely (see especially lines 40–70).

Evoking the link between amorous *simulacra* and desire from Book 4, Lucretius only implies that the magnet's attractive powers are erotic, allowing Belleau to emphasize in his magnet poem what is largely implicit in *DRN*.

> Dans ce vuide aussi tost les premiers élémens
> De ce fer à l'Aymant par doux acrochemens
> Embrassez et collez, comme par amourettes
> Se joignent serrément de liaisons secrettes.
>
> (lines 75–78)

[Instantly in this void, the first elements / Of this Iron are embraced and held by the Magnet / With sweet entanglements, as though with *amourettes* / Closely embracing in secret liaisons.]

The progression of Belleau's poem is pure Lucretius. He begins with a single magnet, which releases a raft of atoms that animate and attract the iron. Drawn to the magnet, the iron fights its way through the (atom–filled) air. In this new *vuide* cleared by the iron, the atoms ("premiers elemens") of the two stones can finally embrace. Their love manifests itself in "doux accrochemens" and a clinging embrace, "comme par amourettes / Se joignent serrément de liaisons secrettes." Lucretian physics becomes an amorous science, and Lucretius a natural philosopher of love.

As in the hymn to Venus, where the goddess seduces warlike Mars to procure peace for mortals, in Belleau's magnet poem this attractive quality is fundamentally pacific, allowing the magnet to subdue bellicose iron.

> Se voit–il rien çà bas plus dur et moins dontable
> Que ce métal guerrier? moins dous et moins traitable?
> Mais en ceste amitié le donteur est donté,
> Et le vainqueur de tout d'un rien est surmonté.
>
> (lines 21–25)

[Is there anything more unyielding and untamable / Than this warrior metal? Less soft and less tractable? / But in this friendship the
tamer is tamed / And the conqueror of all is overcome by a nothing.]

The hymn to Venus illustrates the persuasive power of erotic speech by framing the work of politics as a process of seduction. Just as Venus subdues Mars
with sensuality, the magnet's force of attraction proves to be the force of
peace. Belleau's magnet becomes an emblem for Christian *pax* in a world of
strife. The "noeu d'amitié" (bond of friendship; line 31) that joins magnet to
iron is that which Belleau would hope to see come about in France between
Catholics and Protestants. The magnet is a model for human behavior.

> Invention des Dieux! avoir tiré l'esprit
> D'un cailou rendurci, qui sans sçavoir apprit
> Aux hommes journaliers de tirer un mesnage
> Des jours, des mois, des ans, ruine de nostre âge!
>
>   (lines 175–78)

[Invention of the Gods! To have drawn the spirit / From a hardened
pebble, which unwittingly teaches / Everyday men to form a
household / In these days, months, years, and ruin of our age!]

As Jean Braybrook argues, "Implicit in . . . 'La Pierre d'aymant ou calamite'
is a contrast between the mineral world, united by the magnet, and the
human, in which Catholics and Protestants refuse to be reconciled."[41] The
magnet is the most perfect expression of the divine law of amity that governs
all beings—humans as well as the heavens, animals, stones, and plants—and
a constant reminder that men must respect that law or risk chaos on earth
and divine displeasure. Ever since Adam and Eve ate the apple and intro-
duced pain and death into God's creation, men and women have defied and
destroyed the divine harmony that would ensure their happiness. Humans
fall, but the natural world (here the magnet) always retains the promise of
harmony, a lesson it could teach men if they would only take heed.

The religious and political peace exemplified by the magnet sheds light
on the biblical translations Belleau published with the *Pierres*. Most critics
agree that the texts are linked by more than their publication history, particularly the *Pierres* and the *Discours de la vanité*, which excoriates the pride and
destructiveness of men. Braybrook notes that not only does the terrestrial

splendor of the stones have its moral reversed in the *Discours de la vanité*, but that "in placing his translation and lapidary poems together, Belleau highlights the religious significance of the latter."[42] The religious aura of the stones, however, is not simply derivative: the metamorphoses, particularly that of the ruby, which is associated in Christian lapidaries with blood and thus with Christ's sacrifice, teach Christian lessons of healing and spiritual renewal.[43] For Claude Faisant, the story of the *Pierres* is a "story of Redemption" and Belleau a theological poet, above all.[44] Both critics agree that the main thrust of the *Pierres* is a sophisticated religious moralizing. I argue, however, that the religious component of Belleau's poetry is but one measure of his project, which integrates poetry, religion, and politics.

Establishing French literature as part of French patrimony—as much a national, even natural, resource as France's forests, rivers, and pastureland—Belleau brings Lucretius to bear on this collection to make a point about the relationship between French poetry and French politics. As I have already explained, Lucretius's hymn to Venus politicizes *ataraxia*. When Lucretius prays to Venus for a "quiet peace for Romans," he connects an individual's *ataraxia* to the peace of the Roman state. What motivates this expansion of Epicurean *ataraxia* are the poet's needs: Lucretius requires quiet to write, and peacetime to foster the patronage systems that can bankroll, circulate, and consume his poetry. Venus will persuade Mars to cease war, bringing peace to Rome and thus to Romans: a détente gives the poet time for inspiration and writing, and also grants his patron, Memmius, the free time to pursue not only statecraft but also his cultural pursuits, such as patronizing the arts, supporting poets like Lucretius, and reading their work. This passage, from the hymn to Venus, produces a circuit between national peace (global *ataraxia*), individual peace, and the poet's craft, which converts new Epicureans who will in turn practice *ataraxia*.

It is a singularly practical vision of the conditions necessary to popularize Epicureanism in Rome, but its pragmatism did nothing to limit the implications it had for the construction of Lucretius's poem or its reception in early modernity. Indeed, sixteenth-century French poets were attracted to *DRN*'s association of poetic and political interests within the tropes and language of love poetry. For Lucretius, the disseminator of Epicureanism, the primary purpose of these erotic passages was to illustrate the benefits of *ataraxia*, but Lucretius the poet articulates the paired interests of state and poetry and inserts them into the very heart of Epicurean *ataraxia*. That this is done in his loveliest and most seductive language, in the most gorgeous passages about Venus, desire, and sex, only baited the hook. Early modern poets were only too liable not only to read, treasure, and paraphrase the hymn to Venus but also to soak up its underlying claims about the relationship between poetry and politics.

For Belleau, emphasizing the craft of poetry put poetry into dialogue with political power. Yet while Lucretius does this by glorifying poetry's power, Belleau does so not by elevating poetry above other art forms and handicrafts but rather by situating it among them. Executed correctly, both poetic craft and statecraft glorify God, the author of the entire universe. Of course, they also glorify the representative of God on earth, the king, who is the more immediate dedicatee and recipient of poems and goods that consolidate his might. Of all Belleau's poems, the pastoral collection the *Bergerie* best expresses this node, which sustains and stabilizes the state while encouraging the gentle art of poetry as well as the industrious crafts of the villages. This masterful pastoral poem (the first half of which was published in 1565) depicts an idyllic country house and its surroundings, modeled on Joinville, the home of Belleau's patrons, the Guise family. Life in this house is an idealized rhythm of conversation, recitation, meals, and crafts, as the gentle young ladies work at their needlepoint among marvelous tapestries and are visited by messengers and players who entertain them with poems, masques, and amorous discourse.

The poem is a cornucopia of crafts: it begins with a rapturous description of the tapestries that hang in the great terrace, then moves on to describe the occupations of the "bergeres," the ladies in waiting, and finally the town that sits at the foot of the chateau. The young ladies occupy themselves with genteel handiwork, pretty work intended to attract suitors.[45] The surroundings and nearby town are similarly idealized, and equally full of the products of industrious activity.[46] This profusion of craft has long been cited as evidence of Belleau's mannerism, an expression of his fascination with artworks.[47] Guy Demerson characterizes Belleau's mannerist art in his introduction to the *Bergerie* this way: "What mannerist art strives to emphasize is its technique; the pleasure and goal of art is exhibition. It takes inspiration not from mimesis but from fantasy [*phantasia*], that is, from the imaginative faculty that is able to produce figurations without visible referent."[48] Although this is certainly true, I would argue that Belleau's obsessive descriptions have additional goals: they serve to link high art—particularly poetry—with crafts under the umbrella of state economy, rather than to glorify artworks or subordinate seemingly "realist" descriptions of Joinville to the marvelous register of art.[49] The *Bergerie* draws domestic entertainments, artworks, and crafts into the same orbit of description, intermingling the occupations of the nobility, the craftsmen, and the poet-shepherds. All are expressed through the idea of ingenuity, which is used to describe all the different spheres, and which is the linchpin of the successful economy of the town.

Poetic and technical ingenuity are linked for Belleau. Even the title of *Les petites Inventions* associates poetic *inventio* with technical inventions, describing small crafted objects in careful verse. A number of recent critics such as Claude-Gilbert Dubois, Elizabeth Spiller, and Frédérique Aït-Touati have argued for techniques that link poetry, science, and invention. Dubois explains that "imagination and technique share a common etymological origin: a 'device' [*engin*] is a technical instrument or artifice, but also the spirit of invention: 'ingenuity is more valuable than force' ['*engin vaut mieux que force*']. The inventor and inventiveness in fact come from the same Latin word, *ingenium*, which . . . means 'natural dispositions of the spirit, genius in all senses of the term.'"[50] Belleau's poem "L'heure" in *Les petites inventions* honors Ronsard for the poetic ingenuity he lavishes on ingenious objects. Belleau writes: "Tant fut l'ame curieuse! / Et la main ingenieuse / Pour animer un metal" (The soul was so curious! / And the hand so ingenious, / That they animated a metal).[51] In the same breath, "L'heure" celebrates Ronsard's inexhaustible poetic inventions and the clockmaker's craft, capable of constructing a mechanical marvel. As he will also do in the *Pierres*, here Belleau imagines creation as a type of animation; the clockmaker animates metal in much the same way Ronsard or Belleau animates his poetic material. Claude Faisant has interpreted Belleau's focus on ingenuity as a sort of Neoplatonic poetic practice in which Belleau makes perfect stones from scientific facts through the process of poetic invention. According to Faisant, Belleau renders stones sublime "by bringing them to the point of exemplary perfection. Through the real stone, he aims for the very Idea of the Stone, that of which the natural iterations are but imperfect and ephemeral copies."[52] Faisant is right to emphasize the importance of invention in Belleau's poems, but his focus on the ideal ignores the social and political connections that ingenuity and invention forge in Belleau's poems. However, I see Belleau's emphasis on craft as stemming not from an interest in the ideal but rather from an investment in the entwining of natural and crafted objects in promotion of a robust symbolic and material French economy.

As we see in "L'heure," ingenuity goes hand in hand with curiosity: it is the flip side of that drive that makes philosophers and poets interrogate the bowels of the earth and the expanse of the sky—the urge to create a little world, be it a delicate mechanism, a fine description, or a lavish tapestry. Curiosity, the compulsion to explore things and their causes, leads to the urge to invent. It is this urge that drives the *Pierres*, the 1578 introductory "Discours" to which begins with the words "Recherchant curieux la semence première, / La cause, les effets, la couleur, la matière, / Le vice et la vertu de ce thrésor gemmeux" (Curious, seeking the first seed / The cause, the effects, the color, the material / The vice, and the virtue of the gemmological treasure; lines 1–3), and proceeds to write a whole new world of stones.

As with so many of Belleau's poems, the larger issues at play in the *Bergerie* around natural, creative, and political economies also relate to the specific glorification of Belleau's own patrons. Belleau's circumstantial poetry, which valorizes the life cycles of nobility, is more than an empty patronage-driven tribute—it is a way of articulating the links between those ruling the earth and the earth itself, the health of the king and the health of the land.[53] Poetry, the very medium of the *Bergerie* (but one that is also foregrounded in the frequent compositions and recitations that make up most of the body of the text), is also a craft, one that cements the link between the artisans in the town and the gentle ladies in the castle.[54] With the good management of the noble household mirrored in the well-stocked village, the house and the maidens become an allegory for the state as a whole.

The second day of the *Bergerie* insists upon the idyllic peace that reigns when there is balance between arts, crafts, and *oikonomia*. The "Description de printemps" portrays this harmony.

> Fay donc, Seigneur, que noz Provinces,
> Noz temples, noz feux, et noz Princes,
> Se couplent d'un lien si dous
> Que la paix demeure entre nous,
> Que les querelles domestiques,
> La vengence, ny la rancueur,
> Ou quelque autre importun malheur
> N'offence plus noz Republiques
> Afin que nous puissions, heureux,
> Sans guerre, sans peur, sans Envie,
> Tirer le fil de nostre vie
> Hors de ces troubles orageux.

(lines 81–92)

[O Lord, let our Provinces, / Our temples, our fires, and our
Princes, / Unite in such sweet unity / That peace dwells among us, /
That domestic quarrels / Vengeance, rancor, / And other trouble-
some evils / No longer harm our Republics, / So that we, happy,
can / Without war, without fear, without Envy, / Follow the thread
of our life / Away from these stormy troubles.]

Belleau imitates Lucretius's hymn to Venus. "Effice ut," Lucretius entreats
Venus; "Fay donc," Belleau exhorts God. Like Lucretius, Belleau asks for a
vital springtime whose bounty will heal wounds and bring peace, ushering in
a season that draws French citizens together "d'un lien si dous" (with such
sweet bonds). This passage, like others in the *Bergerie*, refers to France's troubles in the Wars of Religion, but it is images of peace and bounty that control
the collection, dominated by poems about harvest loves and river nymphs.
At stake in this pastoral description of polite conversation, flourishing towns,
and dashing men bearing love poems is ingenuity, that productive drive that
fires France's industry and cements her peace.

The most complete expression of Belleau's Lucretian poetics, the *Pierres*
crown a lifetime's engagement with *DRN*. The collection's dexterous reworking of Lucretian tropes and concepts demonstrates that early modern poets
could not only be attentive to *DRN*'s powerful integration of the interests of
poetry and those of the state, but also were able to adapt Lucretius's lessons
to their own themes and circumstances. Lucretius embedded poetry, its
methods, and its interests into *ataraxia* by framing Epicurean philosophy in
the terms of love poetry. This gave later poets familiar but powerful tools for
envisioning poetry's place in national politics, a particularly pressing question
during the Wars of Religion. Belleau's stone-poems (a category that ought to
include the two poems about Prometheus) hew to Lucretius's vocabulary of
love and his accent on politics but move away from rendering it in love plots
(as in the Ixion poems) to focus on the Venusian power of desire as a pure
force—amorous, pacific, and poetic—that the new styles of Pléiade poetry
could produce and wield. In sixteenth-century France, Lucretius's poem was
far more than a set of static images or tropes; rather, *DRN* was a conceptual
workbook whose virtuosic poetry welcomed imitation, but whose images also
invited new adaptations.

CHAPTER 3

"Like gold to aery thinness beat": John Donne's Materialisms

John Donne's "A Valediction Forbidding Mourning" begins in bed. A death-bed, to be sure, though the virtuous man quietly breathing his last upon it is also a figure for hushed lovemaking and the erotic death of orgasm. The poet exhorts his lover to join him in imitating the dying man: "So let us melt and make no noise, / No tear-floods nor sigh-tempests move: / 'T'were profana-tion of our joys / To tell the laity our love."[1] The lovers' sex is hallowed by their silence. Silent, their love is a mystery, a holy secret inscrutable to "the laity." Silent, their lovemaking is spiritual, a rhythm of souls rather than of bodies. Donne offers a variation on this thought in the next lines: "Moving of th'earth brings harms and fears: / Men reckon what it did and meant; / But trepidation of the spheres, / Though greater far, is innocent" (lines 9–12). For these subtle lovers, the quake of climax is celestial rather than terrestrial ("[m]oving of th'earth" is a literal translation of the Latin *terremotus*, or "earthquake"). Abandoning the tears and sighs that manifest the earth from which their bodies are made (the tears are also floods, the sighs, tempests), they seek to slough off the body's dross and adapt themselves to the heavens.

These lovers pursue the spiritual because they will soon be parted, and if they can learn to love with souls instead of with bodies they will remain united despite any physical distance that might come between them.

> Dull, sublunary lovers' love
> (Whose soul is sense) cannot admit
> Absence, because it doth remove
> Those things which elemented it.

But we, by a love so much refined
That ourselves know not what it is,
Inter-assurèd of the mind,
Care less eyes, lips and hands to miss.

(lines 13–20)

These are hopeful but impossible lines. While the soul-love the couple enjoys is far more "refined" than "[d]ull, sublunary lovers' love," the lovers themselves remain too crude to understand their spiritual love in all its subtlety ("we . . . ourselves know not what it is"). While the love they make is refined, they are not: the ambitious language of the poem has overstepped the boundaries of mortal understanding, and, by the same token, of corporeal possibility. The poem promises more than the lovers can actually achieve. They may "[c]are *less* eyes, lips and hands to miss" (emphasis mine), but they still *care*. The resolutely material register of the famous images that close the poem speaks to the inescapable embodiment of the lovers. In the final image, the poet admits that the lovers' souls may not, as he had previously claimed, be totally unified.

If they be two, they are two so
As stiff twin compasses are two:
Thy soul, the fixed foot, makes no show
To move, but doth if th'other do.

(lines 25–28)

The compasses—vital tools for mapmaking—bring the high-flying poem down to earth by reintroducing a terrestrial imagery that the poem before made such a show of abandoning. Earlier, the speaker rejected the earth for the heavens, abandoning earthquakes to experience a "trepidation of the spheres," but now the lovers' souls are figured by tools used to chart and comprehend the earth.[2]

Though the lovers in "A Valediction Forbidding Mourning" strive toward a perfect, and perfectly spiritual, union, Donne's poem never succeeds in abandoning the body. Instead, it explores the paradoxes and problems of trying to do so, grappling both conceptually and poetically to imagine and depict a perfect and unbreakable union of souls that remain encumbered by bodies. The interdependence of carnal and spiritual love is one of the central concerns of Donne's love lyrics, the poems that in the posthumous 1635 edition of his *Poems* were grouped together and titled the *Songs and Sonnets*. Because the soul and body are only definitively divided at death, what is required to illustrate a mortal yet spiritual love is a theory and imagery of matter that is nearly incorporeal, a matter that approaches or even approximates the incorporeal soul. This is what Donne imagines in the penultimate image of "A Valediction Forbidding Mourning."

> Our two souls, therefore, which are one,
> Though I must go, endure not yet
> A breach, but an expansïon,
> Like gold to aery thinness beat.
>
> (lines 21–24)

In Book 4 of *DRN*, Lucretius describes the extreme subtlety of images (*simulacra*), which are made of the finest, thinnest atoms. *Simulacra* are so "tenvia, quae facile inter se iunguntur in auris, / obvia cum veniunt, ut aranea bratteaque auri" (delicate, they easily stick together when they meet, / As spider webs are wont, or gold to airy thinness beat; *DRN* 4.726–27). In the notes to her splendid English translation of *DRN* (which I use throughout this book), A. E. Stallings does not indicate whether she intends to evoke Donne in her translation of Lucretius.[3] Other translators render the line somewhat differently. In the seventeenth century, Lucy Hutchinson gave "like spiders webs, or leaves of gold," while Thomas Creech has "[a]s threds of *Gold*, or *subtle Spiders* line," and John Evelyn offers "like to Cobwebbs, & leafe-gold they meete."[4] Of course, all of these translators were working decades after Donne wrote this poem; were Donne thinking of Lucretius when he composed "A Valediction Forbidding Mourning," he would have had the original Latin of *DRN* in his head or in a book before him.[5] Whether or not Donne is actually translating Lucretius here, he is certainly thinking like Lucretius about the corporeality of the incorporeal. "A Valediction Forbidding Mourning" conforms in breathtaking ways to Lucretius's erotically charged exposition of the finest forms of matter. In this poem and several other of his love lyrics, Donne's treatment of the balance, in mortals, between body and soul, matter and spirit—what he, in "The Ecstasy," calls "[t]hat subtle knot which makes us man" (line 64)—aligns with Lucretian modes of thinking about the balance in the subtlest forms of matter between corporeality and incorporeality.

Scholars have long argued about what Elizabeth Harvey and Timothy Harrison call the "scientific matter" of atoms meant to Donne.[6] In a famous passage from *The First Anniversary: An Anatomy of the World* (1611, hereafter *FA*), Donne bemoans what he there calls the "new philosophy" (line 205), innovative thinking in astronomy by Copernicus, Kepler, and others that unseated the earth (and thus man) from the center of the universe, calling into question the geocentric world order that had dominated Christendom for over a millenium.[7] The wrenching cri de coeur in *FA*, that this world "[i]s crumbled out again t'his atomies. / 'Tis all in pieces, all coherence gone" (lines 212–13), has dominated the critical conversation and established a baseline assumption that Donne associated Lucretius with fragmented matter, the particles that constitute all things and to which all things return after death. Debate over the role atomism plays in Donne's poetry tends to center on the question of whether the "atomies" of *FA* constitute a desolation or a consolation: Is Donne horrified by the fragmentation entailed by the atomist worldview, or does he find the notion of atoms in some way reassuring? While the prevailing consensus has long been that Donne firmly associates atomist philosophy with desolation, several critics contend that the old and new philosophies populating both the first and the second *Anniversaries* are tools of consolation instead. David Hirsch argues that "scientific matter"—atoms in particular—are a paradoxical solace from death in both Donne's poetry and his sermons. According to Hirsch, atomism's material substructure allayed Donne's fears about the body's resurrection, because although everything will inevitably be "crumbled out again t'his atomies," at least that disintegration will stop at atoms.[8] More recently, Harvey and Harrison have contended that this consolation is produced by the very ideas that provoke the crisis: "Scientific matter furnishes the kernels of elegiac consolation provided by *The Anniversaries*. . . . the 'new Philosophy' (*FA*, 205) simultaneously imperils epistemological stability and sows seeds of coherence."[9]

To this question of desolation or consolation I add a new question: What did Donne consider atomist matter *to be*? As I argue throughout this book, "atomies," atoms swirling in the void, are not the only vision of matter that *DRN* bequeathed to early modernity. The *simulacrum* constitutes a different Lucretian conception of atomist materiality, one that emphasizes the incorporeality of the material. While *simulacra* are made of atoms, and thus emphatically material, they are images of bodies, not bodies themselves, and so manifest, but also skirt, corporeality. If Donne's thinking resonates with

Lucretius's when he tackles the tricky question of the soul's corporeality, or the body's spirituality, it is not only because Lucretius offers a thoroughgoing theorization of the tenuous realms of attenuated bodies or of corporeal fantasies, but also because he does this theorizing in a language of love. For Lucretius, the erotic is the domain par excellence of the *simulacrum*, the site where bodies and fantasy intersect most powerfully, and in Book 4 of *DRN*, he expounds the theory of *simulacra* using examples of sex and love. In a set of important poems from the *Songs and Sonnets*—"A Valediction Forbidding Mourning," "Air and Angels," and "The Ecstasy"—Donne draws on *DRN*'s erotic lessons to think about whether it is possible for lovers to achieve union, physical or spiritual. Using erotic idioms shared with Lucretius, Donne's lyrics ask similar theoretical questions to those Lucretius asks in *DRN* Book 4: How do the corporeal and the incorporeal interact? How can lovers, trapped in bodies, love the incorporeal? For Lucretius, the latter is a question of falling in love with images but making love to bodies. For Donne, it is a question of loving with incorporeal souls while remaining constrained by the body. While Donne's answers to these questions are not strictly Lucretian, he uses Lucretian material(isms) to imagine them.

Lucretius offers Donne multiple visions of matter: not just atomies, but also *simulacra*. Donne introduces further variations by investing these different types of atomist matter with their own multiple meanings. In *FA*, for instance, the vision of atomized matter ("atomies") conveys Donne's anguish at both epistemological and social transformations wrought by changing approaches both to nature and to man's place in it.

> And new philosophy calls all in doubt:
> The element of fire is quite put out,
> The Sun is lost, and th'Earth, and no man's wit
> Can well direct him where to look for it;
> And freely men confess that this world's spent,
> When in the planets and the firmament
> They seek so many new; they see that this
> Is crumbled out again t'his atomies.
> 'Tis all in pieces, all coherence gone,
> All just supply, and all relation:
> Prince, subject, father, son, are things forgot.
>
> (lines 205–15)

In a move typical of Donne's treatment of atomism, the word "atomies" here is given a double meaning. On the one hand, it is a clear reference to Lucretian materialism, as one of the new philosophies unsettling traditional views of matter and the cosmos. On the other, "atomies" serves as a metaphor for any sort of fragmentation—material, political, familial. Donne implies that the material basis of atomism has infected social and cultural formations, fragmenting social bonds. Lucretius, like Epicurus before him, denied that the gods care to govern nature or intervene in human affairs; according to the atomists, everything that comes to be does so thanks to the chance swerve (*clinamen*) of atoms in the void. In Donne's lament, the atomist repudiation of divine control and the fragmentation of matter and of social relations go hand in hand: the former causes the latter. Seeking out new worlds, men lose this one; displaced and abandoned, earth "crumbles out" to the materials from which it was made. Human social forms follow it into the void.[10]

Crucially, in *FA*, the figure of "atomies" stands between a scientific understanding of the world and a description of human relation. When Donne wails that now is "all coherence gone, / All just supply, and all relatïon," he is talking about both the relations between atoms, or between the earth and the sun, and the relations between people: "Prince, subject, father, son, are things forgot." Moreover, while this line focuses on masculine social and familial hierarchies, the poem as a whole is even more interested in relations of love. While there has been a certain scholarly tendency to read Donne's treatment of atomism in the *Anniversaries* as "scientific," the *Anniversaries* are love poems, poems about parents' love for their dead child, about love for the relationship between a body and its soul. All of Donne's poems are love poems in this sense, and this is consistent with a Lucretian worldview.[11] The overriding message of Lucretius's hymn to Venus, which opens *DRN*, is that love is the engine for all life, that love draws things into relation and perpetuates the world.

My claims in what follows are divided into two distinct though related sections. The first discusses several of Donne's love lyrics contained in the *Songs and Sonnets*. In "A Valediction Forbidding Mourning," "Air and Angels," and "The Ecstasy," Donne's thinking on the delicate balance between carnality and spirituality in matters of love and sex conforms to Lucretian thinking on the attenuated materality of *simulacra*. These poems use atomist imagery (both *simulacra* and atomies) to figure not the corporeal but the incorporeal, and to imagine the exchanges between bodies and souls. The second section takes Donne's praise poetry as its point of reference. In a verse letter to the

Countess of Huntingdon ("That unripe side of earth"), Donne associates the fragmented matter of atomism with the fragmentation—of bodies, emotions, and verses—of Petrarchan lyric. Identifying a Lucretian strain within the Petrarchan tradition, Donne makes it a polemical target, skewering Petrarchizing verse that fragments rather than establishes the social relations (between lovers, between poets and patrons) it pretends to seek. Reflecting on the difficulties of securing patrons by dedicating verse to them, Donne, like Lucretius, openly strategizes about which poetic idioms and tactics work most effectively on readers. In a typically double move, even as he leverages Lucretius to critique Petrarchism, Donne also draws on Lucretian imagery to imagine new poetic styles and forms of praise that his poetry might use to compact social relations and gain himself patrons.

As even this brief account should make clear, Donne's response to Lucretian thought is complex, even contradictory. Donne uses the very same atomist images for diametrically opposed purposes in different poems. For example, the atomies in FA figure fragmented matter, but in "The Ecstasy," "atomies" is the word Donne uses to describe the motions and mergers of souls. However, there is consistency even in these diverse uses: in both cases, Donne's atomies are a figure for relation—gaining it or losing it. Read as "scientific matter," the atomies of FA and "The Ecstasy" stand in contradiction to each other. Read as figures for relationality itself, they are in sympathy. Nevertheless, the experience of reading Donne's atomist imagery is of unsettled variability. This variability—the different uses to which Donne puts Lucretius and the different value judgments he attaches to him—can be partially explained by the fact that Donne was writing at the intersection of two very different (but equally important) Lucretian currents in early modernity: the waning of Petrarchism (and thus of the Lucretianizing Petrarchism Donne identifies in "That unripe side of earth") on the one hand, and on the other the rise of scientific atomism (which Donne names in FA). Put another way, Donne responds to DRN on the terms of both the sixteenth and the seventeenth centuries. His poetry looks backward to the way that poets like Pierre de Ronsard and Remy Belleau (the subjects of the first two chapters) used Lucretius in their Petrarchan lyrics, and forward to the epistemological, social, and religious crises that would come to a head in England in the civil war and the scientific revolution (circumstances decisive for the Lucretianism of Lucy Hutchinson and Margaret Cavendish, discussed in Chapters 4 and 5).[12] This chapter therefore functions as what Cavendish, in her book of atomist poems, calls a "claspe," a bridge between two sections of a book. Donne's engagement with Lucretius revolves around the danger and promise of Lucretian erotics: the danger of atomization, which Donne locates in the erotic fragmentations of Petrarchan poetics, and the promise of perfect erotic union, which Donne (perversely, because Lucretius denies the possibility of such erotic satisfaction) locates in the incorporeal corporeality of the Lucretian *simulacrum*.

Of Angels and Beaten Gold

The Lucretian influence on Donne's verse is neither overwhelming nor exclusive, but rather intertwined with other materialist influences. The line from "A Valediction Forbidding Mourning" where Donne describes two souls as being "[l]ike gold to aery thinness beat" (line 24) is an echo of both Lucretius's depiction of *simulacra* and the church father Tertullian's materialist description of how souls grow. In chapter 37 of his treatise on the soul, *De anima*, Tertullian illustrates soul-growth with the image of gold or silver beaten thin.[13] Donne was a thinker and writer both omniverous and syncretic, and we can easily imagine him assimilating the pagan poet's depiction of material images and the church father's materialist metaphors for the soul if it served his poetic purposes.[14] Tertullian himself may have helped Donne to conflate pagan and Christian thought: in *De anima* he discusses Epicurean doctrines on the soul at length, and in one chapter quotes Lucretius on the topic.[15] In "A Valediction Forbidding Mourning," Donne is uninterested in arbitrating the significant doctrinal differences between Lucretius and Tertullian, but wholly invested in the problem of representation (What metaphors best express the finest sorts of matter?) that he shares with both.

While many materialist traditions could have helped Donne to think about the relation between corporeality and incorporeality (whether between the body and soul or internally to the soul), only Lucretian materialism shares Donne's poetic and erotic framework for this work.[16] This is the particularity of the Lucretian contribution to Donne's materialism. In Book 4 of *DRN*, Lucretius presents the gradations of matter—ranging from flimsy *simulacra* to obdurate things—as an erotic problem: of falling in love with images but making love to distressingly unassimilable bodies. Lucretius describes how frenzied lovers bite and claw at each other, desperately (and hopelessly) trying to sate themselves on bodies that they will never be able to consume: "nec satiare queunt spectando corpora coram / nec manibus quicquam teneris

abradere membris / possunt errantes incerti corpore toto" (lovers can't
satisfy / The flesh however they devour each other with the eye, / Nor with
hungry hands roving the body can they reap / Anything from the supple
limbs that they can take and keep; *DRN* 4.1102–4). For Donne, too, the
interplay of the corporeal and incorporeal is an erotic problem, but he
offers a variation on Lucretius's argument: to love the soul, lovers must go
through the body.

In his poems most interested in the love between souls, Donne uses
Lucretian imagery to smuggle the body, and sex, into the conversation. Like
"A Valediction Forbidding Mourning," "Air and Angels" opens with an erotic
scene that is sublimated to the spiritual with the help of religious language.

> Twice or thrice had I loved thee
> Before I knew thy face or name;
> So in a voice, so in a shapeless flame,
> Angels affect us oft, and worshipped be.
>
> (lines 1–4)

The tension in these lines comes from the jarring juxtaposition of "[t]wice or
thrice" and "[a]ngels." Donne's most spiritualizing love poems tend to break
time, with the lovers' union contracting eternity to an instant or swelling an
instant to eternity ("The Anniversary" and "The Sun Rising" both assert
love's control over time). For the speaker of "Air and Angels" to (struggle to)
enumerate the number of times he has loved an angel is both hackneyed and
ungentlemanly. The tonal discrepancy raises questions about the "[a]ngels."
What Donne describes here sounds more like an erotic fantasy than a divine
messenger: twice or thrice I have fantasized about a nameless, faceless creature, twice or thrice I have "loved" her.

The more forthrightly erotic poem "The Dream" uses "angel" in this
way, as a term for an erotic vision. The speaker is wakened from a sensual
dream by his lover, and greets her happily: "My dream thou brok'st not, but
continued'st it" (line 6). He exhorts her to "[e]nter these arms, for since thou
thought'st it best / Not to dream all my dream, let's do the rest" (lines 9–10).
At first, he says, he could not distinguish between his dream of her and the
truth of her coming.

> Yet I thought thee
> (For thou lov'st truth) but an angel at first sight;

But when I saw thou saw'st my heart
And knew'st my thoughts, beyond an angel's art.

(lines 13–16)

In "Air and Angels," the term "angel" obscures the lustiest aspects of the poem, papering them over with religious language.[17] In "The Dream," the erotic context is too obvious to be obscured; it thus casts light on the erotic dynamics of "Air and Angels." Like the adolescent boys in *DRN* Book 4 who are brought to orgasm by nocturnal fantasies generated by the *simulacra* floating free "e corpore quoque" (of some random body or other; *DRN* 4.1032), Donne's speaker in "Air and Angels" fantasizes about, and "loves," "[s]ome lovely glorious nothing" (line 6). Donne's angels in these poems do similar erotic work to that of Lucretian *simulacra*.

In both Donne and Lucretius, fantasies are erotic precisely because they negotiate the corporeal and the incorporeal. This delicate equipoise is the theme of both the end of *DRN* Book 4 and "Air and Angels," which starts at the extreme of incorporeality, and then works toward equilibrium between the embodied and the disembodied. Having begun by adoring "[s]ome lovely glorious nothing," the lover seeks to "ballast Love" (line 15), but quickly finds that he has "Love's pinnace overfraught" (line 18)—he has added too much body. Finally he lands upon angels as a model for the blend of corporeal and incorporeal love that he seeks: "Then, as an angel face and wings / Of air, not pure as it, yet pure, doth wear, / So thy love may be my love's sphere" (lines 23–25). Angels are middle creatures, divine messengers, go-betweens. In this poem they go between gradations of matter, between flesh and the incorporeal, something and nothing. Donne is deeply interested here in *DRN* Book 4's major issue, what I, in the Introduction, called a category mistake: that lovers who are infatuated with images (*simulacra*) must make love to bodies. In Donne, this is reframed as a soul-love that cannot but take bodies: "For nor in nothing nor in things / Extreme and scatt'ring bright can Love inhere" ("Air and Angels," lines 21–22).

Epicureanism has long been (unfairly) associated with hedonism, and Lucretian poetry (somewhat more fairly) with carnality. Donne's love lyrics avoid broad generalizations about the hedonism of materialism, and are remarkably subtle in the way that they exploit these associations. In "Air and Angels" and "A Valediction Forbidding Mourning," Donne smuggles carnal references into ostensibly spiritualizing poems via understated Lucretian imagery. He is equally comfortable, however, spiritualizing Lucretian images.

Like "Air and Angels" and "A Valediction Forbidding Mourning," "The Ecstasy" begins in bed. As in "A Valediction Forbidding Mourning," this setting is disavowed: two lovers lie on a riverbank, "[w]here, like a pillow on a bed, / A pregnant bank swelled up" (lines 1–2). The poem activates a string of sexual images—the cushioned bed, the pregnant belly, the lovers' twisted "eye-beams" (line 7), which conjure entwined limbs—only to deny that any sexual act has taken place. The lovers profess that "t'intergraft our hands, as yet, / Was all our means to make us one, / And pictures on our eyes to get / Was all our propagation" (lines 9–12). The poem goes on to suggest that the lovers' bodies can remain so still because it is their souls that are doing the lovemaking: the souls have left the bodies to parley and mingle in a spiritual ecstasy that supersedes any carnal one. Yet the beginning of the poem also seems interested in the dynamics of erotic fantasy and imagination. While the lovers' immobile bodies and the defused sexual imagery of the first lines are proffered as proof that the love experienced is spiritual, a soul-love (it is a riverbed, not a bed; the bank that is pregnant, not the lady; hands and eye-beams that are intertwined, not legs and arms), the pictures begotten in the lovers' eyes evoke a carnal ecstasy experienced in the imagination (as in "The Dream" or "Air and Angels").

"The Ecstasy" imagines an eavesdropper, someone who is so "by love refined / That he souls' language understood" (lines 21–22), to present the dialogue between the two souls. They declare that their love is not a carnal one.

> "This ecstasy doth unperplex,"
>   We said, "and tell us what we love:
> We see by this, it was not sex;
>   We see we saw not what did move."
>
> (lines 29–32)

Their love demands not a fusion of bodies but rather a mixture or interanimation of souls.

> "We, then, who are this new soul, know
>   Of what we are composed and made,
> For th'atomies of which we grow
>   Are souls, whom no change can invade."
>
> (lines 45–48)

"[A]tomies" here is notable for naming a spiritual rather than a corporeal mixture. Donne appears quite comfortable using pointedly materialist, atomist language for spiritual phenomena. More importantly, the use of "atomies" to describe the combination of souls is exemplary of the way that the poems under discussion here mediate body and soul: through self-undermining disavowals and corporeal, materialist imagery that reintroduces the body into poems from which it was supposedly banished. Like "A Valediction Forbidding Mourning" and "Air and Angels," "The Ecstasy" charts a course from a showy repudiation of the body to an acceptance of the fact that mortals cannot love without bodies. In "The Ecstasy," the lovers realize that "soul into the soul may flow" (line 59) only when routed through the body.

> "So must pure lovers' souls descend
>   T'affections and to faculties
> Which sense may reach and apprehend,
>   Else a great prince in prison lies."

(lines 65–68)

However, even before this turn, even as they make a show of repudiating the body so as to embrace (or embrace with) the soul, these poems introduce the body, physical love, and erotic fantasy with atomist imagery. This imagery— the soul-atomies of "The Ecstasy," the attenuated souls, "like gold to aery thinness beat," of "A Valediction Forbidding Mourning," the angels of "Air and Angels"—is indebted to Lucretius, alongside whom Donne thinks in these poems about the corporeality of the incorporeal and the materiality of the immaterial.

"Wit's mere *atomi*"

Emphasizing the complicity of body and soul in amorous matters, Donne's *Songs and Sonnets* contests Petrarchan influence and seeks a new lexicon for erotic love. Donne's praise poems also meditate on Petrarchism, critiquing Petrarchan ways of writing and offering their own sort of revision. As I have already said, the influence of Lucretius on Donne is neither overwhelming nor exclusive. Not only is it interwoven with other materialist influences, but it also operates less as a direct or obvious influence and more as a sort of background hum, or, to use a different metaphor, a frame of reference, a way of framing questions and a set of images for framing answers to those questions, which Donne shares with Lucretius. In both the *Songs and Sonnets* and in the praise poems, the background hum is loudest when Donne thinks about old and new ways of writing love. At these moments, the poems betray a Lucretian frame of reference, a way of reading lyric traditions through a Lucretian lens, while also using images, concepts, and strategies, held in common with Lucretius, to generate new modes of writing.

In a verse letter addressed to the Countess of Huntingdon probably written around 1605, Donne excavates the latent Lucretianism of common Petrarchan tropes. The poem opens with a description of the New World, "[t]hat unripe side of earth" (line 1) where men live as they once did in Eden.[18] The land "gives us man up now like Adam's time / Before he ate" (lines 2–3). So far from Christendom that news of Adam's expulsion has not yet reached them, these primitive men have heard as little of Christ's coming as they have of Adam's fall. And yet, they only appear to live outside Christian history. Fallen but not yet saved, they live "wanting the reward, yet bear the sin" (line 10). The opening lines' emphasis on distance—both spatial and temporal— informs Donne's appeal to his addressee.

> But, as from extreme heights who downward looks
> Sees men at children's shapes, rivers at brooks,
> And loseth younger forms, so, to the eye,
> These, madam, that without your distance lie,
> Must either mist or nothing seem to be,
> Who are at home but wit's mere *atomi*.
> But I, that can behold them move and stay,
> Have found myself to you just their midway,
> And now must pity them, for, as they do
> Seem sick to me, just so must I to you.
>
> (lines 11–20)

While Donne describes the inhabitants of the New World in terms of temporal remove and horizontal distance (they live on the other side of the round earth), here he emphasizes the countess's elevated position: she looks down "as from extreme heights" upon all that lies below her.

Raised so high, she cannot properly discern what goes on far below. While Donne's English eyes easily make out the New World natives, even from great physical and moral distance, to the countess these minor figures are indistinct, identifiable only through equivocation or analogy—they "either mist or nothing seem to be." In the next stanza, where Donne lists the specific poetic sins that he will avoid in his verse epistle, like playing the groveling Petrarchan lover, it becomes clear that these distant figures, "wit's mere *atomi*," are poets, and that the perspectival scale is that of social standing. It is no wonder that the countess cannot make these scribblers out, given that even in their own place ("at home") they are no more significant than infinitesimal atoms. Donne is evoking the perceptual and epistemological regime of Lucretian atomism, which holds that atoms are invisible to the human eye, and so can only be imagined through analogy. To the countess, these minor wits are truly imperceptible—subvisible or imagined particles —of which she only becomes aware through the medium of Donne's verse, just as a reader of *DRN* understands the motions of atoms by reading Lucretius's poetic analogies to visible things. Donne reworks the Lucretian cosmos of atoms and void into a picture of English society, a spectacle of social proximity and remove that establishes the countess's ascendancy over her literary hangers-on.

Donne's depiction of the countess's superior vantage point also draws on the "Suave, mari magno" passage that opens Book 2 of *DRN*. In those celebrated lines, Lucretius describes the pleasure a spectator feels watching a roiling sea or the tumult of a battlefield from a safe lookout high above.[19] The satisfaction of this view from above illustrates the Epicurean concept of *ataraxia*, mental calm in the face of difficulty and uncertainty. Lucretius shows how the Epicurean believer must be distressed by neither the dramas of human life (war, the pursuit of power), nor the manifestations of nature (the storm at sea), nor the invisible yet violent motions of subvisible atoms (frequently described in *DRN* in martial terms, and thus also figured by the battlefield). Like the Lucretian spectator, the countess "from extreme heights" looks down at the laboring poets with no hint of emotion. The "Suave, mari magno" set piece dramatizes the state not only of humans who have achieved *ataraxia*, but also of the Epicurean gods, who remove themselves from human affairs and persist, forever calm, in the ultimate *ataraxic* state.

This Lucretian imagery resonates with a Christian vocabulary of perspective that Donne employs in other praise poems. In "Obsequies to the Lord Harington, Brother to the Countess of Bedford," he describes how the recently deceased Lord Harington has ascended to a new height from which he still looks up to God, but now also down at humanity.

> Though God be truly our glass through which we see
> All, since the being of all things is he,
> Yet are the trunks which do to us derive
> Things in proportion fit by pèrspective
> Deeds of good men: for by their living here
> Virtues indeed remote seem to be near.
>
>   (lines 35–40)

Donne fixes on Lord Harington as a middle figure, the contemplation of whom will allow those still living—Donne himself—to see things with the clear eyes of the glorified, eyes somewhat closer to God's.[20] The vantage point from which the Countess of Huntingdon gazes, then, absorbs Lucretian imagery into a Christian moral universe, returning "That unripe side of earth" to the themes—Eden, sin, salvation—with which it began.[21]

Just as Lucretian images scaffold Donne's glorification of the Countess of Huntingdon, so do they inform his disparagement of poets and poetic mediocrity. In the next stanza of the verse letter, he bemoans standard modes of poetic praise, all simpering sighs and flaccid moans.

> Yet neither will I vex your eyes to see
> A sighing ode or cross-armed elegy.
> I come not to call pity from your heart,
> Like some white-livered dotard, that would part
> Else from his slippery soul with a faint groan,
> And finally (without your smile) were gone.
>
>   (lines 21–26)

Donne assures the countess that he will not attempt to extract her pity with this sort of verse, which he is sure would only arouse her scorn. Moreover, having just invoked the imperturbable spectator of "Suave, mari magno" to describe the countess, it seems clear that stoking the lady's emotions should not be his goal. Instead, Donne will practice another form of praise, a different sort of love.

> I cannot feel the tempest of a frown:
> I may be raised by love, but not thrown down.
> Though I can pity those sigh twice a day,
> I hate that thing whispers itself away.

Yet, since all love's a fever, who to trees
Doth talk doth yet in love's cold ague freeze.
'Tis love, but with such fatal weakness made
That it destroys itself with its own shade.
Who first looked sad, grieved, pined, and showed his pain,
Was he that first taught women to disdain.

                                                    (lines 27–36)

There are two types of love, one that—with its tempestuous sighs and frowns, its ostentatious grief, and its pining—degrades the lover in the esteem of his beloved, and another that raises him. Donne chooses the latter. This is why, in the first stanza of the verse letter, where poets are compared to invisible atoms, Donne places himself above those infinitesimal wits, between them and the countess: "But I, that can behold them move and stay, / Have found myself to you just their midway" (lines 17–18). Unlike the minor poets, "wit's mere *atomi*" (line 16), whose groveling abases them before their addressee, Donne promises to write a different kind of poetry that will raise him up, bringing him closer to the countess.

The next stanza of the verse letter continues to draw on atomist imagery to illuminate the state of the lover and the nature of love. Donne describes a primordial chaos—part Empedocles, part Ovid—whose elements are sifted and raised from their "vast confusion" by a purifying love.

      As all things were one nothing, dull and weak,
    Until the raw, disordered heap did break,
    And several desires led parts away,
    Water declined with earth, the air did stay,
    Fire rose, and, each from other once untied,
    Themselves unprisoned were and purified:
    So was love first in vast confusion hid,
    An unripe willingness which nothing did,
    A thirst, an appetite which had no ease,
    That found a want, but knew not what would please.

                                                    (lines 37–46)

The description of chaos is meant to illustrate Donne's critique of Petrarchizing love poetry and the poets who write it: the Petrarchan lover "[w]ho first looked sad, grieved, pined, and showed his pain" is like that "raw, disordered heap" of primordial matter. Donne's "sighing ode" and "faint groan" skewer the sighs in the opening of Petrarch's *Rime sparse* ("you who hear in scattered rhymes the sound / of those sighs with which I nourished my heart"), and his "raw, disordered heap" exposes how these amorous symptoms—tears, sighs, roving distraction—fragment the poet's body and verses and evoke the fragmentation of atomist matter.[22] To Donne's mind, this Petrarchan discourse of desire is so fragmented and fragmenting that it becomes ineffectual, driving the beloved away rather than drawing her in, and thus guaranteeing its own failure. The lover's desire goes unfulfilled, "[a] thirst, an appetite which had no ease." Donne declines to play the Petrarchan lover because he doesn't want to "fall apart," to act out in amorous fashion the same jarring fragmentation of matter that he associates with the new world picture of seventeenth-century natural philosophy. The strength of Donne's critique of Petrarchizing praise poetry derives from the way he links the Petrarchan poet's performance of amorous and poetic fragmentation with the fragmentation of atomist matter. Aligned with a bleak atomist physics of chance and transience, Petrarchan verse begins to look like a force of incoherence that endangers the social relations (love, patronage) it is supposed to encourage.

This brings us back to *FA* and its depiction of how decentering and fragmenting the natural world undermine social organizations. There is a strong similarity between the way that the verse letter to the Countess of Huntingdon and *FA* use atomist cosmology as an image of social relations. However, the verse letter to the countess is more directly invested in poetic problems, problems concerning Petrarchan idioms of love and praise. The desolation of atomism in the verse letter to the Countess of Huntingdon is not that the natural world causes the social world to fall apart, but rather that Petrarchism causes both language and social relations to fragment. Petrarchism is a poetic idiom that both thematizes falling apart (the fragmentation of the poet's body and verses) and leads to the disintegration of social relations by driving both lovers and patrons away with its whining.

Donne's conflation of Petrarchism with atomism relies on a reading of literary history; Donne is identifying a Lucretianizing strain of Petrarchan poetry, precisely the strain that I describe in Chapter 1, on Pierre de Ronsard, who reads and writes Petrarchan poetry through the lens of Lucretian atomism, layering atoms swirling in the void onto the turbulent emotions and fragmenting verses of the Petrarchan poet. In the verse letter to the Countess of Huntingdon, Donne positions himself as a literary critic, or theorist, of the legacy of Lucretius in Renaissance poetry and poetics. It is precisely because Donne identifies Lucretian influence as being part of a distinct lyric tradition that he feels compelled to confront it in his own verse. Against what he construes as the pessimism and ineffectiveness of this type of Lucretianizing verse, Donne (as we will see) works to create an alternative model for praise poetry that defuses the threats of lyric and social fragmentation alike, even as it also draws on Lucretius. Thus, in the verse letter to the Countess of Huntingdon, instead of groveling before the countess like a Petrarchan lover, Donne honors her as a quasi-divine figure whose Christian virtue coheres the fragmentation that threatens both the world and poetry. Under the Petrarchan model, love, construed as erotic desire, drives the poet to despair and fragment, producing his scattered rhymes. In Donne's new model, adapted from Christian discourses against atomism, human love is construed along the lines of the divine love that God exerts on the body at the resurrection. In the poem's last lines, Donne describes love as a force of contraction and coherence.

So able men, blessed with a virtuous love,
Remote or near or howsoe'er they move,
Their virtue breaks all clouds that might annoy:
There is no emptiness, but all is joy.
. . . .
Why love among the virtues is not known
Is, that love is them all contract in one.

(lines 121–24, 129–30)

This is a divine love that binds instead of breaks. It is akin to the force Elizabeth Drury exerts in *FA*, where she acts as a sort of world soul, an exemplar of virtue who has the power to consolidate the matter scattered out by the new science. The verse letter implies that just as in *FA*, where God contracts man's body at the resurrection, or Drury "had all magnetic force alone / To draw and fasten sundered parts in one" (lines 221–22), powerful patrons might "contract" socially marginal poets into their employ. In such a model, a virtuous patroness (one completely uninterested in amorous advances from a simpering Petrarchan poet) executes the gesture of social contraction that characterizes patronage. By praising his patrons as paragons of virtue instead of as romantic objects, Donne uses atomist imagery to depict not the fragmentation of literary texts and relationships, but their constitution.[23]

The verse letter adapts Christianized atomist imagery, which Donne also deploys in his sermons, as a positive model for patron-client relations. If atomism's denial of divine intervention into nature and human affairs helps Donne dramatize the chaos of the material world (as in the famous lines from *FA*), the void at the center of atomist cosmology also allows him a certain amount of creative leeway in imagining how Christian forces might reassert the coherence of a fragmenting cosmos. In his sermons and divine poetry, Donne joins the ranks of seventeenth-century thinkers like Nicholas Hill (a copy of whose notorious *Philosophia Epicurea, Democritiana, Theophrastica* [1601] Donne owned) and later Pierre Gassendi, who attempted to Christianize atomism by reinserting divine control at the center of materialist chaos.[24] Donne's sermons contrast the randomness of atomist cosmology with God's divine power over all things. With God presiding over the atomist universe, the threat of materialist disintegration becomes little more than a foil for his power to bring the fragments back together. Donne's Christianized atomist cosmology emphasizes hierarchy, divine power, and the helplessness of atoms—or humans—at the mercy of an all-powerful God.

Donne's favored image for God's divine control over matter is his contraction of the body's scattered remains at the resurrection. In a rather tone-deaf marriage sermon, Donne describes how one's mortal remains, scattered (atomized) though they may be, are mustered together to sit, whole, at God's side in heaven.

> Where be all the splinters of that Bone, which a shot hath shivered and scattered in the Ayre? Where be all the Atoms of that flesh, which a *Corrasive* hath eat away, or a *Consumption* hath breath'd, and exhal'd away from our arms, and other Limbs? In what wrinkle, in what furrow, in what bowel of the earth, ly all the graines of the ashes of a body burnt a thousand years since? . . . What cohærence, what sympathy, what dependence maintaines any relation, any correspondence, between that arm that was lost in Europe, and that legge that was lost in Afrique or Asia, scores of yeers between? . . . [A]nd still, still God knows in what *Cabinet* every *seed-Pearle* lies, in what part of the world every graine of every mans dust lies; and *sibilat populum suum*, (as his Prophet speaks in another case) he whispers, he hisses, he beckens for the bodies of his Saints, and in the twinckling of an eye, that body that was scattered over all the

elements, is sate down at the right hand of God in a glorious resurrection.[25]

With spectacular imagery and repetitive phrasing that piles up like the "[a]toms of that flesh," Donne describes the decomposition of a human corpse by evoking the fragmented matter associated with atomist cosmology. The sermon aligns the body with the material of the cosmos and the soul with God, and atomism functions as a metaphor for the lifeless body after the soul has fled and the flesh has begun to decompose. Where the living body once had "cohærence," "sympathy," "dependence," and "correspondence"—in short, "relation"—dead it becomes atomized, disconnected particles of meat. The sermon deploys the resources of atomist poetics to describe the fear that haunted Donne and many of his contemporaries, that decomposed bodies might not be reassembled at the resurrection.[26] Yet despite the considerable gruesomeness of the sermon's language, its rhetoric tends toward a final resolution: the reassurance of God's power to re-compact any body, no matter how scattered.[27] Though the soul has fled the body, Donne affirms that the flesh still has a center—God: "[A]nd still, still God knows in what *Cabinet* every *seed-Pearle* lies, in what part of the world every graine of every mans dust lies, . . . and in the twinckling of an eye, that body that was scattered over all the elements, is sate down at the right hand of God, in a glorious resurrection." Following his metaphor of human body as the world, Donne has reassured his listeners not only of the body's resurrection but also of God's absolute control over nature, including over those pesky atheistic atoms.

Like his sermons, Donne's praise poetry exploits the vacant center of atomist cosmology. Though the sermons place God at the center of the materialist chaos, Donne's secular verse fills God's place with the men and women who were his patrons and friends, whose virtuous exemplarity, Donne suggests, can be a force of coherence in a fragmenting world. Donne posits a model of literary consolation grounded in a Christianization of atomism, in which a virtuous patron—or verse dedicated to such a patron—can recuperate language and draw the fragments of an atomized nature, or language, back together. This involves a rethinking of the relation between author and text. Atomist cosmology denies that there is any power other than chance bringing atoms together. According to the analogy between atoms and alphabetical letters that punctuates *DRN*, if atoms come together without divine intervention, then the words in a poem also do not require an author. As

P. H. Schrijvers explains, the way that the analogy between atoms and letters linked cosmology and authorship was problematic for the ancient atomists because "the metaphor of composition . . . might easily call to mind an association, unwanted by the atomists, with the concept of an author or creator . . . opponents of Epicureanism were quick to exploit this unintentional association, using the *elementa* analogy in their polemic on the hotly debated question whether our world is a product of chance or of the providence of a divine demiurge."[28]

Like the early opponents of atomism that Schrijvers describes, Donne exploits the Lucretian metaphor of atomic composition to imagine a divine creator for both the world and his poems. Strategically, and rather hyperbolically, Donne pretends that this is not himself, but his patrons. Let us recall how in the verse letter to the Countess of Huntingdon ("That unripe side of earth") Donne describes poets as "wit's mere *atomi*" who "either mist or nothing seem to be" to the quasi-divine countess who sits above them surveying the literary landscape like an Epicurean deity. Donne's sermons use the same language of atomic nothings to compare men to God. The sermon preached on Christmas Day of 1629 on John 10:10 characterizes man, in his smallness, as an invisible atom: "God is too large, too immense, and then man is too narrow, too little to be considered; for, who can fixe his eye upon an Atome? and he must see a lesse thing then an Atome, that sees man, for man is nothing."[29] Man is nothing because he was created out of nothing by God. In a sermon preached at St. Paul's on 2 Corinthians 5:20, Donne thunders: "But shall man, betweene whom and nothing, there went but a word, *Let us make Man*, That Nothing, which is infinitely lesse then a Mathematicall point, then an imaginary Atome, shall this Man, this yesterdayes Nothing, this to morrow worse than Nothing . . ."[30]

Using Christianized atomist cosmology to figure the relation of patron and poet tends toward the extreme glorification of the patron and the diminishment of the poet to nothing at all. Reid Barbour discusses how the anonymous author of "The King and Queenes Entertainment at Richmond" invokes atomism to claim that his piece was written by nobody.

See, Madam, here, what for your sole delight
Is rais'd of nothing to wast out this night.
Scarse is the Author: what he meanes lesse knowne
None will the words, none will the Musique owne.
Yet here it is; and as o'th' world some thought

That it by Atomes of it selfe was wrought:
So this concurring with your high commands
Came to be thus compacted, as it stands.[31]

Although the poet denies his own authorship, he does so in order to depict
the queen as the masque's ultimate author. The queen is called upon to
interject herself into the power vacuum of atomist cosmology (and poetic
composition) to make something out of nothing, a *creatio ex nihilo*. Likewise,
Donne pairs atomism and poetic composition to imply that it is his patrons,
not himself, who are are ultimately responsible for his poems. Another verse
letter to the Countess of Huntingdon ("Man to God's image") suggests that
it is she, not he, who generates the verse that praises her. Because it is from
the countess that "all virtues flow" (line 45), Donne suggests that his poetry
does nothing more than register her qualities.

> So I but your recorder am in this,
>   Or mouth and speaker of the universe,
> A ministerial notary, for 'tis
>   Not I, but you and fame, that make this verse.
>
>   (lines 65–68)

Similarly, at the very end of *FA* Donne will write that "verse the fame enrols"
(line 474), meaning that it is not he, but Elizabeth Drury, who is ultimately
responsible for his poetry. Atomist cosmology is one of the tools Donne uses
to enable this sort of humility topos.

   While the two verse letters to the Countess of Huntingdon are insistent
on their Christianization of atomist cosmology, in his personal correspondence, Donne proves willing to imagine an atomist textual universe that has
no governing deity. In a letter to his friend and frequent correspondent Sir
Henry Goodyer, Donne draws on Lucretius to compare the exchange of
letters to atoms crisscrossing in the void.

> In Letters that I received from Sir H. *Wotton* yesterday from *Amyens*,
> I had one of the 8 of *March* from you, and with it one from M[rs].
> *Danterey*, of the 28 of *January*: which is a strange disproportion. But,
> Sir, if our Letters come not in due order, and so make not a certain
> and concurrent chain, yet if they come as Atomes, and so meet at
> last, by any crooked, and casuall application, they make up, and

they nourish bodies of friendship; and in that fashion, I mean one
way or other, first or last.[32]

Donne transfers the Lucretian analogy between atoms and alphabetical letters
to letters in the epistolary sense. Impressing upon Goodyer how much he
values the friendship evinced by the letters he receives from his faraway corre-
spondents, Donne collapses the Lucretian analogy between atoms and letters:
instead of comparing the way atoms make bodies to the way (alphabetical)
letters make up texts, he asserts that letters (epistles) make up bodies (of
friendship).[33] Mining this new analogy, he invokes the *clinamen*—the chance
horizontal motion that brings free-falling atoms together—to accentuate the
power of epistolary correspondence.[34] Even though the atomist *clinamen*
occurs unexpectedly, with a "casual" instead of a *causal* order, the swerving
atoms still form bodies. In the same way, letters arriving out of order still
sustain a body of friendship.

   Donne is drawing considerable strength from the atomist notion that
most offended the Christian sensibilities of early modernity: the idea that a
random swerve of matter, and not God, dictates the coming into being of
things. The "crooked, and casual application" of letters mimics the haphazard
motion of atoms, and like atoms, the epistles "nourish bodies of friendship"
whether or not they arrive in order. And while Donne's letter discusses not
origins, but rather continuity—"bodies of friendship" that must be
"nourish[ed]"—contrary to all expectation, atomism's disorder, or "strange
disproportion," poses no threat to the unity of Donne's friendships. The
materialism of atomist thought underlies the claim that friendship is a physical as well as spiritual bond (the "body of friendship" formed by letters).

   This thought, which Donne could share with a friend, was not appropriate for patrons. Yet Donne's method of glorifying patrons by comparing
them to God cohering the fragments of atomist cosmology was dangerous in
its own way, because it put too much pressure on the figure of the patron.
Filling the empty center of atomist cosmology with anyone or anything other
than God is heresy. Readers found Donne's conceit in *FA*—that the adolescent Elizabeth Drury was an exemplar of virtue and a figure for cosmological
and moral coherence—overblown and inappropriate to its subject: Ben Jonson famously said that *FA* was "profane and full of Blasphemies," adding that
"if it had been written of ye Virgin Marie it had been something."[35] Donne
himself agreed with Jonson, responding "that he described the Idea of a
Woman and not as she was."[36] Although *FA* is the poem that came in for the

harshest criticism, Elizabeth Drury is not the only of Donne's addresses who got this divine treatment. Donne addressed the same sort of divinizing verse to other women, like the Countess of Huntingdon.

Donne's literary relationship with Lucretius was vexed and complex, but while his arguments about atomism are changeable, there is an imaginative consistency to his thinking when it comes into contact with Lucretius.[37] Donne gravitated toward the eroticism and the danger that Lucretius represented, and together with Lucretius, he thinks about the erotics of matter, the attachments of matter and poetry, and the efficacy of verse. Moreover, like Lucretius, when Donne thinks about matter, he thinks not just about "scientific matter," but about poetic matters. My contention throughout *The Erotics of Materialism* is that early moderns read *DRN* as a treatise on the poetic imagination, initiating an atomist genealogy at the heart of the lyric tradition. My task in the book's first two chapters, on Pierre de Ronsard and Remy Belleau, was to demonstrate the depth and complexity of Lucretian influence on French poetry in a period when poets are generally understood to have recycled a small set of Lucretian clichés without plumbing the depths of Lucretian thought.[38] Moving into seventeenth-century England, my charge is different: to demonstrate the persistent appeal and importance of Lucretian poetics in a period more commonly associated with the rise of modern scientific atomism. Donne is an ideal subject. While he was obviously attuned to the scientific advancements of his day (*FA* makes this clear), he is also remarkably sensitive to the nuances of Lucretian thought on love and sex as well as to the mark that this Lucretian erotics and its attendant poetics left on the foremost lyric tradition of the Renaissance: Petrarchism.

CHAPTER 4

Lucy Hutchinson and the Erotic Reception of Lucretius

Sometime in the 1640s or 1650s, Lucy Hutchinson (1620–1681), the prominent Puritan, translated the full text of Lucretius's *DRN* into English verse. Although the obscure history of the manuscript makes chronologies uncertain, she was probably Lucretius's first English translator.[1] Hutchinson's interest in Lucretius was shared by many of her contemporaries: from the late 1640s onward, England experienced what has been called the "Epicurean revival," an explosion of interest in Epicurean moral philosophy, atomist natural philosophy, and Lucretian poetry that manifested in an array of translations, literary works, and philosophical studies (including those of Margaret Cavendish, discussed in Chapter 5).[2] Amid the ferment of the English Civil War, Protectorate, and Restoration, Epicurean ideas and Lucretian poetics were used to trace major political, religious, and cultural divisions as people from across the political spectrum fought to localize the cultural resonances of Epicurean thought. Was atomist cosmology sympathetic to democratic politics, as Edmund Waller suggested in his commendatory verses for John Evelyn's translation of the first book of *DRN* (1656), punning on the name of the Greek atomist Democritus to declare atomism an "Order Democratical"?[3] Or did Epicureanism's purported hedonism align it with pleasure-seeking royalist poetics and politics?

Whether or not Hutchinson's translation was occasioned by the mid-seventeenth-century Epicurean culture wars, it certainly participated in them. Contemporary critics compare Hutchinson's *DRN* translation to Margaret Cavendish's 1653 collection of atomist poems, the *Poems and Fancies*, which was one of the earliest English publications of the Epicurean craze. Cavendish and Hutchinson lived near each other in the north of England; they were of similar social statures, but held diametrically opposed political commitments. Could Hutchinson have translated *DRN* out of a sense of competition with her royalist counterpart, to reclaim Lucretius from royalist associations? Or perhaps Cavendish's exaggerated professions of untrained ignorance in the prefatory materials to her poems had provoked the extraordinarily learned Hutchinson to assert her mastery of the difficult material.[4] The answers to such questions, however, are less important than the questions themselves, insofar as they reveal the high cultural, religious, and political stakes of Hutchinson's *DRN* translation.

This chapter explores how Hutchinson managed these fraught contexts, particularly the sexual politics of translating Lucretius in mid-to late seventeenth-century England. While English translations of Lucretius soon began appearing in print—Thomas Evelyn's of *DRN* Book 1 in 1656 and Thomas Creech's of the full *DRN* in 1682[5]—Hutchinson's remained unpublished until the twentieth century, though contemporary chatter about a woman translating Lucretius indicates that the work was known, at least in certain circles.[6] In 1675, more than twenty years after the completion of her translation, Hutchinson cites the circulation of an unauthorized manuscript of it as the reason she has complied with Arthur Annesley, Lord Anglesey's request for a copy. She encloses a fresh transcription with a dedication sharply criticizing what she characterizes as a project born of youthful folly, later regretted: "I found I neuer vnderstood him [Lucretius] till I learnt to abhorre him, & dread a wanton dalliance with impious bookes."[7]

Hutchinson's erotic language ("a wanton dalliance") to describe her translation of Lucretius responds to the many different ways in which *DRN* has been eroticized from its composition onward: *DRN*'s own poetics of seduction (discussed in the Introduction), the long history of erotic responses to Lucretian poetry initiated by that erotic poetics, seventeenth-century debates about the propriety of translating Lucretius into English (thus making him more accessible to women, who were less likely to know Latin and be able to read *DRN* in the original), and the association of Lucretius with libertinism, which was especially intense after the Restoration. Hutchinson presents a particularly powerful instance of the erotic reception of Lucretius both because of the intensity of debates around Lucretius in her time, and because she was a woman. *DRN* is an overtly erotic poem whose erotics have always influenced the nature and terms of its reception. The erotic associations of Lucretian poetry were particularly charged for early modern women writers, who were vulnerable to attacks that associated the circulation and availability of their texts with sexual promiscuity. In what follows, I establish erotics as an important framework for Hutchinson's career-long engagement with Lucretius. Through a reading of Hutchinson's translation and then repudiation of *DRN*, and then of her late poems, the *Elegies* and *Order and Disorder*, I locate the particular resonances the erotics of Lucretian reception had for early modern women.

Burning (for) Lucretius

While Hutchinson vigorously repudiates her Lucretius translation in her dedication to Lord Anglesey, that repudiation uses an erotic register shared with *DRN* as well as with a long history of eroticized receptions of Lucretius. Hutchinson's "repudiation" of Lucretius is thus an instance of her reception of Lucretian erotics rather than a straightforward denunciation. The dedication frames the Lucretius translation as the product of misguided youth and inscribes it in a redemptive narrative of Hutchinson's literary career. By 1675, Hutchinson was the author of a wide range of both published and unpublished works, including (in rough chronological order) her biography of her husband, the *Memoirs of the Life of Colonel Hutchinson*; her *Elegies*; parts of her monumental biblical epic, *Order and Disorder* (hereafter *OD*); a translation of the prominent Puritan theologian John Owen's *Theologoumena Pantodapa*; and a treatise on religion addressed to her daughter. Denouncing the impieties of her Lucretius translation allowed Hutchinson to frame the explicitly religious output of the 1660s and 1670s, articulating a trajectory from pagan error to Christian salvation. The preface to *OD*, written around the same time as the dedication to the *DRN* translation, makes this explicit: Hutchinson writes that *DRN* had "filled my brain with such foolish fancies, that I found it necessary to have recourse to the fountain of Truth, to wash out all ugly wild impressions, and fortify my mind with a strong antidote against all the poison of human wit and wisdom that I had been dabbling withal."[8]

Hutchinson's repudiation of her translation does more to inscribe *DRN* in a narrative of her literary career than to efface it; the same is true of her claims about the circulation of both the translation and *OD*. *OD*'s first five cantos were published anonymously in 1679 (the only publication during Hutchinson's lifetime of the poem, which in its final form comprises twenty cantos), with a preface indicating that the text was "not at first designed for public view, but fixed upon to reclaim a busy roving thought from wandering into the pernicious and perplexed maze of human inventions; whereinto the vain curiosity of youth had drawn me to consider and translate the account some old poets and philosophers give of the original of things."[9] Hutchinson's biblical epic, that is, atones for her youthful translation of a pagan epic. To understand such claims, however, readers would have had to be familiar with her *DRN* translation, know who its translator was, and also be able to identify that translator as the author of *OD*. Thus, while Hutchinson claims that neither the translation of *DRN* nor *OD* were intended for public consumption, both did circulate, probably intentionally, and readers were expected to be able to identify their author. The prefatory materials to both the translation of *DRN* and *OD* rely on such knowledge as they lay out a developmental narrative within which readers ought to understand both texts.[10]

The prefatory materials to *OD* and to the *DRN* translation also announce the evolution of Hutchinson's textual hermeneutic. The younger Hutchinson saw little danger in reading romances or translating Lucretius, which she claims in the preface to the *DRN* translation to have done "only out of youthfull curiositie, to vnderstand things [she] heard so much discourse of at second hand," because she believed that such a translation would not necessarily "propagate any of the wicked pernitious doctrines in it."[11] However, the mature Hutchinson, whose religious convictions intensified over the course of her marriage and after her husband's death in 1664, would write in the preface to *OD* that it is "a very unsafe and unprofitable thing for those that are young, before their faith be fixed, to exercise themselves in the study of vain, foolish, atheistical poesy."[12] In the dedication of her *DRN* translation, she warns the reader to "let none, that aspire to eternall happines, gaze too long, or too fixedly on that Monster, into which man by the sorcerie of the devill is converted, least he draw infection in att his eies, and be himselfe either metamorphosed into the most vgly shape, or stupified and hardned against all better impressions."[13]

Hutchinson's warnings about reading pagan texts reflected more than just her own religious evolution: unlike in the 1650s, when the political associations of Epicureanism were not yet fixed, by the 1670s, Lucretius had come to be inescapably associated with a royalist libertine milieu that Hutchinson would have found repugnant, despite being related by ties of blood and friendship to the prominent Lucretian libertine, the notorious Earl of

Rochester.[14] While the Epicurean experimenters of the revival years were usually anxious about the sexual politics that could be extracted from *DRN*, Restoration libertines embraced a hedonism derived from Epicureanism and *DRN*'s sexually charged poetics. The sexualized vocabulary Hutchinson uses in her 1675 dedication to vilify her *DRN* translation thus evokes a contemporary libertine Lucretian milieu.

That sexualized language exists in an uneasy tension with the translation itself. Hutchinson declined to translate the most sexually explicit section of *DRN*, the end of Book 4, yet the account of erotic fascination and sexual dalliance she omits from the body of her translation supplies the vocabulary and framing for her dedication's retrospective account of the translation project. Furthermore, the present absence of *DRN*'s most erotic passages appears to be intentional: in the manuscript copy Hutchinson sends to Lord Anglesey, Book 4 is the only book in the manuscript with line numbers (marked every ten lines), and at line 1084 someone (perhaps Hutchinson, who wrote marginal comments into the book herself) has drawn a thick line on top of the ruling for lines to indicate the missing text.[15] It is possible that Hutchinson added line numbers so that readers could refer back to the Latin to read in the original what was omitted in the translation. This suggests that she wanted readers to notice the glaring absence of the untranslated lines.[16] If this wasn't enough to send readers back to the Latin original, Hutchinson certainly would have titillated those readers' interest with the marginal annotation marking the place she breaks off translating, where she notes in an arch tone that "[t]he cause & effects of Loue which he makes a kind of dreame but much here was left out for a midwife to translate whose obsceane art it would better become then a nicer pen."[17] The omitted passage's description of sensuality and fruitless obsession pervades the dedication's disapproving account of her attraction to and eventual rejection of the Lucretian text, which Hutchinson describes as a sort of sexual dalliance: "I found I neuer vnderstood him till I learnt to abhorre him, & dread a wanton dalliance with impious bookes."[18]

What Hutchinson characterizes as an illicit youthful fascination with Lucretius has transformed, she claims, into an equally burning distaste. Though her dedication acknowledges the immense labor of the translation—the untold hours Hutchinson spent in her children's schoolroom grappling with Lucretius's notoriously difficult Latin—it disavows any lingering attachment to the work. Had an unauthorized manuscript copy of the translation not already been circulating, even Lord Anglesey's request for the manuscript could not have saved it: "[E]uen your Lordships comand, wch hath more authority with me, than any humane thing I pay reverence to, should not haue redeemd it from the fire."[19]

Hutchinson's threat of fire speaks to a Lucretian reception history as fixated on the flames of desire as on the bonfires and pyres of the Inquisition. In threatening to burn her translation, Hutchinson takes her place in a line of early modern Lucretians who burned for—and burned—*DRN*, among them such towering figures as the fifteenth-century Neoplatonist Marsilio Ficino, who claimed to have burned his youthful treatise on Lucretius when he realized the errors of Epicurean philosophy, and Giordano Bruno, the Dominican friar-philosopher who was burned at the stake in 1600 for his Lucretian heresies.[20] Ardor, both for and against Lucretius, has played an outsized role in Lucretian reception history. While the number (and vehemence) of Renaissance anti-Lucretians is in itself amazing,[21] the rhetoric used by those readers, imitators, translators, and editors who don't reject Lucretius outright, but turn away from *DRN* after initially appreciating it, is even more explosive.[22] The renunciations Renaissance readers perform of Lucretius could be explained by the content of *DRN*; after all, Epicureanism maintains that atoms coming together randomly in the void, and not God, or the gods, were responsible for all creation. Yet although we usually assume a direct relationship between Lucretius's denial of the immortality of the soul and divine Providence, and Christian poets' renunciation of his work, other pagan poets (Ovid, for example) did not necessitate the same ritual purging.

As I explain in the Introduction, *DRN*'s poetics is as much to blame for this explosive reception as its philosophical content; *DRN* produces the erotic overtones—including fiery repudiation—of its own reception by theorizing its poetics of seduction. The poem declares its intentions early, showing through a series of vignettes—the invocation of Venus as poetic muse, Venus seducing Mars, a doctor tricking a child into drinking medicine by smearing the cup with honey—how the poem's pleasures will seduce a reluctant Roman audience into accepting Epicurean philosophy. Like a lover so boldly confident of her charms she spells out her plans for seduction ahead of time, the text declares its intentions openly: its gorgeous poetry will seduce the reader, who will embrace Epicurean philosophy wholesale in a haze of poetic ravishment. Responding to the poem's pressures, readers of Lucretius perform their own seduction, or instead fight back against Lucretius's proclaimed efforts to ravish them with his seductive verse. Furthermore, because Lucretius's erotic imagery is so explicit, both overt submission to and vigorous renunciations of *DRN* tend to use imagery drawn from *DRN* itself. In this sense, even the repudiations like Hutchinson's don't cut ties with *DRN* but, paradoxically, strengthen them.[23]

By calling attention to its seductive poetics, *DRN* produced readers attuned to both the dangers of poetic seduction and the potentially dangerous effects of Epicurean philosophy. Because of this, tropes of desire became prominent in *DRN*'s reception, as readers responded fiercely to what the text announced as its temptations and dangers. Such readerly anxieties manifest themselves in *DRN*'s early modern reception in narratives about both Lucretius as a poet and also early moderns as readers. In these accounts, *DRN*'s metaphors for poetic persuasion—honey and wormwood, Mars's seduction—are repurposed as tropes for both composition and reception. Lucretius, we are told, was the victim of a love potion that drove him mad and eventually killed him; *DRN* was written in the intervals of his madness. Readers like Hutchinson, we learn, were seduced by *DRN*'s honeyed verse, only coming to their senses when they came to recognize the poison poetic language had rendered so appealing. Love and pleasure become important ways to describe any interaction with Lucretian poetry, but this amorous vocabulary is frequently accompanied by its violent opposite: the hostile imagery and vocabulary of the "ex," the angry dupe disillusioned with a former lover, furious with themselves for falling for such cheap charms.

Because *DRN* presents itself as a kind of all-or-nothing relationship, those who backpedal must do so in an explicit fashion. Consequently, the idea of commitment has been particularly important in *DRN*'s reception history. Like early modern readers, modern critics often approach Lucretian reception through the lens of commitment, focusing on the dangers and problems early modern readers and writers faced in committing to an author whose poem endorses a philosophy so difficult to assimilate to Christian beliefs. In the case of Hutchinson, questions of gender, religion, and politics, combined with her own language of sexual dalliance, inflect scholarly accounts of her translation. Hutchinson's "wanton dalliance" suggests a romantic plotline and a colloquial idiom—"What was a nice Puritan doing with a naughty pagan like Lucretius?"—as though translating Lucretius were, in fact, to dally with him. The association with Lucretius besmirches Hutchinson's otherwise perfect reputation, solidified in the nineteenth century when her biography of her husband made both her and him into Puritan saints. Unlike Plato, early modernity's pagan good boy (because his thinking was so easily assimilable to Christian thought), Lucretius is not the one you take home to the parents; he is the "other woman," the youthful crush you lust after and burn for, but would never marry. Much of Hutchinson's textual output is oriented around her family: the "Defence" and *Memoirs* of her husband, the *Elegies* upon her husband's passing, and *On the Principles of the Christian Religion, Addressed to her Daughter.* Framed as an extramarital dalliance, the Lucretius translation undermines the coherence and orientation of Hutchinson's textual corpus.

Contemporary critics follow their early modern objects of study by implying that readers of *DRN*—both early modern and contemporary—must either be "all in" or all out, either fully committed to or utterly indifferent to Epicurean philosophy. Stephen Greenblatt's popularizing account of Lucretius and Renaissance Europe, *The Swerve*, models a version of "all in." For Greenblatt, the rediscovery of Lucretius sparked modernity itself. Greenblatt's zeal is yet another episode in *DRN*'s erotic reception, characterized by rapturous embrace or violent repudiation. Greenblatt opens his book with an account of erotic fascination around his youthful discovery of *DRN*: browsing a bookstore discount pile, he chooses a paperback with an "extremely odd" book cover featuring a painting by Max Ernst, two pairs of legs under a crescent moon "engaged in what appeared to be an act of celestial coition."[24] Like so many readers, Greenblatt is initially skeptical about a poem on materialist cosmology ("Ancient physics is not a particularly promising subject for vacation reading") but buys *DRN* for its cover.[25] The young Greenblatt is drawn into the text by the "ardent hymn to Venus" that opens the poem, then devours the vision of Mars and Venus. When he gets to the "lengthy exposition of philosophical first principles" he is too far gone to lose interest.[26]

The crucial moment in the long history of erotic attraction to and repulsion for *DRN* is Saint Jerome's brief mention of the poet in his *Chronicle*, where he twists *DRN*'s seductive poetics into a slanderous biography. Though she likely knew better than to believe it, Lucy Hutchinson reproduces the story to criticize *DRN*'s irregularity, writing in the margins of the manuscript of her translation: "Here is one of the Poets abrupt Hiatus for he was mad with a Philtrum his wife gaue him & writt this booke but in the intervals of his phrenzie."[27] Even before Jerome established the erotic terms of Lucretian reception, ancient poets were already loving and leaving Lucretius. Both Horace and Virgil perform a turn to and then away from Lucretius, a turn both they and their critics articulate in terms of poetic influence and maturity, part of a necessary philosophical and literary development. Apocryphal stories reinforce this narrative: Virgil, it is said, came of age on the day Lucretius died, implying that Lucretius had to be decisively overcome before the younger poet could come to maturity.[28] Philip Hardie explains that attraction to and rejection of Lucretius become something of a trope in later Roman literature: "Horace's anti-conversion in Odes 1.34 purports to be a personal confession, but could almost be a blueprint for a dominant strand in the response to the *DRN* in later antiquity and beyond."[29] The only poet to break what has been called the "conspiracy of silence"—the refusal of the Augustan poets to name Lucretius directly—was Ovid, whose debts to Lucretius are immense, and who mentions "sublime" (*sublimis*) Lucretius in his list of poets in *Amores* 1.15.[30] Suggestively, Ovid's reputation also suffered for his overtly erotic poetry: his racy *Ars amatoria* was said to have offended Emperor Augustus and led to the poet's exile.[31]

Both classical and early modern repudiations of Lucretius evoke the genre of the palinode, a poem that retracts views expressed in an earlier poem. The first palinode was written by Stesichorus (sixth century BCE), who is said to have been blinded after insulting Helen of Troy in an earlier poem. Stesichorus's recantation of his insult in another ode to Helen apparently won the poet back his sight. Early modern readers would have been even more familiar with Augustine's and Petrarch's recantations—both in and out of verse—of juvenile erotic experience, from which they turn to a religious maturity. As Ayesha Ramachandran has argued, by the sixteenth century, the palinode "contained the promise of deliverance from the blindness of erotic seductions both literal and poetic."[32] This promise would have been particularly appealing to readers of Lucretius, fearful as they were of *DRN*'s promised seductions.[33]

Those lovers of Lucretius who did not recant their dalliances with *DRN* often met with grim ends invented or embellished by their biographers to recall the dangers of *DRN* (recall the stories about Michael Marullus and Thomas Creech, discussed in the Introduction). Even more significant, however, is the precedent set by Ficino, who took control of his own *DRN* narrative and modeled for later readers how to leave Lucretius once you had loved him. The Italian humanist, so important to the Renaissance as the father of Renaissance Neoplatonism, began his philosophical career with a commentary on Lucretius, a work he repudiated and claimed to have burned later in life.[34] Although Ficino renounced Epicureanism, Lucretius lives on in his texts as a counterexample to Platonism, and Ficino cannot resist quoting Lucretius on love in his *Libro dell'amore* (1469).[35] Ficino is particularly important for the early modern reception history of Lucretius because he exemplifies Renaissance and early modern narratives about Lucretian reading: a youthful dalliance with *DRN*, followed by eventual renunciation and commitment to another, more powerfully Christian, philosophy, in this case—as in many others—Platonism. It may also be that readers like Ficino, who turn away from *DRN*, are Lucretius's most apt pupils, absorbing all too well the lessons Lucretius taught about avoiding erotic desire and abjuring the "sweetness" of a poem that is itself conflicted in its ethics of eroticism. Although Lucretius staunchly defends his use of verse to popularize Epicurean philosophy, he seems to recognize that the uneasy proximity *DRN* establishes between rhetorical and sexual pleasure not only unsettles the role pleasure plays in Epicurean moral philosophy, but also implicates poetry in precisely the sorts of negative affects Epicureanism strives to avoid.

Like Ficino, Marullus, Creech, and others, Hutchinson draws upon *DRN*'s erotics to characterize her own engagement with *DRN*. Her translation of Lucretius, she writes to Lord Anglesey, is inexpert, a juvenile effort that reeks of the schoolroom in more ways than one: "I did not employ any serious studie in [it], for I turnd it into English in a roome where my children practizd the severall qualities they were taught, with their Tutors, & I numbred the sillables of my translation by the threds of the canvas I wrought in, & sett them downe with a pen & inke that stood by me."[36] The assertion is a striking one. Hutchinson infantilizes herself by association with her own children—as they do their lessons, she, too, numbers syllables. Moreover, the domestic scene feminizes her: translation work is associated here with women's work, the embroidery whose threads and canvas serve as props for composition. The translation, she seems to be saying, is no finer than women's piecework or exercises in a child's lesson book. Hutchinson stages what critics most feared about English translations of pagan texts: that they would be brought into the home, becoming part of the fabric of domestic life, infecting both women and children.

The place where Hutchinson translates—the schoolroom where her children study—heightens the sexual stakes of her "dalliance" with pagan books, suggesting marital infidelity or misguided maternal devotion to textual offspring rather than to her own flesh and blood. Yet although Hutchinson's account of her "dalliance" implies a pleasure in translation, her description of numbering syllables in her children's schoolroom does not sound indulgent in a hedonic sense; she may be whimsical to choose Lucretius, but the domestic labor of supervising tutors and counting stitches that frames her translation does not pose translation as a particularly pleasurable or sensual endeavor.[37] Hutchinson, that is, may be riffing on the dual meaning in the period of women's "work," a word used to denote both needlework and sex. While she is translating, Lucretius feels like work—needlework—but upon learning to "abhorre him," Hutchinson retroactively sees her translation as the second sort of work, a "wanton dalliance."[38]

Hutchinson's account of her translation, however, is in conversation with Lucretian poetics and cosmology in several ways: it links the misguided, casual way Hutchinson claims to have translated the poem to the looseness of Lucretian cosmology, which she describes in terms similar to those used to describe the haphazard motion of atoms in the void. In her dedication to Lord Anglesey, she twice calls the motion of atoms a frivolous "dance," describing the "Casuall, Irrationall dance of Attomes" as well as the "foppish casuall dance of attoms."[39] The key term is "casual," which reminds the reader that the atomist universe is governed by chance rather than divine reason; the near identity of the words "casual" and "causal" ironizes the radical difference between a cosmos with God and one without. "Foppish," however, lends a silly, social tone to the fall and swerve of atoms in the void, and aligns the loose motion of atoms with the loose morals of seventeenth-century libertines, so often described as fops, and also frequently associated with Lucretius.[40] By turning atoms into casual fops, Hutchinson critiques *DRN*'s readers for allowing themselves to be so easily led away from the true faith by alluring Lucretian heresies, for being governed not by divine will but by the casual winds of chance. Hutchinson may also be taking direct aim at Margaret Cavendish, who in her *Poems and Fancies* describes atomist motion as a dance in poems like "Motion directs, while Atomes dance." (Cavendish's atomist poetry is notable for its avoidance of the topic of God.)

Furthermore, Hutchinson's comparison of translation to both needlework and sex reiterates Lucretius's own poetics.[41] Lucretius also describes his poem as threads of a cloth and his own mode of composition as weaving. Drawing his images from the spider's handiwork, Lucretius figures his poem as a web or woven design, made up of threads of images and arguments. "Sed nunc ut repetam coeptum pertexere dictis" (To pick up the thread where I left off; *DRN* 1.418), he writes, resuming a thread of thought.[42] Both Hutchinson's and Lucretius's imagery reinforces one of the grounding principles of *DRN*, the analogy between atoms and alphabetical letters. In Lucretius's terms, alphabetical letters, like atoms, are building blocks of composition— one for texts, the other for matter. Hutchinson adapts the metaphor from Lucretius to a domestic and feminine context: her embroidery, thread on thread, seems to degrade her scholarly achievement, but her chosen imagery actually (or also) brings her closer to the poetic principles of the poet she translates.

Women and Lucretius in Seventeenth-Century England

Hutchinson's dedication participates in a tradition of erotic responses to *DRN* stretching from antiquity onward, and she was also actively engaged with contemporary conversations around Lucretius that also linked Lucretian poetry to questions of sex and gender. The erotic discourse surrounding *DRN* made the poem a lightning rod for early modern debates about women and reading. Anxiety over the morally corrupting influence of reading texts perceived as dangerous—particularly pagan literature and sexually suggestive genres like romance or love lyric—was exacerbated in seventeenth-century England by the increasing availability of texts in English, both translations of classical and continental texts and homegrown English renderings of classical and continental genres and styles. English-language texts came under particular suspicion because women, who were far less likely than men to have been taught foreign languages, especially ancient languages like Latin or Greek, could read them. Large sections of *DRN* were first made available to English-speaking audiences in John Florio's translation of Michel de Montaigne's *Essais* (1603), which contains approximately one-sixteenth of *DRN* in quotation. Because it was dedicated to a group of aristocratic women, Florio's translation was understood to be directed toward a female audience. Reid Barbour and David Norbrook argue that Florio's petition to women followed a pattern set by earlier French editions of the *Essais*: "Montaigne's first editor, Marie de Gournay, was a champion of women's learning, establishing a pattern in which Epicurean ideas showed a strong appeal to female readers."[43]

While Florio's "englishing" of the classical authors, including Lucretius, quoted by Montaigne was remarked upon by readers and critics, English translators who tackled the entire *DRN* came under stronger fire. English translations of *DRN*, a notoriously atheistic and hedonistic text, were attacked as being expressly designed to seduce women. Thomas Creech encountered a barrage of criticism for his translation, some focused on the dangers an English Lucretius posed to the gentler sex. An anonymous detractor raged that "'[t]was enough that M[r] Hobbs seduced the Men [with atomist ideas]; too much that M[r] Creech should debauch the Women with those corrupt Notions of a Deity, & by his soft Translation of a rough Piece melt the Ladies into admiration first of the Poetry & then of the Opinion."[44] Other commentators, however, applauded Creech for the very same reason. In her commendatory poem on Creech's *DRN*, "To the Unknown Daphnis on his Excellent Translation of Lucretius," Aphra Behn praises the translator for rectifying gender inequality—he "Equall'st Vs to Man!"—by making the important classical text available in English.[45] Behn boldly embraces the sexualized vocabulary associated with *DRN*, writing in the same poem that in Creech's translation "Reason over all unfetter'd Plays, / Wanton and disturb'd as Summers Breeze."[46] While Behn agrees with Hutchinson that *DRN* is "wanton," she celebrates such wantonness as liberatory for women; Hutchinson would have strongly disapproved.

Seventeenth-century dialogues about the particular danger Lucretius posed to women intersected with ongoing debates about gender and style. The anonymous critic's description of Creech's *DRN* as a "soft Translation of a rough Piece" suggests that poetic style is gendered, a "rough" style masculine, a "soft" one feminine. Lucretius's jagged, archaizing Latin verse was considered distinctly masculine, a style his English translators were accused of softening into femininity with smooth diction, meter, and rhyme. As a woman translating such a "masculine" classical author, Hutchinson was implicated in this discussion. In 1658, Sir Aston Cokain wrote a letter to his friend Alexander Brome, who was apparently planning a Lucretius translation, telling him not to worry about competition from Hutchinson, because her gender made her unfit to translate the Roman poet.

> I know a Lady that hath been about
> The same designe, but she must needes give out:
> Your Poet strikes too boldly home sometimes,
> In geniall things, t'appear in womens rhimes,
> The task is masculine, and he that can
> Translate *Lucretius*, is an able man.[47]

As Cokain puts it, a woman could never really translate Lucretius because his treatment of sex—"geniall things"—renders him inappropriate for a woman's pen. If a lady managed to translate *DRN*, she would betray her very gender, proving herself not an able translator, but an able man.[48]

Hutchinson seems to have agreed with Cokain that some sections of *DRN* were too sexually explicit for a lady to translate, though in the margins of Book 4 she avers that a midwife, rather than a man, would be most fit for the task. However, she had little patience for crude equations of gender and style. A profoundly skilled and principled reader, writer, and thinker, Hutchinson was more than happy to criticize other writers for having a weak, soft style, but she did so based not on their gender but rather on the quality of their craft and the firmness of their ideological convictions. Hutchinson attacked male poets linked to other Lucretius translations with charges of vanity and weak style, questioning the male poets' political and literary motives using language borrowed from standard critiques of women writers. In the dedication to her *DRN* translation, for example, she disparages John Evelyn, who had been vain enough to appear in an engraving on the frontispiece to his translation of *DRN* Book 1 wreathed in laurels.[49] Hutchinson remarks ironically that although she is ashamed to have translated a heretical text such as *DRN*, "a masculine Witt hath thought it worth printing his head in a lawrell crowne for the version of one of these bookes."[50] Hutchinson's ostentatious humility pokes fun at Evelyn's inflated sense of accomplishment for his lesser achievement—the translation of just one book of *DRN* to her six.

Though she does not address the quality of Evelyn's translation, an earlier attack on Edmund Waller in her unpublished reply to his "A Panegyrick to my Lord Protector" indicates the nature of Hutchinson's literary values. Her "To M:ʳ Waller vpon his Panegirique to the Lord Protector" (1655), a line-by-line satirical rewriting of Waller's encomium on Cromwell, accuses Waller of writing sickeningly sweet poetry whose softness does not betray his gender but rather reveals his flattering, servile spirit.[51]

> Whilst with a smooth but yet a servile Tongue
> You Court all Factions, and haue sweetly sung
> The Triumphs of yoʳ. Countreys Overthrow
> Raysing the Glory of her treacherous Foe.
>
> Let partiall Spirits praise alowd the verse
> And with like flattery yoʳ. soft lynes Rehearse.[52]

Hutchinson disliked Cromwell, whom she felt was a tyrant, but her real target is Waller, who had only recently switched allegiances to Cromwell from the king, whom he had been equally quick to praise. Waller's nimble change of political orientation enraged royalists and commonwealthers alike, few more than Hutchinson, who saw in Waller's "soft lynes" a weak and wavering spirit. As David Norbrook argues, in Hutchinson's verse attack, the "duplicitous smoothness of Waller's language" is "a symptom of the corruption of language and mores by tyranny. His servility is frequently linked with the smoothness, sweetness, and softness of his verse."[53] Hutchinson objects to both Evelyn's translation and Waller's poem because of their motives, in Evelyn's case, for poetic fame, in Waller's, for political favor. The animosity Hutchinson felt toward Waller in the 1650s would have been exacerbated in the 1670s by his entry into the cold war between Lucretius translators, with his commendatory verses for Evelyn's translation of *DRN* Book 1, where he calls atomism an "Order Democratical."[54] Hutchinson would have had little patience—or sympathy—for Waller's facile wordplay, which could be seen to betray the political two-facedness that allowed him to easily change sides from royalism to parliamentarianism.

For Hutchinson, then, poetic style has no necessary relation to gender: "softness" is a category she applies comfortably to male poets, implying that a woman such as herself could have a stronger style than a man (without, moreover, rendering herself unwomanly, as Cokain had quipped). This does not mean, however, that Hutchinson shied away from using gendered language to attack stylistic or ideological weakness in poets. She feminizes Evelyn and Waller by calling them vain and their writing smooth, but is equally quick to discredit her own translation of Lucretius by characterizing herself as a foolish, wanton woman. Hutchinson seems to untether gender from biology, and makes it function as a moral and aesthetic category: the category of "woman" becomes something applicable to both women and men, particularly those whose moral weakness leads them to dally with pagan texts like Lucretius.[55]

Lucretian Desires in Hutchinson's Later Poetry

In the 1675 dedication to her *DRN* translation and in her poetry written in the late 1660s and 1670s (*OD* and the *Elegies*), Hutchinson persistently associates Lucretius with wayward desire. In her dedication of *DRN*, this is rendered in biographical terms, but Hutchinson's characterization of her translation as a "wanton dalliance" with "impious books" also activates contemporary associations of Lucretius with the textual seduction of vulnerable women as well as with libertine culture. Hutchinson presents herself as a young woman (though she was probably in her thirties when she translated

Lucretius, not young in the terms of the time) briefly seduced by the tempting pagan Lucretius, who atones for her error by applying herself in her later poetry to a devout, biblical poetics. However, although Hutchinson's prefatory materials make strong claims for a strict opposition between *OD* and *DRN*, with *OD* acting as a religious purification after her dalliance with the pagan Lucretius, the epic's strict biblical hermeneutics and Genesis narrative unequivocally overcoming *DRN*'s wanton poetics and haphazard chaology, *DRN*'s influence persists in *OD*.[56] Although Hutchinson frames her trajectory from the *DRN* translation to *OD* as one from wanton error to textually faithful devotion, from the disorder of the Lucretian cosmos to the divine order of Genesis, the account she gives of her authorial development obscures important Lucretian legacies in her later work, which confutes, but also assimilates, *DRN*.

Hutchinson integrates a wide range of Lucretian conceits into *OD*. Not only are there moments when *OD* has a distinctly Lucretian quality—a feel for the natural world that goes beyond that of the biblical stories that form the epic's backbone, or moments when the poem's voice veers into a description far more passionate than the restrained explanatory or didactic mood that dominates—but there are also specific Lucretian touchstones to which Hutchinson returns over and over: Lucretius's denunciations of worldly ambition; the famous "Suave, mari magno" passage that opens Book 2, which illustrates mental calm and the retreat from public life; and Book 4's account of perception and dreaming. Hutchinson unites these diverse Lucretian echoes within *OD* by using them—albeit in different ways—to represent the pitfalls of fallen consciousness. *OD*'s most pointed uptake of *DRN*, which is central to its depiction of the difference between mortal and heavenly orders, lies in its representations of love and desire, particularly as part of women's experience. While the preface to *OD* minimizes the particularity of both gender difference and pagan philosophy, *OD* itself is notable for its focus on female experience in its depiction of biblical women.[57] Although neither *DRN* nor gender is Hutchinson's focus in *OD*, indeed, even though she rather insistently moves beyond minor distinctions about more or less heretical texts, and more or less vulnerable readers, to treat the grand theme of the fall of humanity, these themes persist into *OD* as illustrations of the fallen condition. In *OD*, women's desire, as illustrated through Lucretian tropes, exemplifies the fallen will.

What is important here is not that the influence of Lucretius persists in Hutchinson's later poetry, but rather how it persists: in representations of fallen desire and in stories about women, both the Old Testament women Hutchinson describes in *OD*, and, in the *Elegies* written to mourn her husband's death, herself. Perhaps owing to the erotic charge surrounding Lucretius in England in the 1660s and 1670s, perhaps to the added freight of translating Lucretius as a woman, perhaps simply to the irresistible pull of Lucretius's seductive poetics, Hutchinson's later poetry is marked by the erotics of Lucretian materialism. Both *OD* and the *Elegies* draw on the very sections of *DRN* that Hutchinson omits from her translation and which color her dedication—the passages at the end of Book 4 describing insatiable lust and tormenting desires. These Lucretian lusts and desires help Hutchinson to depict fallen psychology. In *OD*'s accounts of female desire and the pains of motherhood, Hutchinson departs from her biblical material and interpolates strong authorial additions, which contain the most striking Lucretian elements in *OD*. In the *Elegies*, Lucretian images surface to describe her desire for her husband. And although *OD* and the *Elegies* thematize women's experience, in both Lucretius ultimately serves not to characterize women alone, or to differentiate between women and men, but rather to highlight the divide between the fallen and unfallen orders, mortal disorder and heavenly order. Hutchinson makes desire, drawn with Lucretian lines, the figure for all human desire, and *DRN* a synecdoche for all seductive pagan texts.

Like Petrarch, who in the *Rime sparse* bemoans his youthful errors even as he records them in obsessive detail, in *OD* Hutchinson relegates her Lucretian fancies to her errant youth while retaining those fancies as a part of her mature poetic and moral universe. The preface to *OD* sharply differentiates the biblical epic's imaginative economy from that of the Lucretius translation. *OD*, with its Christian cosmology and fixed, orderly biblical poetics, is supposed to supersede *DRN*, with its wanton atoms, elements not just of an atomist chaology but also figures for a loose and disorderly pagan poetics. *DRN*, Hutchinson writes in the preface to *OD*, had "filled my brain with such foolish fancies, that I found it necessary to have recourse to the fountain of Truth, to wash out all ugly wild impressions, and fortify my mind with a strong antidote against all the poison of human wit and wisdom that I had been dabbling withal."[58] Because *OD* is supposed to wash away the traces of *DRN*, Hutchinson is careful to differentiate her biblical poetics from the wanton ethics of translation she practiced with Lucretius. Although during the seventeenth century *DRN* was considered to be an exceptionally dangerous pagan text for the way it contradicted central tenets of Christian belief (most importantly the immortality of the soul and divine providence), as

Hutchinson presents it here, *DRN* is no more poisonous than any other text born of "human wit and wisdom." The elision of *DRN*'s particular dangers serves to emphasize what for Hutchinson is a far more fundamental distinction, between divine and mortal orders of knowledge and creativity. Unlike Milton, who presumed to "justifie the wayes of God to men" in *Paradise Lost* (whose composition was roughly contemporaneous with *OD*'s), Hutchinson maintains that human creativity has nothing to contribute to scripture.[59] Mankind should adore rather than explain God, and readers abjure the temptations of all texts save the Bible. Hutchinson's own textual salvation, *OD* is the fruit of her realization that "I found I could know nothing but what God taught me."[60]

Both *OD* and Hutchinson's *Elegies* map the topography of fallen desire, *OD* through its retelling of Genesis, the *Elegies* in a more personal key. The poems stage the continual and powerful threat of the fallen order and the promise that it could be overcome—against all odds, and after much suffering—by divine forces of salvation. As emblematic of the disorder threatening divine order, *DRN* haunts *OD* and the *Elegies* as that which must be continually overcome, continually overwritten. Thus, although Lucretian ideas and images generally operate as negative—because mortal and fallen—counterpoints to divine salvation and heavenly pleasures, Lucretian psychology is an essential component of Hutchinson's vision of a Christian universe. While any good Christian seeks to eventually overcome the mortal condition, it is not a stage you can skip. Both *OD* and the *Elegies* reprise and adapt elements from the most erotically charged sections of *DRN* and from the long erotic reception of Lucretius, which Hutchinson so adeptly manipulates with the sexualized frame her dedication imposes on both her translation and her repudiation of *DRN*. Just as *DRN* Book 4's description of obsessive desire is a present absence in Hutchinson's translation of *DRN* and its dedication, *DRN* is a present absence in *OD* and the *Elegies*: a symbology of sinfulness, a handbook of poetic images for fallen human fancy and deranged human understanding that Hutchinson continually draws upon so that human errors can be exposed. Indeed, it is precisely the omitted sections of *DRN* Book 4—the account of the desperate and insatiable lovers unable to consume their beloved object—that Hutchinson wields in *OD* and the *Elegies* as a vision of the threat of mortal desire.

Lucretius's scandalous description of insatiable sexual desire (the lines from Book 4 of *DRN* that Hutchinson refuses to translate) is an implicit touchstone for *OD*'s account of fallen psychology. Erotic fantasy is the object

of some of Lucretius's greatest poetry but also his sternest warnings. He
describes how sleep revives the activities and concerns of the waking hours—
lawyers dream they plead cases in court, sailors imagine they wage war with
the winds, hounds snuffle after their prey, and the poet himself has reveries
of composing *DRN*. For the young, however, sleep comes bearing sensual
fantasies.

> tum quibus aetatis freta primitus insinuatur
> semen, ubi ipsa dies membris matura creavit,
> conveniunt simulacra foris e corpore quoque
> nuntia praeclari vultus pulchrique coloris,
> qui ciet irritans loca turgida semine multo,
> ut quasi transactis saepe omnibu' rebu' profundant
> fluminis ingentis fluctus vestemque cruentent.
>
> (*DRN* 4.1030–36)

[For those in adolescence's riptide, [into whom / Seed is penetrat-
ing] for the first time—then images invade, / Images of some random body or other—bringing news / Of a lovely face and radiant
complexion's rosy hues. / This irritates and goads the organs, swollen hard with seed—/ Such that frequently, as if he'd really done
the deed, / A youth floods forth a gush of semen so he stains the
sheet; translation modified]

Hutchinson adapts these lines in her portrayal of the overabundant and self-
destructive passions that are consequences of the fall, which she depicts as a
fall into insatiable, conflicted appetite. "The never-failing consequents of
sin," Hutchinson writes in *OD*, is a "civil war" between "Reason and sense,"
"th'aversion and the appetite, / Which led two different troops of passions
out."[61]

> The less world with the great proportion held:
> As winds the caverns, sighs the bosoms filled;
> So flowing tears did beauty's fair fields drown,
> As inundations kept within no bound.
> Fear earthquakes made, lust in the fancy whirled,
> Turned into flame and, bursting, fired the world:
> Spite, hate, revenge, ambition, avarice

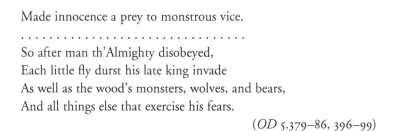

Made innocence a prey to monstrous vice.
. . . .
So after man th'Almighty disobeyed,
Each little fly durst his late king invade
As well as the wood's monsters, wolves, and bears,
And all things else that exercise his fears.

(*OD* 5.379–86, 396–99)

The fall, which rends the fabric of the created world, stirs up a matching ferment within the human breast, as the disorder among the natural elements—"all things without them jar" (5.373)—is matched by the "civil war" of passions within the human heart. As she writes elsewhere, in the *Elegies*:

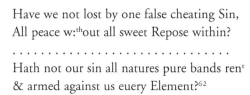

Have we not lost by one false cheating Sin,
All peace w:ᵗʰout all sweet Repose within?
. . . .
Hath not our sin all natures pure bands renᵗ
& armed against us euery Element?⁶²

Lapsed psychology is a maelstrom of fear and desire, mutually constituting emotions that feed off and reinforce each other even at the level of Hutchinson's imagery: "Fear earthquakes made, lust in the fancy whirled" (*OD* 5.383). These last lines channel Lucretius, who characterizes fear and lust as the greatest threats to human happiness. Moreover, Hutchinson's earthquakes and swirling fancy have parallels in *DRN*: Book 6's lengthy explanation of possible causes for earthquakes, and Book 4's account of erotic fancy. In the fourth canto of *OD*, Hutchinson describes Noah's drunken lust and wretched slumber.

Nor give tired Nature the relief of sleep
Till they their brains in their crowned goblets steep,
When the wine, working with wild fancy, makes
False dreams of pleasure, horrid sad mistakes.

(*OD* 9.75–78)

If the Lucretian explanation of dreaming and erotic fixation is a submerged reference point for *OD*'s depiction of fallen psychology, it surfaces, briefly, here, in *OD*'s account of Noah's drunken lust. Noah is not simply an example of sinfulness, but also of how hedonic indulgence encourages degraded fantasy, and moreover, how "false dreams of pleasure" can become "horrid sad mistakes."

While Noah's drunken lust, which leads him to sleep with his daughters, is a particularly disturbing instance of desire, Hutchinson is quite clear that desire is a threat even within the confines of lawful marriage. In *OD*, Hutchinson indulges an almost Donnean fascination with the paradoxes of human desire and the institutions of human love. Marriage is her particular focus. On the one hand, marriage is essential to salvation: after the fall, marriage alone ensures the endurance of humanity, through children, and promises salvation and eternal life, with the eventual birth of Christ the savior. On the other hand, both marriage and children are sources of immense suffering and temptation. In canto 3 of *OD*, Hutchinson explains both marriage's importance as a stop against "death and solitude," and also the ways in which it is "accursed."

> Thus God did the first marriage celebrate
> While man was in his unpolluted state,
> And th'undefilèd bed with honour decked,
> Though perverse men the ordinance reject,
> And, pulling all its sacred ensigns down,
> To the white virgin only give the crown.
> Nor yet is marriage grown less sacred since
> Man fell from his created excellence:
> Necessity now raises its esteem,
> Which doth mankind from death's vast jaws redeem,
> Who even in their graves are yet alive
> While they in their posterity survive.
> In it they find a comfort and an aid
> In all the ills which human life invade.
> This curbs and cures wild passions that arise,
> Repairs time's daily wastes with new supplies;
> When the declining mother's youthful grace
> Lies dead and buried in her wrinkled face,
> In her fair daughters it revives and grows
> And her dead cinder in their new flames glows.
> And though this state may sometime prove accursed,

For of best things, still the corruption's worst,
Sin so destroys an institution good,
Provided against death and solitude.

(*OD* 3.433–56)

Marriage is the most important mortal estate, an "institution good" that instantiates mortal order so as to prepare for the divine order yet to come. And yet, in both the *Elegies* and *OD*, it is clear that marriage also produces profound temptations and traumas.

Although marriage, as Hutchinson claims, "curbs and cures wild passions that arise," in addition to repairing "time's daily wastes with new supplies," it is also a venue for fallen desire. The fifth canto of *OD* rewrites Eve's curse as not just pain in childbirth, but also as the pain of desire.

Alas! How sadly to this day we find
Th'effect of this dire curse on womankind;
Eve sinned in fruit forbid, and God requires
Her penance in the fruit of her desires.
When first to men their inclinations move,
How are they tortured with distracting love!
What disappointments find they in the end;
Constant uneasinesses which attend
The best condition of the wedded state,
Giving all wives sense of the curse's weight,
Which makes them ease and liberty refuse,
And with strong passion their own shackles choose.
Now though they easier under wise rule prove,
And every burden is made light by love,
Yet golden fetters, soft-lined yokes, still be
Though gentler curbs, but curbs of liberty,
As well as the harsh tyrant's iron yoke;
More sorely galling them whom they provoke
To loathe their bondage, and despise the rule
Of an unmanly, fickle, froward fool.

(*OD* 5.127–46)

Here, Hutchinson engages in a profound reflection upon what it means to desire something that causes you pain and fundamentally compromises the structures of personal—and implicitly political—autonomy. Hutchinson depicts desire as politically dubious, almost monarchical, because it leads to subjection. And although Hutchinson focuses on the horrors of being married to an unworthy husband, "an unmanly, fickle, froward fool," she implies that not only is all desire torture—women are "tortured with distracting love!"—but that the desire for the subjection that comes with marriage may not even be justified by the character of a good husband.

Most strikingly, she dwells at length on the fruits of lust—children. A mother of nine, she makes the horrors of childbirth and parenthood vivid in her lines about the particular torture of having and raising children.[63]

> How painfully the fruit within them grows,
> What tortures do their ripened births disclose,
> How great, how various, how uneasy are
> The breeding-sicknesses, pangs that prepare
> The violent openings of life's narrow door,
> Whose fatal issues we as oft deplore!
>
> (OD 5.149–54)

The passage continues in a similarly negative vein, with Hutchinson noting that even after they have made their way, violently, through "life's narrow door," children continue to pain their mothers with their disobedience. And even when they do behave, mothers are tormented with worry over their children's safety and livelihood.

Yet even this is not marriage's greatest danger. To be sure, marriage is the venue for the execution of Eve's curse as Hutchinson presents it: in the pains of childbirth, as well as in the horrors of subjection to a husband. Yet marriage's worst temptation is that its mortal pleasures—fraught and fallen as they are—can be mistaken for, or prioritized over, divine ones, mortal love placed above divine love, love for a husband above love of God. Marriage, after all, is a brief oasis—a dream, even—of stability in the storm of mortal life, a stopgap against the ravages of fallen existence that is useless if it does not train the soul for the eternal pleasures of union with God. The *Elegies*, more than *OD*, shine a light on this temptation. While *OD* explores the tension between mortal and divine attachments through figures like Lot's wife, who cannot resist turning back toward Canaan against God's express orders, or Abraham, who manages to master his will and subordinate his attachment to this life (in the form of his son) to his obedience to God, the

Elegies focus on Hutchinson's own despair after the death of her husband, and her mighty struggles against what she recognizes is a misguided longing for her husband to return to earth from Heaven. Hutchinson knows that it is the ultimate vanity to want to snatch her husband from the bliss of salvation for what would be nothing more than a fleeting, fallen pleasure in each other's company. She also knows that her own desire for her husband misdirects toward an incorrect object, or even forecloses, what should be her own desire for salvation.

In Hutchinson's desperation after her husband's death, even her children cannot assuage her grief and relieve her longing for the deceased John. The poet who could write in *OD* that a child's fresh face "revives and grows" the cinders of a parent's long-dead youthful grace finds no comfort in the "disperst Image" the father leaves in the faces of his children.

> Where ere I goe affliction Still
> Takes vpe my walkes & Still I find
> Something That calls my losse to mind
> His disperst Image which I see
> Amoungst his Children Joyes not me
> Whoe pine with an vnfilld desiere
> W:ch Seekes him in each one entier.[64]

In this moment, the resemblance of a child to her parents becomes something like another part of Eve's curse, because the partial resemblance, the "disperst Image" of the father, cannot fulfill the bereaved wife's "vnfilld desiere." Hutchinson may be channeling Lucretius's account of a lover whose desire cannot be fulfilled by images of the love object. Trapped in the cycle of unfilled desires, the very thing that should redeem life's finitude—children—produces only despair. Hutchinson's longing for her husband is a mistaken desire, one that seeks to combat finitude (in this case her husband's death) not in the continuance of his line in their children, but by keeping him by her side forever, ripping him from heaven and dragging him back down to fallen earth, whatever it costs his—or her—soul.

OD powerfully echoes the *Elegies*' lesson about the pitfalls of clinging to mortal things in its recounting of the story of Lot's wife, who disobeys God's orders to flee Sodom without looking back, and is punished for her disobedience by being turned into a pillar of salt. Because she illustrates the most basic and important sin, that of refusing divine salvation, Lot's wife is a

singularly important negative example: she fails to shift her orientation away
from the mortal realm of goods and earthly attachments toward the divinely
appointed path.

> But for example to her sex remained,
> Teaching how curious minds should be restrained
> And kept within the Lord's prescribèd bound,
> Which none e'er passed but swift destruction found.
>
> (*OD* 13.173–76)

Hutchinson identifies with Lot's wife. As Norbrook points out, these lines
about the negative example she sets strongly recall both Hutchinson's "con-
cluding remarks upon her husband's death: 'God had removed me that I
might not tempt him [to] look back upon this world as a flaming Sodom
while the angels [were] carrying him to the mountains of rest and safety' (*M*
337), and her apology in the Lucretius dedication for 'the defects and errors
of my vainly curious youth' (*L* 27)."[65] Hutchinson associates the temptation
of the Lucretius translation with the temptation of her love for her husband.
Both are trespasses of mortal, fallen desire of the sort exemplified by Lot's
wife. Moreover, *OD* and the *Elegies* make it clear that Hutchinson conceives
of this desire—both her youthful desire for Lucretius and her longing for her
husband—in terms of the erotic obsession and insatiable longing that Lucretius illustrates so forcefully in *DRN* Book 4.

While Hutchinson's mature poetic works primarily associate *DRN* with
the dangers of fallen desire, they also sometimes use *DRN* to depict positive
moral orientations. Hutchinson juxtaposes her struggles to transcend her
mortal attachments to her husband's ability to transcend mortal constraints.
As she presents him in the first of the *Elegies*, John Hutchinson, imprisoned
for his political views, finds spiritual freedom in physical confinement. By
Love's "Great power he free in prison remaned / And in y^e *Bloody Tower*
with triumph reignd / Dispising his oppressors rage while They / By lusts
enslaued in sadder [Thralldome] lay."[66] Rising above a landscape of the
passions—the wrath, grief, and fear of his opponents—John Hutchinson
emerges as a pillar of calm, savoring the sweets of divine love though locked
in a wretched prison. This passage strongly evokes the infamous "Suave,
mari magno" passage that opens Book 2 of *DRN* and represents the negative
pleasures of *ataraxia*, freedom from pain.[67]

While Lucy Hutchinson grapples with what she presents as a fruitless (and dangerous) desire for her husband, even in life John Hutchinson is able to free himself from mortal passions. His self-discipline in prison, which leads him away from the cares of this world toward the delights of the next, offers a foretaste of the sweet joys that await him in Heaven. Just as mortal life was framed through the question of desire and satiety, paradise, as Hutchinson depicts it in *OD*, is a place of desires ever sated and ever renewed.

> Although the paradise of the fair world above,
> Each-where perfumed with sweet-respiring love,
> Refreshed with pleasure's never shrinking streams,
> Illustrated with light's unclouded beams,
> The happy land of peace and endless rest
> Which doth both soul and sense with full joys feast,
> Feasts that extinguish not the appetite,
> Which is renewed to heighten the delight.
>
> (*OD* 1.185–92)

Heaven, like earth, is a place of perpetual appetite, but with a crucial differ-ence: here the soul's hunger is endlessly renewed so that it can be endlessly fulfilled, and the celestial feast is one of desire sprung from satiety rather than insatiability. Psalms 16:11, cited in the margins of this passage, reads: "Thou wilt shew me the path of life: in thy presence is fulness of joy; at thy right hand there are pleasures for evermore." While the Psalms passage stresses eternal pleasure, Hutchinson emphasizes eternal appetite as well. Although in canto 1 of *OD* Hutchinson makes paradise a place of endless appetite, she is quite clear in canto 3 that the endless appetites of Heaven do not foreclose divine fulfillment. The life of man "is but a progress of desire, / Which still, enjoyed, doth something else require, / Unsatisfied with all it hath pursued / Until it rest in God, the sovereign good" (*OD* 3.33–36). Having lost their share of Heaven until Christ returns it to them, humans must wait until the afterlife to find any satisfaction. Life, then, "is but a progress of desire," in which no earthly satisfaction will suffice. The insatiability that is constitutive of mortal experience will be sated in Heaven.

In spite of Hutchinson's protestations in the preface to *OD* and the dedication to the *DRN* translation to have overcome the influence of pagan literature, a strong Lucretian presence remains in Hutchinson's mature poetry. Her pointed omission of the end of Book 4 from the *DRN* translation emphasizes rather than suppresses the passages Lucretius dedicated to obsessive, unrequited passion, and they resurface in not just the later dedication of the translation to Lord Anglesey but also the *Elegies* and *OD*, in depictions of fallen psychology. Like so many before her, Hutchinson dramatized her response—both attraction and repulsion—to *DRN*'s erotic poetics, a poetics that has shaped the poem's reception since its composition. This erotics was a crucial framework for the early modern reception of *DRN*. Hutchinson's translation and then repudiation of *DRN* help to locate the particular resonances the erotics of Lucretian reception had for early modern women. Moreover, the traces of Lucretius that remain in Hutchinson's *Elegies* and *OD* show how the erotics of Lucretian poetics and Lucretian reception leave their mark not just on Hutchinson's translation and framing of that translation, but also in her poetry.

Lucretian Poetics and Women's Writing in Margaret Cavendish's *Poems and Fancies*

The first book Margaret Cavendish (1623–1673) published was the 1653 *Poems and Fancies* (hereafter *P&F*),[1] a collection of lyrics that versifies the atomist underpinnings of the cosmos in imitation of *DRN*.[2] Like Lucretius, who formalizes the bond between poetry and matter through a repeated analogy between atoms and alphabetical letters, Cavendish links the fanciful variety of her poems to the profusion of nature itself.[3] Until recently, *P&F*'s bewildering variety, which seems to bespeak serious flaws in the collection's formal concept, has deterred scholarly study.[4] Because *P&F* is both Cavendish's only book of poetry and her most important atomist work, the critical fate of *P&F* has downgraded the status of atomism and poetry alike in the Cavendish corpus.[5] Cavendish herself has also played an important role in the sidelining of her first published work. Soon after composing her atomist poems, Cavendish apparently became troubled by the idea that dead atoms form the basis of all life, and in the *Philosophicall Fancies* published alongside *P&F* in 1653 explains that she does not believe that inanimate particles of matter constitute the actual grounds of matter.[6] However, as I will argue in what follows, Cavendish learns from *DRN* not only a theory of matter but also an argument about the connection between poetry and philosophy.[7] Although Cavendish's views on matter evolved away from the classical atomism espoused in *DRN*, other Lucretian principles—about the fundamental unknowability of nature's foundations and the sympathy between nature and the imagination—stay with her throughout her career.[8] Drawing on Lucretian ideas about the relationship between natural and poetic creativity, the inscrutability of nature's internal workings, and the usefulness of poetry for philosophy, Cavendish conceives of poetic fancy—the imaginative expression of the natural and variable motion of thoughts—as an invaluable tool for carrying out the work of natural philosophy. And while she claims in a later natural philosophical work to "Wave the Opinion of Atoms"[9]—that is, the idea that discreet and indivisible particles constitute the fundamental structure of matter—she never forswears the fanciful Lucretian epistemology she develops in *P&F*.[10] Cavendish appropriates Lucretian suspicion about the knowability of the universe to her own seventeenth-century purposes, establishing a natural scientific practice based in the potentialities of poetic fancy rather than the certainties of experiment.

In the prefatory epistles, the author seems to encourage disregard for her atomist poems by apologizing repeatedly for the haphazard products of her fickle, untrained, female brain. The poems, Cavendish writes in her prefatory epistles, "An Epistle to Mistris Toppe" and "To Naturall Philosophers," are the product of "Thoughts which run wildly about," which she composed in verse because "Errours might better passe there, then in Prose."[11] Indeed, the poems are likely to be error-ridden because, she writes, "I never read, nor heard of any English Booke to Instruct me."[12] Whatever she does know about atomist philosophy or Lucretius's poem has been learned secondhand in conversation with her husband, brother-in-law, and other family members,[13] yet even these ideas Cavendish claims to have not "throughly reason'd on."[14] The only faint praise she has for her own book is that the poems are "harmelesse Fancies,"[15] though even this is cause for regret: "I wish heartily my Braine had been Richer, to make you a fine Entertainment."[16] However, Cavendish's seemingly negative assessments of herself—and her poems—are neither biographical truths nor frank critical assessments of her work, but rather a Lucretian strategy. Her negative self-representations in *P&F*'s dedicatory epistles are part of her Lucretian project: Cavendish invokes gendered stereotypes of women as flighty and ignorant to illustrate the principle that nobody, male or female, is capable of discerning nature's inner workings. She does not represent her poetry as the errant fancies of a flibbertigibbet (my term) because it—and she—is one, but because the notion of fancy she establishes through those self-representations elucidates a skepticism, which she shares with Lucretius, about the capacity of humans to distinguish truth from error.

Like so much of Cavendish's writing, *P&F* is strongly feminized. The prefatory materials make much of the author's gender, and the poems focus on female characters and draw their governing metaphors from the feminized domestic sphere. Cavendish's feminization of her own writing is undeniably bound up with her personal circumstances, but it is also programmatically linked to *DRN* and its feminine imagery. *DRN* opens with the striking hymn to Venus, which hails the goddess as *genetrix* (*DRN* 1.1), who inspires all living things to procreate and persist, and Lucretius begs her to inspire him to write his poem of nature. Venus embodies the principles of natural and poetic abundance and poetic seduction that are essential to both Lucretius's natural philosophy and his defense of didactic poetry. Cavendish also invokes a powerful female deity to oversee her atomist universe. Introducing a long series of poems on the workings of the atomist universe (with titles such as "Of Aiery Atomes," "The bignesse of Atomes," "What Atomes make Change," "Of Sharpe Atomes," "Of Vacuum"), *P&F*'s first poem, "Nature calls a Councell," sets the stage for the natural philosophical poems to follow with a personified Nature assembling her handmaidens Motion, Figure, Matter, and Life to "advise about making the World." Nature declares her purpose.

> Besides it is my nature things to make,
> To give out worke, and you directions take.
> And by this worke, a pleasure take therein,
> And breed the Fates in huswifery to spin,
> And make strong Destiny to take some paines,
> Least she growe idle, let her Linke some Chaines:
> Inconstancy, and Fortune turne a Wheele,
> Both are so wanton, cannot stand, but reele.
>
> (lines 9–16)

Whereas the Lucretian Venus is an exuberant earth mother, stirring a yearning for life in all things, Cavendish's Nature is the lady of a great house, directing her staff in busy "huswifery" to keep them from idleness. She is a careful mistress, choosing tasks for her subordinates that suit their characters: the Fates will spin, strong Destiny link chains, and even reeling Inconstancy and Fortune are not chastised for their wantonness but rather instructed to put it to good use turning a wheel.

Cavendish takes sly pleasure in transforming the magnificent Lucretian Venus into a housewife. In another poem from *P&F*, "The Fairy Queen," she jokes that

> Yet Venus is a Tinkers wife, we see,
> Not a goddesse, as she was thought to be;

When all the world to her did offerings bring,
And her high praise in prose, and verse did sing:
And Priests in orders, on her Altars tend,
And to her Image all the wise heads bend.
But to vain wayes that men did go,
To worship gods they do not know.

(lines 73–80)[17]

The hymn to Venus has always been controversial: Why does Lucretius, who argues so vehemently and eloquently against the mystifications of religion, begin his poem by praising one of the divinities he urges readers to disregard? "The Fairy Queen" takes aim at the contradictions inherent in the Lucretian position and turns *DRN*'s critique of religion back on its author: here is Lucretius, singing Venus's "high praise in . . . verse," another of those pagans worshipping "gods they do not know."

Although Cavendish pokes fun at Lucretius for his pagan allegorizing and reduces his glorious Venus to a "Tinkers wife" (her husband, the divine blacksmith Vulcan, is the tinker), the personified Nature that appears again and again in *P&F* resembles the Lucretian Venus and serves a similar function. Both *DRN* and *P&F* set out to versify the subvisible atomic workings of nature; to expound what cannot be seen, they both rely on analogy. *DRN*'s hymn to Venus is a naturalistic encomium, but the springtime phantasmagoria of ardent animals, rushing rivers, and bursting blossoms is also intended to illustrate the subvisible dance of atoms.[18] The passions that Venus stirs in the hearts of all nature's creatures, driving them to come together and procreate, present in familiar mythological guise the mysterious swerve and embrace of atoms in the void that, Lucretius argues, brings the hymn's tumbling calves and swooping birds into being. Like *DRN*'s Venusian passions, the busy domesticity of Cavendish's Nature allegorizes the motions of matter. As Cavendish puts it in "Natures Grange," "Nature in this Housewifry doth take / Great pleasure, the Cloath of Life to make" (lines 17–18).

The connection between "Housewifry" and the subvisible motions of matter is made explicit in *P&F*'s "Motion makes Atomes a Bawd for Figure," where Cavendish personifies Motion as a paramour greedy for new lovers. The poem plays on the multivalent word "figure" (*figura*), important in *DRN* as a term for the forms taken by groupings of atoms, but current in both Lucretius's Latin and seventeenth-century English to designate the form and appearance of bodies.[19] Delighting in change, Motion presses atoms into service as his bawd "That Figures young he might have to imbrace" (line 8). Switching pronouns—now Motion is a "she"—Cavendish describes Motion's greedy lust.

> For some short time, she will make much of one,
> But afterwards away from them will run.
> And thus are most things in the World undone,
> And by her Change, do young ones take old's roome.
> But 'tis butt like unto a Batch of Bread,
> The Floure is the same of such a Seed.
> But Motion she a Figure new mould, bak'd,
> Because that She might have a new hot Cake.
>
> (lines 9–16)[20]

While the first half of the poem is governed by sexual metaphors, the second revolves around baking. Cavendish compares the ever-changing figures of atoms to baked goods and the atomic Bawd of the poem's title to a cook who forms her matter, "Floure" and "Seed," into new figures, fresh treats to feed a household hungry for "a new hot Cake." The turn to the kitchen mirrors the development of *P&F* as a whole. The collection's first section, *Poems*, describes the motions of atoms, while the final section, *Fancies*, similizes these motions, often to domestic, feminized, household spaces and activities: poems such as "Natures Cook," "Natures Oven," "A Hodge-Podge for Natures Table," "Natures House," "Natures Grange," and more.

While the sexualized language in the first half of "Motion makes Atomes a Bawd for Figure" channels the voluptuous sensuality of *DRN*'s hymn to Venus, like "The Fairy Queen" it reframes *DRN*'s eroticized Nature as domestic economy, while retaining some of its key characteristics. Like Lucretius's sensual Venus, Cavendish's housewife Nature characterizes her work as a labor of pleasure, and the pleasures that permeate *P&F* translate the Venusian *voluptas* of *DRN*. In the opening lines of *DRN*, Venus is hailed as "Aeneadum genetrix, hominum divumque voluptas / alma Venus" (Life-stirring Venus, Mother of Aeneas and of Rome, / Pleasure of men and gods; *DRN* 1.1–2). It is with pleasure that she drives the motions of all nature: "omnibus incutiens blandum per pectora amorem / efficis ut cupide genera-tim saecla propagent" (your delicious yearning goads / The breast of every creature, and you urge all things you find / Lustily to get new generations of their kind;" *DRN* 1.19–20). Cavendish shifts perspective somewhat, focusing

not on the pleasure Nature produces in her creations, but rather on the
pleasure Nature herself takes in her work. In "Nature calls a Councell,"
Nature declares that "it is my nature things to make, / To give out worke,
and you directions take. / And by this worke, a pleasure take therein" (lines
9–11). In "Natures Grange," "Nature in this Housewifery doth take / Great
pleasure, the Cloath of Life to make" (lines 17–18). In "A Dialogue betwixt
the Body, and the Mind," the Mind describes how the Body takes pleasure
in fighting: "And so of every thing that Nature makes, / By my direction you
great pleasure takes" (lines 45–46).

The idea that pleasure accompanies all nature's motions, which Cavendish adapts from *DRN*'s hymn to Venus, helps her establish a continuum
between the natural world and the world of her poetry. In *DRN*, Venusian
inspiration ties words to things: the goddess inspires natural motions as well
as the poet's verses.

> quae quoniam rerum naturam sola gubernas
> nec sine te quicquam dias in luminis oras
> exoritur neque fit laetum neque amabile quicquam,
> te sociam studeo scribendis versibus esse
> quos ego de rerum natura scribendis versibus esse.
>
> (*DRN* 1.21–25)

> [Because alone you steer the nature of things upon its course, / And
> nothing can arise without you on light's shining shores, / And noth-
> ing glad or lovely can be fashioned, I invite / You Goddess, stand
> beside me, be my partner as I write / The Nature of Things, these
> verses I am striving to set down.]

Implicit in this appeal is the idea, which Cavendish foregrounds, that letters
and atoms, the poem of nature and nature itself, are of a piece. Pleasure in
P&F reinforces this Lucretian point: that mental fancies participate in the
same material motions as all other things. In "The Reason why the Thoughts
are onely in the Head," Cavendish makes it clear that the brain's fancies are
just as material as something more obviously corporeal, like the bones of a
foot. The brain knows the pain felt by the foot because it is made of the same
stuff.

> Yet tis not Sympathy, but tis the same
> Which makes us thinke, and feele the paine.

For had the Heele such quantity of Braine,
Which doth the Head, and Skull therein containe;
Then would such Thoughts, wich in the Braine dwell high,
Descend downe low, and in the Heele would lye.
. . . .
Had Sinewes roome, Fancy therein to breed,
Copies of Verses might from the Heele proceed.

(lines 9–14, 21–22)

A Brain and a Heel differ primarily in terms of the quantity and placement of their materials: if there were more space for brains in the heel, feet would write poetry.

For Cavendish, the pleasure associated with mental motions is the greatest pleasure of all, and she gives poetry pride of place in the realm of pleasure. In "Poets have most Pleasure in this Life," she writes:

Nature most Pleasure doth to Poets give;
If Pleasures in Variety do live.
There every Sense by Fancy new is fed,
Which Fancy in a Torrent Braine is bred.
Contrary is to all that's borne on Earth,
For Fancy is delighted most at's Birth.

(lines 1–6)

The production of verses gives poets as much pleasure as Nature gets from forming a new creature, and bawdy Atomes from making a new "figure" or a "new hot Cake." Nature's pleasure is in creation, and the poet's "Torrent Braine" is the best breeder.

The language of pleasure that permeates *P&F* and characterizes Cavendish's understanding of matter is indebted to *DRN*'s erotic poetics. Yet although Cavendish speaks of bawds and wantonness when she describes the motions of matter, her reference point is the verdant spring of the hymn to Venus rather than the sexual decadence of *DRN* Book 4. Lara Dodds argues that the tropes of bawd and housewife in Cavendish's writing can be seen as figures for writing. The bawd "is a trope that is open and, somewhat ironically, endlessly fertile" that "stands in contrast to the housewife not only as a moral emblem, but also as a resource for literary invention. Where the one stands as a metaphor for the containment of meaning, the other shows this to be impossible."[21] Nevertheless, in *P&F* the housewife "ushers in her own kind of figurative excess" and "the metaphorical transformations elsewhere attributed to the bawd are performed under the sign of the housewife."[22] Indeed, as demonstrated in "Motion makes Atomes a Bawd for Figure," where sexual imagery easily becomes domestic imagery, and atoms transform from panders to pastry chefs, *P&F* establishes a continuum between bawds and housewives, sex work and housework. Cavendish neither emphasizes nor underplays this potentially explosive comparison, but, as I will show in what follows, subtly employs it to argue against those who would criticize women's writing as wanton or sexually suspect. In "Nature calls a Councell," Inconstancy and Fortune are "so wanton, [they] cannot stand, but reele," but this is easily absorbed into the household economy as they are made to "turne a Wheele" (lines 12, 11). Similarly, in the "Epistle Dedicatory" to *P&F*, Cavendish figures her own writing as "Spinning with the braine," something that could turn to wantonness if left unchecked, but if managed correctly functions as a labor appropriate to a virtuous woman.[23]

P&F's gendered imagery generates a thought about women and makes strategic interventions into seventeenth-century English gender relations. Since antiquity, Epicureanism has been perceived as particularly welcoming to women.[24] Diogenes Laertius, whose *Lives of Eminent Philosophers* was translated into Latin in the fifteenth century (and into English in 1688) and quickly gained currency as an authoritative account of the ancient schools, starts his report on Epicurus by noting that he received women (and slaves) at his school in Athens.[25] In *DRN*, Lucretius lends a distinctly feminine aura to Epicurean philosophy and Lucretian poetics alike with his insistent invocations of Venus. Finally, Lucretius's skepticism about humanity's ability to know anything of nature beyond the fundamental principles of atomic motion meant that education and expertise were not prerequisites for understanding—or practicing—atomist philosophy or poetry. All of this made atomism (at least rhetorically) more accessible to women readers. Thus for Cavendish, writing at a time when few women were well educated or granted access to a male-dominated intellectual scene,[26] *DRN*, as the most important text of Epicurean ethical and physical thought, not only welcomed women into its teachings, but modeled a way for women to practice natural philosophy—in poetry.[27]

Lucretius emphasizes the power of poetry because he is acutely aware of the limitations the invisibility of atoms places on Epicurean philosophy's persuasive power. While one of the central principles of Epicureanism is the reliability of the senses,[28] as the editors of the recent Oxford edition of Lucy Hutchinson's translation of *DRN* point out, "Epicurean epistemology (founded on the reliability of the senses) and physics (founded on the existence and properties of invisible atoms) are so clearly at odds that '[t]he only possible method of argument then is from the perceptible to the imperceptible, i.e. by analogy.'"[29] While Lucretius takes as unassailable Epicureanism's dogmatic claims about the atomic underpinnings of nature, he is equally adamant that these claims must be accepted without proof because human senses are too weak to discern the causes of things.

As a poet, Lucretius has at his disposal a whole toolbox of poetic tropes—metaphor, sound effects, wordplay, and so on—with which to illustrate by analogy the way atoms move in space. Yet these very tools also exacerbate atomism's uneasy pairing of dogmatism about the material substructure of nature with skepticism about the human capacity to know through sense perception. Even as analogical and poetic language do crucial explanatory work, the very need for such tools draws attention to the inadequacies of the senses, potentially intensifying doubt.[30] Lucretius's protestations that Epicurean philosophy needs poetry to be understood and accepted—that the wormwood of philosophy needs poetry's honey to seduce readers—also drew attention to the absence of decisive visible proof for Epicurean beliefs about nature.[31]

Cavendish's adaptation of Lucretian natural philosophical poetry in *P&F* is closely attuned to this intersection between epistemological skepticism and poetic bravado in Lucretian poetry. Like Lucretius, Cavendish maintains that nature's causes are unknowable, with humans privy only to effects: "Understanding runs in a levell course, that is, to know in generall, as of the Effects: but to know the Cause of any one thing of Natures works, Nature never gave us a Capacity thereto."[32] Lucretius took the invisibility of the atom, which renders the physical grounds of natural phenomena inaccessible to human perception, to mean that Epicurean philosophy needed poetic methods, analogy, and persuasion to be grasped and adopted. From a similarly skeptical position, in *P&F* Cavendish launches a robust defense of poetry's capacity to practice, and not just explicate, natural philosophy. While early modern scientific epistemology would come to be founded upon the elimination of error, Cavendish domesticates error through the topoi of modesty and fancy. She affirms that poetic fancy and natural philosophy go hand in hand precisely because poetic fancy does not pretend to rest upon or achieve a fundamentally inaccessible knowledge.[33]

P&F amplifies the elements of Lucretian atomism that bring it into conversation (or productive confusion) with skepticism: an emphasis on the limitations of human knowledge, multiple explanations, and dialogism. From its focus on the nonhuman in poems about animals and fairies (such as "The Hunting of the Hare" and "The Fairy Queen," among others) to the shocking—for conventional understandings of lyric—scarcity of the word "I" in the collection, and a persistent focus on multiple voices in either cacophony or dialogue, *P&F* undermines certainties of any kind by decentering the perspective of both the speaker and the reader.[34] Instead of certainty or a fixed perspective from which to interpret the world, Cavendish offers an assortment of fancies, imaginative explorations of the infinite possibilities inherent in this world (and others).

The claim that poetic fancy is the firmest ground for philosophical thought delivered a powerful challenge to the developing English scientific establishment, consolidated in 1660 in the form of the Royal Society. Though the pillars of England's burgeoning scientific establishment also embraced doubt and humility, they appealed to method and experiment, rather than fancy, to bring themselves closer to the truth.[35] These men would become Cavendish's targets in *The Blazing World* (1666), where she represents the members of the Society as foolish animals who carry out failed experiments under the disdainful gaze of a powerful female ruler. Having despaired of the ability of her animal virtuosi to give her answers about the nature of the universe and abandoned her attempts to construct a world based on the world systems of the ancients, the Empress of the Blazing World eventually opts to construct the world through the imagination rather than exploring or experimenting upon it in real life. Though the Royal Society didn't yet officially exist during the years of *P&F*'s composition, it was certainly in formation in groupings of virtuosi. Cavendish's encounter in 1667 with the newly formed Society, which welcomed her as a noble patroness while barring her as a natural philosopher, throws into relief the ways *P&F*'s poetic natural philosophical method stood against the values of erudition, scientific methodology, and truth that would be propounded by the Society.[36] Both *P&F* and Cavendish's later natural philosophical works allow her to entertain a debate about the appropriate methods for natural philosophy.

Thus, despite calculated comments to the contrary—indeed, built on such comments—Cavendish's early atomist poetry offers a vision of how poetry might constitute a natural philosophical method, even at a time when

the rise of empirical scientific methodologies downgraded the human imagination's capacity to conceive of and explain natural phenomena.[37] Cavendish
argues that because nature's inner truths are fundamentally unknowable,
fancy is a legitimate speculative practice: to use the terms of Cavendish's
Observations upon Experimental Philosophy (the first edition was published in
1666, a second in 1668), while fancy does not partake of sense perception,
like reason it is a product of the rational part of matter. By pitting her fanciful
methodology against methodologies (empiricism and experimentalism) that
make claims to truth, Cavendish establishes ignorance as a defensible epistemological posture.[38] Her manipulation of gender stereotypes, in her showy
modesty and ostentatious professions of ignorance, is essential to this goal.
She subverts the conventional modesty topoi that are so central to early modern women's writing in order to establish epistemological modesty—
skepticism—as the hallmark of genuine natural philosophy. Though writers,
including women, have always smuggled hubris into their texts under the
guise of modesty, Cavendish flips the script entirely, redefining the project of
natural philosophy as a modest one that seeks not truth but the "probability
of truth,"[39] rather than feigning modesty about her capacity to follow a
method that required training and expertise very few women of her time
could claim.[40] As she writes in *Observations upon Experimental Philosophy*,
"that I am not versed in learning, nobody, I hope, will blame me for it, since
it is sufficiently known, that our sex being not suffered to be instructed in
schools and universities, cannot be bred up to it."[41] This, however, is more
than a defense of one woman's capacity to practice natural philosophy: Cavendish not only positions herself as a thoroughly qualified practitioner of
natural philosophy, but takes a strong stand for epistemological skepticism
in general. As she puts it quite forthrightly in the chapter of *Observations
upon Experimental Philosophy* entitled "Of the Doctrine of the Sceptics concerning the Knowledge of Nature," "When sceptics endeavour to prove, that
not anything in nature can be truly and thoroughly known; they are, in my
opinion, in the right way."[42] Cavendish's reflections on her own education
are more than personal positioning: they expound an epistemological skepticism that undergirds her natural philosophical and poetic practice alike.

For Lucretius, as for Cavendish, the principle of both nature and writing
is variety—the innumerable arrangements of *elementa*: letters and atoms. In
DRN, this produces both formal effects (for example, spectacular punning
on words with similar letters, such as the explanation of how fire, *ignis*, comes
from wood, *lignum*) and philosophical ones (for example, the principle of

multiple explanations, whereby Lucretius offers a range of plausible explanations for natural phenomena instead of asserting a single truth).[43] *P&F* also stresses variety and change; yet however much Cavendish's versification of an endlessly shifting, combinatory, and pleasurable atomist cosmos in *P&F* takes inspiration from *DRN*, there are important differences between the two. Stylistically, *P&F* diverges sharply from *DRN*. While both are didactic, *P&F* eschews *DRN*'s epic for shorter lyric forms better suited to what Cavendish describes as her hurried, unplanned compositions. In "The Poetresses hasty Resolution," she writes that when Reason begged her to reconsider publishing her verses, "Then all in haste I to the Presse it sent, / Fearing Perswasion might my Book prevent" (lines 19–20). Though Cavendish's deprecating accounts of her own work ethic should never be taken at face value, her prolific publication history does suggest that she wrote quickly. Furthermore, her frequent revisions to her early works demonstrate a willingness to revise after as well as before publication. Indeed, revision and refinement seem to be part of her philosophy as well as her work.[44]

Though both *DRN* and *P&F* emphasize variety, the breathless velocity of Cavendish's lyrics diverges from *DRN*'s more obviously calibrated and emphatic style, which—as befits epic—builds more slowly on larger units of text. In contrast, some of the poems in *P&F*, such as the four-line "Of Loose Atomes," are as minute as atoms themselves.

> In every Braine loose Atomes there do lye,
> Those which are Sharpe, from them do Fancies flye.
> Those that are long, and Aiery, nimble be.
> But Atomes Round, and Square, are dull, and sleepie.
>
> (lines 1–4)

The poem's insistent rhyme bespeaks the rapid unspooling of thoughts and fancies, while also giving the short poem a propulsive quality. Taken singly, the poems of *P&F* can feel hurried and unfinished, single atoms spinning in the void. But at the level of the entire collection they coalesce into a more commanding whole—a chaos, perhaps, but nevertheless a cosmos. In this sense, Cavendish's lyrics are more formally appropriate to atomist cosmology than Lucretius's epic, though the criticisms of disorganization leveled at the collection, or which she claims were leveled at the collection, indicate that her attempt at didactic lyric may have mirrored the chaos of atomist cosmology all too convincingly.

Even those critics who identify the principles of variety and profusion motivating *P&F* have tended to dismiss the poems because of that very variety and profusion, reading the collection as a breakdown of poetic method rather than the expression of a stated poetics.[45] Instead of judging *P&F* according to Cavendish's stated poetics of variety, the poems are evaluated on completely different terms: strict organization and discipline. Measured by this ruler, Cavendish's poetry looks artless, chaotic, anarchic, and formless, leading most critics to see it as a failure at order rather than a success at fancy. Cavendish's own seemingly negative assessments of her verse encourage this argument. Perpetually unwilling to grant the interpretation of her texts to anyone but herself, Cavendish stipulates readings of her own work, demanding that it be read as a domestic textual production born of a woman's boredom, idleness, and fancy, seemingly in order to preclude hostile reactions to a woman writer writing herself into the masculine public sphere.

Even though Cavendish herself does not encourage such a reading, many scholarly accounts are just as quick to dismiss her atomism as either a childish phase or trendiness, following the scientific crazes of her time unthinkingly. In the 1640s, the Cavendish house in Paris was a hub for thinkers interested in atomism, and *P&F* played a part in bringing atomist ideas to England and stoking what has been called the "Epicurean revival," an explosion of interest in Epicurean moral philosophy, atomist natural philosophy, and Lucretian poetry that manifested in an array of translations, literary works, and philosophical studies.[46] The trendiness narrative reads Cavendish's atomism as a minor side effect of a larger historical phenomenon. For example, in an early article on Cavendish's natural philosophy, Lisa Sarasohn argued that *P&F*'s atomism was little more than a phase brought on by the omnipresence of mechanical science during Cavendish's lifetime: "As a scientific philosophy, Margaret Cavendish's materialism is an interesting, but unimportant by-product of the Scientific Revolution."[47] Sarasohn reads Cavendish's atomism as a symptom of contemporary philosophical trends, notable not in itself but because it demonstrates the influence of the Epicurean revival. Anna Battigelli's assertion that *P&F* "reviewed Gassendi's revival of Epicurean atomism in a series of poems" succinctly expresses the way that reading Cavendish's atomism as a historical by-product forecloses both interpretations that take seriously her philosophical engagement with atomism, and formal readings of her verse.[48] The word "review" makes both Cavendish's poetry and her thought seem dilatory: the verse form is incidental to content, and the philosophical thought merely broadcasts someone else's ideas.

However, as I have been arguing, although Cavendish's views on matter evolved away from the classical atomism espoused in *DRN*, she retains the Lucretian principle that nature and the imagination share the same materials. Her turn after *P&F* toward a vitalist materialism signals not an abandonment of atomism, but its rewriting: the abandonment of lifeless atoms could speak to an intensified commitment to a form of imaginative materialism springing from *DRN*'s vibrant account of a lively, ever-shifting nature.

In *The Blazing World*, Cavendish gives a comical, fictionalized account of her philosophical development that implies that any rejection of atomism on her part springs as much from a decision to abjure previous natural philosophical models altogether as from quarrels with atomist ideas. Along with the Empress, the ruler of the Blazing World, the Cavendish character sets out to construct a world within herself. She makes several attempts, according to the models first of Thales, then of Pythagoras, Plato, and eventually Epicurus, but "she had no sooner begun, but the infinite atoms made such a mist, that it quite blinded the perception of her mind; neither was she able to make a vacuum as a receptacle for those atoms, or a place which they might retire into; so that partly for the want of it, and of a good order and method, the confusion of those atoms produced such strange and monstrous figures as did more affright then delight her, and caused such a chaos in her mind, as had almost dissolved it."[49] Having next attempted and then abandoned the systems of Aristotle, Descartes, and Hobbes, "the Duchess saw that no patterns would do her any good in the framing of her world; she resolved to make a world of her own invention, and this world was composed of sensitive and rational self-moving matter."[50] This passage is a veritable allegory of leaving behind mechanical atomism for a fanciful, imaginative, and vitalist one.

While *The Blazing World* revels in its depiction of female authority, *P&F*'s defense of women's writing is couched in what at first glance seems like a narrow vision of women's social role. In the epistles dedicatory to *P&F*, and elsewhere, Cavendish argues that poetry, like traditional busywork, reinforces domestic virtue because it keeps women quietly occupied at home instead of gossiping or gallivanting about. This is not a transparent rendition of social reality, but rather harnesses a set of tropes and terms that were particularly charged in the 1650s because of the many supporters of the monarchy who went into exile or were dispossessed of their estates during the English Civil War and interregnum. Evoking the idleness of exile while also associating idleness particularly with women, Cavendish writes that she "Print[s] this Book, to give an Account to my Freinds, how I spend the idle

Time of my life, and how I busie my Thoughts, when I thinke upon the Objects of the World. For the truth is, our Sex hath so much waste Time, having but little imployments, which makes our Thoughts run wildly about, having nothing to fix them upon, which wilde thoughts do not onely produce unprofitable, but indiscreet Actions; winding up the Thread of our lives in snarles on unsound bottoms."[51] The poems both use up "the idle Time" of Cavendish's life—they are something upon which to fix her wild thoughts that is neither unprofitable nor indiscreet—and give a public account of that time. Although we know that early modern women of all classes worked remarkably hard, and while male writers of the period also declare idleness to be the occasion for their writing, Cavendish claims "waste Time" as a particularly female problem.[52] However, this misrepresentation of women's work and the gendering of idleness has an important payoff in her defense of women's writing.[53]

Defying those who would urge her, as they did Mary Wroth, to "Work Lady Work, let writing Books alone, For surely Wiser Women ne'r writ one,"[54] Cavendish expands on her justification of women's writing in the *Sociable Letters* (1664), apologizing for her lack of facility in traditional women's work while defending writing as a valid substitute: "My Lord, I cannot Work, I mean such Works as Ladies use to pass their Time withall."[55] In the absence of natural skill at such "work," women's employments like spinning or embroidery, but also the fact that she had no children, or an estate upon which to exercise the traditional feminine management skills because she lived for much of her married life in exile, Cavendish turns to poetry: "I have no Children to imploy my Care, and Attendance on; And my Lords Estate being taken away, had nothing for Huswifery, or thirsty Industry to imploy my selfe in; having no Stock to work on."[56] The formal characteristics of a poem, organization and parsimony, make it a fertile comparison to housekeeping:[57] "It is just as in Poetry: for good Husbandry in Poetry, is, when there is a great store of Fancy well order'd."[58] Cavendish claims to exercise her wifely duties in the composition of her verse, while also rhetorically expanding the range of traditionally female activities to encompass poetic activity.[59] Moreover, during a period in which experimental science was expanding, activities like needlework, spinning, kitchen work, and other forms of housework were all being reconfigured as tropes for the sorts of laboratory activities undertaken by virtuosi in the pursuit of the new science.[60] This happened both in attacks on the effeminacy of experiment and in encomiums of the usefulness of experiment. By disassociating herself from such "work," Cavendish both claims poetry as women's work and distances herself from the experimentalism of which she was a vociferous critic throughout her career.

Cavendish's account of poetry as female housework authorizes an epistemological and ontological argument about the affinity between poetry and women's bodies: she defines poetry as a female activity by positing a fundamental kinship between different kinds of women's work and the very structure of women's minds. The "Epistle Dedicatory" that opens *P&F*, addressed to her brother-in-law Sir Charles Cavendish, is typical of Cavendish's prefatory materials, in which she frequently establishes controversial points through disavowal: "True it is, Spinning with the Fingers is more proper to our Sexe, then studying or writing Poetry, which is the Spinning with the braine: but I having no skill in the Art of the first . . . made me delight in the latter; since all braines work naturally, and incessantly, in some kind or other."[61] Although she prudently puts the distaff before the pen, Cavendish characterizes writing as little more than a different medium for "Spinning," which makes poetry, spinning with the brain, a viable alternative to the distaff, spinning with the fingers.[62] Both forms of spinning, Cavendish claims, are appropriate female activities because they mirror the motion of women's brains.

> Poetry, which is built upon Fancy, Women may claime, as a worke belonging most properly to themselves: for I have observ'd, that their Braines work usually in a Fantasticall motion, as in their several, and various dresses, in their many and singular choices of Cloaths, and Ribbons, and the like; in their curious shadowing, and mixing of Colours, in their Wrought workes, and divers sorts of Stitches they imploy their Needle, and many Curious things they make, as Flowers, Boxes, Baskets with Beads, Shells, Silke, Straw, or any thing else, besides all manner of Meats to eate: and thus their Thoughts are imployed perpetually with Fancies. For Fancy goeth not so much by Rule, & Method, as by Choice.[63]

Having linked women and poetry through appeals to normative values of order—domestic parsimony and well-managed time—Cavendish exploits the wonderfully multivalent term "spinning" to defend women's writing according, instead, to principles of feminine extravagance, even disorder.[64] Developing another of her preferred metaphors, clothing, Cavendish notes that women's preference for ribbons, bows, and all sorts of sartorial frippery also inclines women to poetry. Fanciful garments belong to women in the same way poetry is "a worke belonging most properly to themselves," according to an analogy that runs off the fantastical motion of their minds. (This argument, moreover, is not an abstract one: Cavendish herself was notorious for wearing outlandish clothing.)[65]

The rhetoric of feminine pastime in the prefatory materials to both *P&F* and the *Sociable Letters*—recall that the poems are an account of how Cavendish "spend[s] the idle Time of [her] life," while the writing of the *Sociable Letters* is a replacement for women's work, "such Works as Ladies use to pass their Time withall"—connects Cavendish's thinking on women's writing and poetic fancy to the skeptical epistemology of atomist natural philosophy. On the one hand, a lady's pastimes indicate her virtue, because the object of a woman's "Fantasticall" mind is a choice. As Cavendish notes, "Fancy goeth not so much by Rule, & Method, as by Choice."[66] Time can be passed well or ill, but it must be passed: women choose the objects upon which they fix their thoughts, and that choice determines the quality of their behavior. It is an act of virtue and temperance to choose well, of vice to choose ill. As we have seen, Cavendish argues in *P&F* and *Sociable Letters* that poetry is as suitable a pastime for a woman as spinning or fashion, because poetic fancy, too, has a kinship with the fantastical and fanciful nature of the female mind.

On the other hand, Cavendish's skepticism about the ability of humans to know the truth about nature means that pastime also has traction as an epistemological concept. Cavendish believes that the world's causes are unknowable: humans are only privy to their effects, which means that nobody can really judge between true and false. In "An Epistle to Mistris Toppe," which precedes *P&F*, Cavendish couches her choice of genre within an epistemological frame concerning the unknowability of nature: "[T]here are as few meer Fools, as wise men: for Understanding runs in a levell course, that is, to know in generall, as of the Effects: but to know the Cause of any one thing of Natures workes, Nature never gave us a Capacity thereto. Shee hath given us Thoughts which run wildly about, and if by chance they light on Truth, they do not know it for a Truth."[67] Because humans can't know causes, every person's thoughts, not just women's, are spinning wheels with nowhere to stop but where that person chooses for them to stop. Human knowledge, like feminine pastime, depends on individual choice and has no essential connection to truth. In this sense, all thought is "fancy," and every product of fancy is a "pastime."

"Pastime" was a charged word for Cavendish to use in this context. In the sixteenth and seventeenth centuries, "pastime" could be used to describe a whole range of agreeable recreations. Sixteenth- and seventeenth-century publications with the word "pastime" in their title include stories, songs, and plays about knights errant; books for children's religious or moral instruction; and guides for hunting, fishing, and other ways to pleasantly, but also profitably, pass the time. "Pastime" was also associated with the traditional holiday pastimes Charles I tried to reinstitute with his 1633 *Book of Sports*, as well as the cavalier poetics that defended that and similar royal policies.[68] Experimentalists critiqued aristocratic leisure and articulated their experimental ethos in contrast to aristocratic idleness, urging gentlemen to choose activities for their leisure hours that would not merely pass the time, but rather educate them to usefulness. As Joanna Picciotto recounts, Robert Boyle urged gentlemen to fill "their 'vacant houres' by learning a skill like limning, watchmaking, gardening, 'or som manuall Vocation, or other': 'I know that this will be spurn'd at by all our Gallants as a Proposition fit to be made rather to blue Aprons than to skarlet Cloakes. But sure it is not so much below a gentleman to do something, as it is below both a Man and a Christian to be Idle.'"[69] Indeed, experiments became something of an aristocratic pastime, with many nobles—including Margaret Cavendish's husband, William Cavendish—establishing laboratories in their homes.[70]

Margaret Cavendish makes natural philosophy into a pastime by associating it with poetic pastimes. In so doing, she also calls the truth claims of natural philosophy into question. She openly admits that the arguments in her *P&F* could as easily be false as true: "But amongst many Errours, there are huge Mountaines of Follies; and though I add to the Bulke of one of them, yet I make not a Mountaine alone, and am the more excusable, because I have an Opinion, which troubles me like a conscience, that tis a part of Honour to aspire towards a Fame."[71] Because Cavendish vindicates the foolishness and ignorance of an uneducated woman, such as she represents herself to be, as a particularly defensible epistemological posture, her "many Errours" and "huge Mountaines of Follies" do nothing to indict her poems. Cavendish pits fancy against method, the ignorant, fanciful woman against educated male philosophers and scholars.[72]

Ignorance, particularly what she presents as her own linguistic ignorance, is a central trope in Cavendish's fanciful epistemology. She claims a great aversion to (or inability to learn) languages, not only foreign or ancient ones such as French, which she claims to never have learned despite her five years living in France, or Latin, which would have been useful for her philosophical studies, but even English. In *P&F*, she insists that whatever education she has was gained as a casual onlooker in familial conversations, not from books:

> [F]or I never read, nor heard of any English Booke to Instruct me: and truly I understand no other Language; not French, although I was in France five yeares: Neither do I understand my owne Native Language very well; for there are many words, I know not what they signifie; so as I have only the Vulgar part, I meane, that which is most usually spoke. I do not meane that which is us'd to be spoke by Clownes in every Shire, where in some Parts their Language is knowne to none, but those that are bred there. And not onely every Shire hath a severall Language, but every Family, giving Marks for things according to their Fancy. But my Ignorance of the Mother Tongues makes me ignorant of the Opinions, and Discourses in former times; wherefore I may be absurd, and erre grossely.[73]

Her ignorance of books and languages, Cavendish argues, makes her unschooled in all but the commonplace elements of English. While she distances herself from those peasants who speak a dialect so local that they are incomprehensible to anyone not bred in their neighborhood, Cavendish's insistence that she knows no "Mother Tongues" associates her with a partial, localized knowledge. She seems to have believed that people can only really know their immediate environs: they might gain a local familiarity, but could never extrapolate those local ways of knowing into a system of knowledge that enabled, for example, familiarity with foreign cultures or the acquisition of foreign languages.[74]

This ignorance, however, is a boon for the fanciful poet-philosopher. According to Cavendish, the mind we are born with is as wise as the learned mind, because our natural, childlike mind is nature's mind, and our most familiar language is nature's language, which no amount of learning can enrich. If anything, learning, custom, and affectation will detract from or ossify our natural state and language, or simply waste our time.[75]

> Greek and Latine, and all other Languages are of great ornament to Gentlemen, but they must spend so much time in learning them, as they can have no time to speak them, and some will say it is a great advancement to wisdom, in knowing the natures, humours, laws,

and customs of several men, and nations; which they cannot do,
except they understand their several Languages to answer that,
although al Languages are expressed by four and twenty letters, yet
there is no Language which will not take up an age, to learn it
perfectly as to know every circumstance; and since mans life is so
short, and learning so tedious, there wil accrue but little profit for
that laborious pains, so that the benefit that should be made will
come too late, but surely these men are wise enough which understand the natures, laws, and customs of their own country, and can
apply them to their right use.[76]

It is well nigh impossible ever to master the language and customs of another
people, because of the great time and effort involved. Furthermore, drawing
a distinction between language learning as an "ornament" to gentlemen and
as "a great advancement to wisdom" (presumably to scholars), Cavendish
implies that there is more wisdom in understanding and putting to "right
use" the language and customs of one's own country than those of others. It
is in this sense that Cavendish advertises her ignorance of languages and
books even when that ignorance is belied by the learnedness of her work. A
frontispiece first used for *The Philosophical and Physical Opinions* (1655) bears
this inscription:

> Studious She is and all Alone
> Most visitants, when She has none,
> Her Library on which She looks
> It is her Head, her Thoughts, her Books.
> Scorninge dead Ashes without fire
> For her owne Flames doe her Inspire.

The author is vehement that her fame will be won by herself alone, not
through any debt to another text or thinker.[77] Instead of books, she has her
own thoughts, natural and self-generated. This living library—"her owne
Flames," perhaps a reference to the sharp fire-atoms that in *P&F* are said to
make up thoughts—makes a mockery of the "dead Ashes" of book learning.

Cavendish figures her propensity toward poetry and philosophy as natural gifts, not acquired by training, but also not a result of inspiration. Cavendish writes that "it pleased God to command his Servant Nature to indue me
with a Poetical and Philosophical Genius, even from my Birth; for I did write

some Books in that kind, before I was twelve years of Age."[78] Her youthful writings attest to the innateness of her gift. This casts light on the importance of Cavendish's earliest notebooks. In the *Sociable Letters* she writes that what she calls her "baby-Books" have "neither Beginning nor End, and [are] as Confused as the Chaos, wherein is neither Method nor Order."[79] Instead of an infirmity, the lack of method and preponderance of chaos in Cavendish's juvenilia attest to her natural gifts. That she was so early a "natural" poet is only proper, when it is the gifts of nature rather than the acquisitions of learning that make a poet.

Cavendish's persona—isolated, ignorant, naive, and melancholic—is a strategy that serves a dual purpose. On the one hand, it fixes her within the domain of feminine decorum by depicting a modest and retiring lady. On the other hand, it is programmatic, fleshing out her conception of a natural poetry that reproduces the varieties and pleasures of nature. Cavendish, who constantly describes herself as reclusive and melancholic, had as great a passion for publishing her texts as she did for "publishing" herself, dressing with a singularity and ostentation in her public appearance that made her name circulate like wildfire in the talk—and type—of British society. Cavendish figures herself as ignorant and secluded not because she actually was, but because ignorance and seclusion marked her as a writer of natural poetry inspired by nature and her own mind rather than by textual precedents.

As I have already suggested, Cavendish's poetics and her conception of the natural world are mutually constitutive. Her valorization of fancy over empiricism relies upon a specific conception of nature that finds itself reflected in the workings of the human mind and the forms of the written text. The human mind—when unspoiled by pretension, too much learning, or painstaking artifice—is not just *like*, but rather *is*, nature. Its fanciful motions share in nature's very flux and flow, which means that the fancies of an unmediated mind produce a variety and *copia* in writing that do not merely represent but rather partake in nature. What Cavendish calls "natural" poetry has the same goal as natural philosophy (to bring the human mind closer to nature's secrets), but instead of trying to crack nature's structures to find its hidden truths, natural poetry replicates nature in the human mind and human art forms, manifesting its structures in the forms of poetry.

Although Cavendish vehemently asserts her singularity, her self-representations are in fact normative and serve to establish her as part of a class of natural poets. What she often describes as circumstances of her personal development or character traits—haphazardness, impatience, a quick mind—exemplify the common characteristics of these natural poets. She uses "natural poetry" as a rubric with which to judge other poets, and by establishing herself as such a poet she situates herself in a literary genealogy encompassing both her contemporaries and the titans of the classical period. Because natural poetry emphasizes untutored ease, we must look for the tenets of this school in the place we would logically least expect to find them: Cavendish's professions of ignorance of literary history. Natural poets, as Cavendish describes them, create rather than imitate, inviting their material forth from their fecund fancy: "Natural poets . . . are far beyond Artificial Chymists, their Creation of Fancies is by a Natural way, not an Artificial."[80] They are also more likely to represent themselves as natural and naive than as inspired by the work of other writers. In order to emphasize her own naturalness, Cavendish stressed her seclusion and naivete, emphasizing her ignorance of literary traditions and incapacity to read foreign languages.[81] Early in her career, Cavendish denied that she consulted a library or was at all influenced by any other writer, but denying such influence was a way of asserting the naturalness so important to her poetics.

Cavendish is most explicit about the fact that natural poetry constitutes a school rather than a style exclusive to herself when she praises the Roman poet Ovid. In the *Sociable Letters*, Cavendish applies the category of natural poet to the author of the *Metamorphoses*. Responding to her interlocutor's question of which is her favorite Latin poet, Virgil or Ovid, Cavendish decides for Ovid without hesitation. His great strength is what she often apologizes for as her greatest stylistic weakness: haphazardness and variety: "[H]aving more Variety," Ovid's poetry is "Brief, and yet Satisfactory."[82] That is, he writes much and in pieces, but each piece is in itself full and sufficient, and furthermore the collection of fragments benefits more than loses from their relative brevity (and possibly even incoherence). Ovid does not "spend his Reason, Judgment, Wit, and Fancy, on One Tedious Feigned Story, but on Hundreds of Stories, and Express'd himself in his Metamorphosis, as much a Moral, and Natural Philosopher, a Courtly Lover, an Heroick Souldier, a Valiant and Prudent Commander, a Politick States-man, a Just Governour and Ruler, a Wise and Magnificent Prince, a Faithful Citizen, a Navigator, Fortificator, Architect, Astronomer, and the like, as also a Learned Scholar."[83] Rather than artificially limiting the scope of his work or the range of his style, Ovid's work covers a vast span of topics. The implications of this emerge when Cavendish compares his work to Virgil's. The alternative to Ovid's roving poetic eye is the sort of ambitiously program-matic poetry Virgil wrote. To make her point, Cavendish repeatedly contrasts Ovid with Virgil in terms of their relationships to the state. This creates a surprising moment when Cavendish—so often characterized as writing with a finely tuned awareness to politics and with political motives—criticizes Virgil for writing to please Caesar rather than to do justice to nature: "I give my Opinion, That Virgil was the Craftier, but Ovid the Wittier man, that Virgil was the better Flatterer, but Ovid the better Poet."[84] His dedication to nature cost Ovid dear, and he was exiled. (A royalist exile herself, Cavendish must have felt a double kinship with the exiled Ovid.) Nevertheless, Nature kept him in her favor: "Though [Ovid] was not one of Augustus Caesar's Favorits, yet he was Nature's Favourite . . . [a] Natural Poetical Birth."[85] In Cavendish's account, Virgil is a good poet whose art is undermined for being in the service of mere politics, instead of in the service of nature.

Like Ovid, Cavendish is a child of nature. What appears in her work as modesty topoi—ignorance, monolingualism, bashfulness, and so on—manifests her commitment to the practice of natural poetry. The frequent exclamations of her own ignorance, lack of training, and haphazard poetic compositions serve to present Cavendish as a natural poet, untutored by culture but attuned to nature: "[F]or though I am a Poetess, yet I am but a Poetastress, or a Petty Poetess, but howsoever, I am a Legitimate Poetical Child of Nature, and though my Poems, which are the Body of the Poetical Soul, are not so Beautiful and Pleasing, as the rest of her Poetical Childrens Bodies are, yet I am neveertheless her Child, although but a Brownet."[86] This directly recalls her description of Ovid, "Nature's Favorite . . . [a] Natural Poetical Birth."[87] Cavendish excuses herself for her poetic failings by claiming the equality of her creations as poetical children. However mean she is, she is nevertheless a "Legitimate Poetical Child of Nature," and her poems legiti-mate poetical children.

While in the *Sociable Letters* Cavendish focuses her attentions on Ovid as an exemplary natural poet, the way she describes natural poetry suggests that Lucretius, the great poet of nature who inspired the vivacious variety of her early natural philosophical poetry, is also central to her understanding of what it means to be a natural poet. Cavendish's valorization of linguistic incompetence—both her inability to learn languages and her bad handwrit-ing, which, as she writes in the autobiographical "A true Relation of my Birth, Breeding, and Life," "is so bad as few can read it"[88]—has Lucretian underpinnings—namely, in the Lucretian analogy between atoms and letters that Cavendish evokes throughout her work.[89] As in her discussion of women's writing, where she develops Lucretian skepticism to support a defense of her atomist poetry, when Cavendish discusses natural poetry, she pairs Lucretian concepts with gendered self-deprecation to subtly make positive claims for what she claims are unique character traits but which in fact represent a veritable poetic school.

In *DRN*, letters relate to each other within texts the same way atoms relate to each other in nature. The Lucretian analogy formalizes the bonds between poetry and matter, the Lucretian poem and the atomist cosmos it describes, while emphasizing the variety of both words and things. In *The World's Olio*, Cavendish expresses this Lucretian principle in her own terms, adding a comparison to musical notes.

> As eight notes produce innumerable tunes, so twenty four letters produce innumerable words, which are marks for things, which marks produce innumerable imaginations, or conceptions, which imaginations or conceptions begets another soul which another animal hath not, for want of those marks, and so wants those imaginations and conceptions which those marks beget; besides those marks beget a soul in communitie; besides words are as gods that give knowledge, and discover, the mindes of men.[90]

For Cavendish, as for Lucretius, everything springs from changing the interactions and variations in placement of literary *minima*. However, whereas in *DRN* Lucretius emphasizes the superior variety of atoms, Cavendish focuses on letters and words, the way they generate "innumerable imaginations," which discover not just "the mindes of men" but also the motions of nature.[91] Ultimately, Cavendish's cosmos is more textual, and imaginative, than Lucretius's.

While Lucretius stresses the expressivity of letters, Cavendish points to the way words, like things, can decompose and atomize. The cause of her problems with language, she writes, is a tendency to break language down into its component parts, particularly in moments of stress. Her bashfulness "[d]isturbs the Thoughts so much, as the Thoughts are all in a Confused Disorder, and not any one Thought moves Regularly, neither will they Suffer the Words to pass out of the Mouth, or if they do, they are Uttered without Sense, nay, sometimes in no Language, being but Pieces of Words, or Pieces of the Letters of Words."[92] The proliferative variety of Cavendish's textual productions finds its counterpoint in the collapse of her private speech. Cavendish establishes a Lucretian foundation shared by both her modesty and her variety, her incoherence and her creativity.

The Lucretian grounding for Cavendish's self-representations and poetic fancy casts new light on the apology for verse in *P&F*'s "To Naturall Philosophers." The epistle reads as an apology for the flaws in Cavendish's writing, but is really an apology for poetry in the vein of Sir Philip Sidney's, which is to say, a justification.

> And the Reason why I write it in Verse, is, because I thought Errours might better passe there, then in Prose; since Poets write most Fiction, and Fiction is not given for Truth, but Pastime; and I feare my Atomes will be as small Pastime, as themselves: for nothing can be lesse than an Atome. But my desire that they should please the Readers, is as big as the World they make; and my Feares are of the same bulk; yet my Hopes fall to a single Atome agen: and so shall I remaine an unsettled Atome, or a confus'd heape, till I heare my Censure. If I be prais'd, it fixes them; but if I am condemn'd, I shall be Annihilated to nothing: but my Ambition is such, as I would either be a World, or nothing.[93]

Cavendish claims to know how male natural philosophers would respond to her poems, and takes a stance they might understand, pleading "poetry" to their charge of "error." Yet in the context of her critique of truth claims in the other prefatory materials, where she recalibrates the balance between "Errours," "Truth," and "Fiction," the letter to natural philosophers is a disingenuous apology.[94] When Cavendish says that errors might better pass in poetry than in prose, she echoes Sidney, who writes that the poet "nothing affirms, and therefore never lieth."[95] Yet her poetics is much more affirmative and ambitious than either Sidney's or Lucretius's. She affirms, contra Sidney, that poetry participates materially in the natural world, but also—pressing Lucretius, who sometimes (as in the honey and wormwood passage) admits to nothing more than writing poetry to sweeten bitter philosophical truths— that poetry is not a superficial inducement to natural philosophical insight but rather fundamental to its practice. That her poems are "small Pastime[s]" makes them no less capable of making a world. In fact, the construction of the final sentences repeatedly links the single atom to the whole world, although, as per usual, under the veil of disparagement.

The rhetorical opposition between reason and fancy that Cavendish makes in *P&F* does not, however, mean that fancy cannot partake of rationality, quite to the contrary. Cavendish's point is not that men are rational and women are not, or that experiment is rational and fancy is not. Rather, fancy is a rational method (although one with no claim on truth), while experiment is nothing more than the delusion that method produces truth. Fifteen years after *P&F* was published, Cavendish would write, contra Aristotle, who argues in *De anima* that the imagination is neither knowledge nor intelligence, that "fancy or imagination is a voluntary action of reason, or of the rational parts of matter."[96] In *The Blazing World*, she will also be careful to justify her fanciful method: "The end of reason, is truth; the end of fancy, is fiction; but mistake me not, when I distinguish fancy from reason; I mean not as if fancy were not made by the rational parts of matter; but by reason I understand a rational search and enquiry into the causes of natural effects; and by fancy a voluntary creation or production of the mind, both being effects, or rather actions of the rational parts of matter."[97] Though they operate in different modes—reason inquires, while fancy creates—both are rational, and as such, complement each other. Cavendish's publication record bears out her conviction that fancy and reason could and should work in concert: *P&F* and *Philosophicall Fancies* were intended as companion pieces, which indicates, as Lisa Walters writes, that "generic mixing could inform and elucidate meaning for her readers."[98] Not only is fancy rational; it is also optative, going not by chance, but by choice. The rational intentionality of fancy empowers poetry by gesturing toward an agency inherent in poetic composition. What in Cavendish's poetry is often construed as a lack of order is in fact fancy, disorder not as lack but as choice. Cavendish inverts the argument that haphazardness constitutes a falling-off from a state of order: to her, the originary state—of nature, of the mind—is variety, fancy (which looks like disorder). Eradicating this originary variety would be a mistake, because although Cavendish's fanciful poetics is a manifestation of her skepticism about the human capacity for knowing, it is also fundamentally optimistic, embracing and promoting an infinite human capacity for creative imagination.

This Is Our Venus

"*Naked* she lay clasp'd in my longing Armes."[1] John Wilmot, Earl of Rochester's "The Imperfect Enjoyment" begins where most love poems only dream
of ending: with the lovers nude and entwined, "[b]oth equally inspir'd with
eager fire" (line 3).[2] Yet while the poem's exultant first word—*Naked*—
crackles with erotic triumph, the "longing Armes" that close the line indicate
that satisfaction has not yet been realized. These lovers aspire to something
beyond embrace, a superior union brought about by "[t]he all dissolving
Thunderbolt beloe" that the man is still preparing "to throw" (lines 10, 9).
He imagines climax as a dissolution that will break down all boundaries
between himself and his partner such that they might recombine as one, in a
perfect fusion. Rochester offers a bawdy parody of Donne's "The Ecstasy,"
in which two souls, having departed their chaste bodies, break down to "atomies" as a preamble to merging together as one new, enlarged soul: "Love
these mixed souls doth mix again, / And makes both one, each this and that"
(lines 35–36). While Donne's lover declares that "th'atomies of which we
grow / Are souls, whom no change can invade" (lines 47–48), Rochester's
"all dissolving Thunderbolt" is decidedly less spiritual: "that part / Which
shou'd convey my soul up to her heart" (lines 13–14) is the speaker's penis.
"Seeds" (*semina*) is one of Lucretius's favored terms for atoms, as well as his
term for ejaculate (*DRN* 4.1034); keeping both Lucretian usages in mind,
Rochester pivots on Donne's "atomies" from souls to semen.

Rochester knew *DRN* well. He was first cousin once removed to Lucy
Hutchinson, who was probably *DRN*'s first English translator. Rochester
himself translated two brief passages from the first book of the poem (*DRN*
1.1–4 and 1.44–49), and his own poetry is shot through with Lucretian images

and ideas. "The Imperfect Enjoyment" hits several Lucretian notes, ulti-mately combining them into a neo-Lucretian chord. The beginning of the poem draws on moments from *DRN* Book 4's explanation of the mechanics of sex and the dangers of erotic obsession. Lucretius describes lovers who do each other harm in their frenzied attempts to gain satisfaction from each other's bodies, "premunt arte faciuntque dolorem / corporis et dentis inlidunt saepe labellis / osculaque adfligunt" (so closely pressing / What they long for, that they hurt the flesh by their possessing, / Often sinking teeth in lips, and crushing as they kiss; *DRN* 4.1079–81). Like Lucretius's lovers, Rochester's couple interlace their bodies, "[w]ith Armes, Leggs, Lipps, close clinging to embrase" (line 5), but—again like Lucretius's lovers—frustrate themselves by aiming beyond fleeting pleasures for something more. For Lucretius, the impossibility of sexual satisfaction is constitutive: lovers "nec satiare queunt spectando corpora coram / nec manibus quicquam teneris abradere membris / possunt errantes incerti corpore toto" (can't satisfy / The flesh however they devour each other with the eye, / Nor with hungry hands roving the body can they reap / Anything from the supple limbs that they can take and keep; *DRN* 4.1102–4). Rochester's bawdy farce, by contrast, makes the problem out to be one of timing. The "lesser lightening" (line 7) of the lady's tongue preempts the man's "all dissolving Thunderbolt" (line 10), and his premature ejaculation frustrates their mutual ecstasy.

His misplaced bolt evokes another moment from *DRN* Book 4: the arresting account of wet dreams. Adolescent boys receive nocturnal visitations from gorgeous, free-floating *simulacra* generated "e corpore quoque" (by "some random body or another"; *DRN* 4.1032). These visions rouse the sleep-ers: "qui ciet irritans loca turgida semine multo, / ut quasi transactis saepe omnibu' rebu' profundant / fluminis ingentis fluctus vestemque cruentent" (This irritates and goads the organs, swollen hard with seed—/ Such that frequently, as if he'd really done the deed, / A youth floods forth a gush of semen so he stains the sheet; *DRN* 4.1034–36). Rochester's lover endures a similar mishap; even though he has a real woman between his sheets, he still spends his seed on nothing.

> In liquid raptures I dissolve all o're
> Melt into sperm and spend at every pore.
> A touch from any part of her had don't
> Her hand, her foot, her very look's a C—t.

> (lines 15–18)

Dissolution is what the lovers sought, and here they are indeed dissolved, but into sex, not soul. He is all Pr—ck, she all C—t. Rochester's speaker ungenerously blames his partner: it is her overwhelming sensuality, dispersed through every part of her, that so disperses him.

Sex in "The Imperfect Enjoyment" is a "liquid rapture," a seeping, swelling, spurting sensuality that melts, dissolves, overflows, and overwhelms the body. This same liquidity characterizes Rochester's translation of the opening of *DRN*'s famous hymn to Venus. For Lucretius's four taut Latin lines, Rochester gives eight English ones.

> Greate Mother of Eneas and of Love
> Delight of Mankinde, and the powers above,
> Who all beneathe those sprinkl'd dropps of light
> Which slide upon the face of gloomy night,
> Whither vast regions of that liquid world
> Where groves of shipps on watry hill's are hurl'd
> Or fruitfull earth, do'st bless, sinc 'tis by thee
> That all things live, which the bright sunn do'es see
>
> (lines 1–8)

The overwhelming liquefaction of these lines is not present in Lucretius's original.[3] Rochester allows one image—Lucretius's *mare navigerum* from line 3, which A. E. Stallings translates as "ship-freighted sea"—to infect the others, so that what in *DRN* are "sliding constellations" (*labentia signa*) and "fruited earth" (*terras frugiferentis*) become in Rochester's rendering "sprinkl'd dropps of light" in "vast regions of that liquid world" (the sky), and trees morph into "groves of shipps on watry hill's." The thrust of the Lucretian hymn is that the nature of things is love; all the creatures of the earth and seas and skies come into being and procreate under the sign of Venusian pleasure (Lucretius's *voluptas*, Rochester's "Delight"). In his translation, Rochester renders this pleasurable, generative Venusian power as pervasive liquid. The stars, the sky, the hills, melt under the influence of the goddess of love into one swirling mass. There is something of this liquid, Lucretian Venus in the woman in Rochester's "The Imperfect Enjoyment," the woman who elicits "liquid raptures" because her sensuality is so suffused through her body that her "hand . . . foot . . . very look's a C—t" (line 18). One reading of Rochester's poem is that it imagines what it would be like to make love to Lucretius's Venus.

The Venus of *DRN* is multifaceted. She is first and foremost the fecund springtime goddess of the hymn, *alma Venus* (*DRN* 1.2), whose pleasures drive all things under the sun to flourish and reproduce. This goddess was well known and well loved in the Renaissance and early modernity, when the hymn generated myriad imitations. However, the cruel seductress who pushes lovers to madness in Book 4 is also Venus: "This is our Venus" (Haec Venus est nobis, *DRN* 4.1058), Lucretius writes, as he describes how "Veneris dulcedinis" (Venus's honey) inevitably turns to "frigida cura" (Icy Care) when lovers find themselves trapped in amorous obsession (*DRN* 4.1059, 4.1060). Though these are two sides of the very same goddess of love, in *DRN* Lucretius separates these two aspects of Venus as much as he can, quarantining them in different books and ascribing to them different values. To the first we owe everything that lives, but sterility and despair are said to follow in the wake of the second. Rochester, however, telescopes these Venuses to one point—sex—assimilating the sensual naturalism of *DRN* Book 1's hymn to Venus to the erotic instruction contained at the end of *DRN* Book 4.

"This is our Venus" would have been an appropriate rallying cry for libertines like Rochester, who made *DRN* Book 4 central to their adaptations of Lucretian thought. From the mid-seventeenth century onward, *DRN* was an important point of reference for libertine writers in both France and England. They embraced Lucretius's critique of religion as well as his erotic articulation of philosophical issues. In Book 4, Lucretius warns that love is dangerous and ultimately unfulfilling: dangerous because erotic fixation brings pain, and unfulfilling because love will find no satisfaction in sex (lovers may "devour each other with the eye," but "hungry hands" cannot "reap / Anything from the supple limbs that they can take and keep"; *DRN* 4.1102–4). However, Lucretius advises that love's pains can be avoided through promiscuity. He exhorts his (male) readers to "iacere umorem collectum in corpora quaeque . . . si non prima novis conturbes vulnera plagis / vulgivagaque vagus Venere ante recentia cures" ("spend the fluids that collect / On any body") because you have to "reopen the first wound with new cuts while it's still fresh / And with the Venuses of Easy Virtue cure the flesh"; *DRN* 4.1065, 4.1070–71). Natania Meeker emphasizes the centrality of this advice to libertine thought: "Passed through the filter of libertinism, Lucretius's apparent endorsement of infidelity blossoms into a physical and philosophical program—a training in self-management that morphs readily into a form of voluptuous education."[4] For Lucretius, promiscuity is a form of moderation. He recommends it as a means of curbing love (a far greater danger than dispassionate sex).

Libertine Lucretians modify these lessons, taking Lucretius's argument for promiscuity as a practice of emotional moderation and transforming it into an ethos of sexual excess. For libertines, Meeker writes, "*De rerum natura* enables (and, to a certain extent, models) this kind of slippage from a materialist endorsement of pleasure, through a critique of theological dogmatism, and into a focus on sexual promiscuity as a crucial means by which satisfaction (not to mention the ideal of *voluptas*) might be reached. This Enlightenment recuperation of Lucretius allows him to emerge as the poet *par excellence* of libertine *inclination*."[5]

Although the hapless male speaker of "The Imperfect Enjoyment" imagines that shared climax will bring about some sort of higher union between himself and his partner, the true protagonist of Rochester's poem—the recalcitrant member the lover excoriates as "Thou Treacherous base Deserter of my Flame" (line 46)—proudly flies the flag of libertine inclination. *He* knows better than to love, and adheres to the licentious Lucretian advice about promiscuity. "So true to Lewdness, so untrue to Love" (line 49), he never fails a tryst, but refuses "great Love" (line 60). The disappointed lover thunders his displeasure.

> What Oyster, Cynder, Beggar, Common whore
> Did'st thou ere fayle in all thy life before?
> . . . .
> Even so thy brutall vallour is display'd,
> Break'st every stew, doest each smale whore invade,
> But when great Love the onsett does Command
> Base Recreant to thy Prince thou durst not stand.
>
> (lines 50–51, 58–61)

Lucretian erotology emphasizes the impossibility of higher-level satisfaction. Sex brings pleasure, but it will never fulfill love. The unruly male member acts accordingly, taking his pleasures when he can, but never rising to Love. The lesson here: accept the pleasure of climax, but do not pretend that it will be an "all dissolving Thunderbolt."

I close *The Erotics of Materialism* with this case study in libertine poetry to show how different the Lucretian erotics of the libertines is from that of any of the poets discussed earlier in this book. Rochester wrote "The Imperfect Enjoyment" sometime after 1670, either before or around the same time that his cousin Lucy Hutchinson was composing a scathing repudiation of her translation of *DRN*. Hutchinson had translated *DRN* decades earlier, when the meanings and fortunes of *DRN* were not yet fixed, but by the mid-1670s, she felt compelled to disavow her earlier work on the poem. In all likelihood, this is because she was repelled by the now-fixed association between libertinism and Lucretianism effected by writers like her cousin. Libertinism marks a decisive shift in the possibilities for Lucretian poetics, and Lucretian erotics, in early modernity. The age of Enlightenment is the period toward which much of the scholarship on early modern Lucretian reception tends, because it is only in the Enlightenment that the radical potential of Lucretian thought is given free rein—the frank sexuality, the austere materialist vision of nature, the functional atheism.[6] In *Reading Lucretius in the Renaissance*, Ada Palmer asks why, although *DRN* was rediscovered in 1417, there are no "Epicureans" until Pierre Gassendi (1592–1655), whose mid-seventeenth-century publications on Epicurus were part of an ambitious project to revive and popularize atomist philosophy.[7] *DRN* was in wide circulation by the end of the fifteenth century; why did it take over a hundred and fifty years for the intellectual climate to shift such that Lucretius could be read for his radical thought? Palmer finds the cause of "this strange conjunction of fast dissemination and slow intellectual reception" in humanist educational agendas.[8] Renaissance readers sought to "absorb useful classical language regardless of content," and humanist reading practices "acted as a filter that dominated the reading experience, and thereby limited the capacity of atomism . . . to circulate in Renaissance Europe even as the texts that contained them circulated broadly."[9] Humanists were able to read *DRN* comfortably because their "moral filter" allowed them to tune out the heretical ideas and focus on philological and poetic issues.

According to Palmer, the breakdown of this moral filter began in the second half of the sixteenth century "as the purpose of reading turned from resurrecting lost ancients toward a new emphasis on science, method, and innovation."[10] One way of thinking about the work of this book is that it explores what happened in poetry influenced by Lucretius from the time this filter begins to break down (Ronsard's first book of *Amours* is published in 1552) until the dawning of the Enlightenment (the latest works I consider are Hutchinson's *Elegies*, *OD*, and dedication of her *DRN* translation, all from the 1670s), when that filter breaks down entirely. Scholarship on the reception of *DRN* in roughly the three centuries after the poem's recovery in 1417 tends to gravitate, both historically and conceptually, toward the pole of Renaissance rediscovery or that of the Enlightenment. *The Erotics of Materialism* works against the illusion that either Renaissance humanism or Enlightenment radicalism exhausts what we can know of Lucretius in the Renaissance and early modernity. The poets studied in this book neither produce faithful imitations of a small number of Lucretian commonplaces, nor are they proto-Enlightenment radicals.

What was it like to write with Lucretius between approximately 1550 and 1675? Lucretius wrote with Venus. In the opening lines of his poem, he asks the goddess to be his muse: "te sociam studeo scribendis versibus esse / quos ego de rerum natura pangere conor" (I invite / You Goddess, stand beside me, be my partner as I write / *The Nature of Things*, these verses I am striving to set down; *DRN* 1.24–25). Lucretius asks Venus to join him in his endeavors "quae quoniam rerum naturam sola gubernas / nec sine te quicquam dias in luminis oras / exoritur neque fit laetum neque amabile quicquam" (Because alone you steer the nature of things upon its course, / And nothing can arise without you on light's shining shores, / And nothing glad or lovely can be fashioned; *DRN* 1.21–23). The goddess animates nature, and she will animate the poet of nature as well. The power she wields, over both nature and poetry, is erotic. The birds and beasts of the hymn are "perculsae corda tua vi" (struck with your [Venus's] power through the heart; *DRN* 1.13), and Lucretius must have imagined that he would be like those animals, "ita capta lepore / te sequitur cupide quo quamque inducere pergis" (Caught in the chains of love, and follow you wherever you [Venus] lead; *DRN* 1.15–16). Lucretius embraces this seduction. When he writes of Mars lying in Venus's lap, he perhaps imagines himself in the god's place. He tips back his head and lets the goddess's honeyed words, her honeyed kisses, drip into his mouth. He will use those words, in images that conflate poetic persuasion and sexual seduction, to write a honied poetry that mimics Venus's power, that also seduces as it animates. Though Venus inspires Lucretius to writing, not rutting, Lucretian poetry is imbued with Venusian eroticism.

From late antiquity onward, critics of Epicureanism turned *DRN*'s erotics against Lucretius, twisting Lucretian images for poetic seduction—Venus seducing Mars, honey rimming a wormwood cup, the sensual frenzies of Book 4—into figures for the failures and dangers of Epicurean thought and Lucretian poetry. Lucretian poetry is Venusian; it aims to strike its readers through the heart, to catch them in chains of love. Lucretian writing is seduction that invites a reading that is desire, a believing that is love. In the sixteenth and seventeenth centuries the erotic language that Lucretius used as a theoretical idiom for his poetics was weaponized by his critics to tar both himself and his work with charges of hedonism and impiety. Those who wrote with Lucretius in this period were fortified against pagan heresy, well defended against the seductions of Lucretian poetry. They do not tilt back their heads, expose their creamy throats, and invite the poet and his goddess to do their worst. These readers espy the filaments of what Lisa Robertson calls the "supple snare" of Lucretian poetry and are wary. And yet, as I have shown throughout this book, even though they were highly sensitized to the long-established and much-advertised dangers of Lucretian erotics, sixteenth- and seventeenth-century poets were alert to the potential of Lucretian poetics. They recognized that in *DRN*, Lucretian thinking on erotics and Lucretian thinking on poetry occupy the same theoretical terrain, so that accounts of the former—in *DRN*'s most gorgeous poetic set pieces, the hymn to Venus, the honey and wormwood passage, and the end of Book 4—illuminate Lucretian thinking on the latter. Tentatively, aware of the danger, yet not immune to the seduction, they engage both erotics and poetics. Thinking with Lucretius, writing with Lucretius, these poets meditate on the seductive potential of poetic language, the materiality of fantasy, and the kinship of words and things. The Lucretian promise is to illustrate the nature of things; for these poets, Lucretius also illuminates the nature of poetry.

NOTES

INTRODUCTION

Note to epigraph: Robertson, *Nilling*, 39.

1. "Marullo's corrections circulated in several different versions in the Renaissance and were widely used by scholars and publishers, exerting a huge influence on the early form of the text" (Palmer, *Reading Lucretius in the Renaissance*, 81–82). Marullus's commentary is in part preserved in Pietro Candido's notes to his 1512 Florentine edition (Gillespie and Hardie, *The Cambridge Companion to Lucretius*, 186).

2. *DRN* 1.17–20, translation modified. All quotations from *DRN* in the Latin original are cited from the edition by Cyril Bailey; English translations are from Stallings, *The Nature of Things*. Henceforth citations will be provided in the text. Because Stallings makes every effort to match the lines of her translation to the Latin original, I do not give separate line numbers for the English translation.

3. Like his corrections to *DRN*, Marullus's hymns were influential in the Renaissance. They are newly available in English translation in Marullus, *Poems*.

4. Because it does not deny the existence of the gods, Epicurean philosophy is not atheist, but insofar as the gods are not essential to the functioning of the atomist universe, it is functionally atheist. The leap from Epicureanism to atheism is an easy one.

5. "fere plus aequo"; quoted by Hopkins, in Gillespie and Hardie, *The Cambridge Companion to Lucretius*, 257.

6. In Jerome's Latin translation of Eusebius's lost *Chronicon* (fourth century CE), the church father writes: "Olympiade 171 Titus Lucretius poeta nascitur, qui postea amatorio poculo in furorem versus, cum aliquot libros per intervalla insaniae conscripsisset, quos postea emendavit Cicero, propria se manu interfecit, anno aetatis quadragesimo tertio" (In the second year of the 171st Olympiad Titus Lucretius the poet was born, who was later driven mad by a love potion, and having written some books in the intervals of his insanity which Cicero later corrected, killed himself in his forty-fourth year; quoted in Palmer, *Reading Lucretius in the Renaissance*, 106).

7. Hopkins, in Gillespie and Hardie, *The Cambridge Companion to Lucretius*, 257. At the time of Creech's death a bizarre pamphlet (Bodleian Bliss B 366) circulated against his character; the pamphlet was titled "A Step to Oxford: or, a mad essay on the reverend Mr. Thomas Creech's hanging himself, as it is said, for love: with the character of his mistress. In a letter to a person of quality." It claimed that Creech "lov'd Women better than Wives, and was so expert in the *Art of Love*, that he would *praise a Lady's Vertue till he got to Bed to her*." David

Norbrook suggests that the pamphlet was perhaps authored by John Oldmixon (Norbrook, in Norbrook, Harrison, and Hardie, *Lucretius and the Early Modern*, 66–67).

8. On what she calls "proto-biographies" of Lucretius, see Palmer, *Reading Lucretius in the Renaissance*, 97–139.

9. Epicurus's vast corpus now exists only in fragments. *DRN* likely draws on Epicurus's lost prose work *On Nature*.

10. These are all ninth-century manuscripts, two complete and one fragmentary. On these, see Butterfield, *The Early Textual History of Lucretius' "De rerum natura,"* 5–13.

11. The text entered wide manuscript circulation about forty years later. On Poggio's rediscovery of *DRN*, see Gordan, *Two Renaissance Book Hunters*. On the textual history of *DRN* before that rediscovery, see Butterfield, *The Early Textual History of Lucretius' "De rerum natura."* On the Renaissance manuscript circulation of *DRN*, see Palmer, *Reading Lucretius in the Renaissance*. On early printed editions of *DRN*, see Gordon, *A Bibliography of Lucretius*. While the narrative of loss and rediscovery is the received history of *DRN*'s transmission and Renaissance reception, some scholars argue that *DRN* was more available during the medieval period than we think. See Lokaj, "Strepitumque Acherontis avari." On attested traces of Lucretius in the Middle Ages, see Michael Reeve's chapter "Lucretius in the Middle Ages and Early Renaissance," in Gillespie and Hardie, *The Cambridge Companion to Lucretius*, 205–13; also Butterfield, *The Early Textual History of Lucretius' "De rerum natura."*

12. Epicureanism has always been associated with sensuality: the Epicurean directive to seek out the negative pleasure of *ataraxia*, or mental calm, was easily and frequently mischaracterized as an encouragement to hedonism. In early modernity, Epicureanism's denial of an afterlife was taken to encourage sexual degeneracy in this life because the lack of a posthumous punishment for bad behavior was seen as encouragement to sin. Moreover, by the latter half of the seventeenth century, Epicureanism became associated with libertinism (see Chapter 4 and the Epilogue).

13. Only a handful of editorial introductions from the sixteenth and seventeenth centuries do not mention the love potion (Palmer, *Reading Lucretius in the Renaissance*, 97–139)

14. Gerard Passannante has argued that *DRN* "is a poem that . . . theorizes its own receptions" (*The Lucretian Renaissance*, 5). Focusing on the humanist discipline of philology, he shows how in the Renaissance the Lucretian analogy between atoms and alphabetical letters "[became] meaningful for the development of textual criticism, for thinking about the transmission of ancient knowledge in print, [and] for understanding the Renaissance itself as a material relation to a classical past" (Passannante, 4).

15. On Epicurean philosophy as cure, see Nussbaum, *The Therapy of Desire*.

16. The full honey and wormwood passage reads: "primum quod magnis doceo de rebus et artis / religionum animum nodis exsolvere pergo, / deinde quod obscura de re tam lucida pango / carmina, musaeo contingens cuncta lepore. / id quoque enim non ab nulla ratione videtur; / sed veluti pueris absinthia taetra medentes / cum dare conantur, prius oras pocula circum / contingunt *mellis dulci* flavoque liquore, / ut puerorum aetas improvida ludificetur / labrorum tenus, interea perpotet *amarum* / absinthi laticem deceptaque non capiatur, / sed potius tali pacto recreata valescat, / sic ego nunc, quoniam haec ratio plerumque videtur / tristior esse quibus non est tractata, retroque / vulgus abhorret ab hac, volui tibi *suaviloquenti* / carmine Pierio rationem exponere nostram / et quasi *musaeo dulci contingere melle,* / si tibi forte animum tali ratione tenere / versibus in nostris possem, dum perspicis omnem / naturam rerum qua constet compta figura" (Because I teach great truths, and set out to unknot / The mind from the tight strictures of religion, and I write / Of so darkling a subject in a poetry so bright,

[touching all with the Muse's charm.] / Nor is my method to no purpose—doctors do as much; / Consider a physician with a child who will not sip / A disgusting dose of wormwood: first he coats the goblet's lip / All round with *honey's sweet blond stickiness*, that way to lure / Gullible youth to taste it, and to drain the *bitter cure*, / The child's duped but not cheated— rather, put back in the pink— / That's what I do. Since those who've never tasted of it think / This philosophy's a bitter pill to swallow, and the throng / Recoils, I wished to coat this physic in *mellifluous* song, / To kiss it, as it were, with the *sweet honey of the Muse*. / That is the purpose of my poetry, as you peruse / My lines, to try to keep your mind's attention, while you start / To understand the framework at the universe's heart; *DRN* 1.931–50, emphasis mine, translation modified).

17. "efficé ut interea fera moenera militiai / per maria ac terras omnis sopita quiescant. / nam tu sola potes tranquilla pace iuvare / mortalis, quoniam belli fera moenera Mavors / armipotens regit, in gremium qui saepe tuum se / reicit aeterno devictus vulnere amoris, / atque ita suspiciens tereti cervice reposta / pascit amore avidos inhians in te, dea, visus, / eque tuo pendet resupini spiritus ore. / hunc tu, diva, tuo recubantem corpore sancto / circumfusa super, suavis ex ore loquelas / funde petens placidam Romanis, incluta, pacem" (Meanwhile, Holy One, both on dry land and on the deep, / Make the mad machinery of war drift off to sleep. / For only you can favour mortal men with peace, since Mars, / Mighty in Arms, who oversees the wicked work of war / Conquered by Love's everlasting wound, so often lies / Upon your lap, and gazing upwards, feasts his greedy eyes / On love, his mouth agape at you, Famed Goddess, as he tips / Back his shapely neck, his breath hovering at your lips. / And as he leans upon your holy body, and you reach / Your arms around him, Lady, sweet-talk him with honeyed speech, / Pleading for a quiet peace for Romans; *DRN* 1.29–40).

18. As Philip Hardie puts it, "the *De Rerum Natura* is a poem of confident certainties. . . . but to this is added a didactic voice that projects what might be called a rhetoric of uncertainty" (*Lucretian Receptions*, 231).

19. In different ways, both Jonathan Goldberg and Wendy Beth Hyman have emphasized the importance of erotics to the early modern reception of Lucretius. Goldberg stresses "the relationship of sexuality to philosophical materialism" in early modernity, arguing for "the many ways in which the writers' engagement with materialism necessarily implicates gender and sexuality" (*The Seeds of Things*, 3). Hyman links erotic lyrics to Lucretian materialism, arguing for a "revolutionary intervention of materialist philosophy upon erotic literature specifically" (*Impossible Desire*, 19). Daniel Tiffany's study of what he calls "the iconography of materialism" in lyric poetry was also an important influence on this book, though Tiffany focuses his analysis on Heronic rather than Lucretian materialism and on modern rather than early modern poetry (*Toy Medium*, 6).

20. On the force of the Lucretian honey and wormwood passage in Counter-Reformation Europe, see Prosperi, *Di soavi licor gli orli del vaso*. On analogy in *DRN*, see particularly Schrijvers, "Le regard sur l'invisible"; Hardie, *Virgil's Aeneid*; Schiesaro, *Simulacrum et imago*; and Passannante, *The Lucretian Renaissance*.

21. Robertson, *Nilling*, 39.

22. Robertson, 22.

23. Goldstein, *Sweet Science*, 3–4.

24. Goldstein, 6. Goldstein continues: "Lucretian materialism . . . granted substance to tropes and tropic activity to nonverbal things" (Goldstein, 7).

25. Of the fifty-two manuscripts Palmer studies (the total number of extant manuscripts of *DRN* from the period after 1417 until the end of the fifteenth century is fifty-four), this

section "is marked in sixteen copies, 33 percent of the total. Notes here tend to be conspicuous, with labels in block capitals, long brackets marking entire pages, brackets on both sides of the text, or large *manicula* for added emphasis" (*Reading Lucretius in the Renaissance*, 70).

26. "Two other sections often annotated by those who left the rest of the text blank are IV 1030–1287 (on love) and VI 1090–1286 (on the cause of plague and the Athenian plague)" (Palmer, *Reading Lucretius in the Renaissance*, 52). Palmer is describing the annotations in fifteenth-century manuscript copies of *DRN*, but my informal survey of annotations in about seventy-five sixteenth- and seventeenth-century print copies of *DRN* indicates that later readers were equally unlikely to read beyond the famous opening lines of the poem. In the summer of 2017 I looked at the majority of the fifteenth-, sixteenth-, and seventeenth-century *DRN* editions in the holdings of the Bibliothèque Nationale, British Library, Bodleian Library, Cambridge University Library, Staatsbibliothek (Berlin), and Folger Shakespeare Library. Judging from annotations in these editions, sixteenth- and seventeenth-century readers seem to have been just as likely as their predecessors to focus on Book 4.

There are many reasons why readers of Lucretius may have been drawn to *DRN* Book 4. The inescapable story of Lucretius and the love philter likely led readers to interpret Book 4 biographically. Renaissance humanists considered authorial biography to be an important reading tool: early print editions of classical texts were prefaced by biographies that defended the author's virtue and explained the relation between the author's life and text in order to reassure the reader that they would be educated rather than endangered by reading the text (Palmer, 98–99). Although the story of the love philter certainly would not have reassured readers of Lucretius's moral character, it may have established his credentials as an expert on love and led them to *Rebus Veneriis*. Readers may also have sought out the end of Book 4 because Epicureanism was irrevocably (though mistakenly) associated with sensualism and hedonism, themes dramatically illustrated there.

27. To my knowledge, no other critics of early modern literature have emphasized this section of *DRN*. The *simulacrum* has been of greater interest to philosophers and critical theorists than it has to literary critics. Of these, Gilles Deleuze's work on the concept of the *simulacrum* in *Difference and Repetition* and *The Logic of Sense* (and its appendices) is most pertinent to this project. On this, see Hock, "A Broken Line."

28. Many contemporary theoretical and philosophical accounts focus on the *clinamen*, that chance swerve of matter in the void. In a late essay, "The Underground Current of the Materialism of the Encounter," Louis Althusser theorizes the *clinamen* as encounter (*Philosophy of the Encounter*, 167). Starting from a similar point as Althusser—the "rain" of atoms—Michel Serres develops a different model of Lucretian physics based around liquidity and what Serres calls "laminar flow" (*The Birth of Physics*, 5). Meanwhile, literary critics as diverse as Harold Bloom, Jacques Lezra, and Stephen Greenblatt have used the *clinamen* to theorize aspects of literary history. For example, in *The Swerve*, his popularizing account of *DRN's* rediscovery and influence in early modernity, Greenblatt associates Lucretius with a historical swerve, or *clinamen*, toward modernity, embodied in the values of secularism and science (Greenblatt, *The Swerve*; see also Bloom, *The Anxiety of Influence*; Lezra, *Unspeakable Subjects*).

Other literary critics focus on different tropes. In her monograph on the influence of *DRN* on Romantic poetry and science, Amanda Jo Goldstein attends to the honey and wormwood passage, which she argues bequeaths to the Romantics a "sweet science" that refuses divisions between poetry and philosophy (*Sweet Science*). Gerard Passannante focuses on the analogy between atoms and letters to give a brilliant reading of "the ways in which the dynamic, invisible world of *De rerum natura* came to reflect ideas about the production of literature and knowledge" in early modernity (*The Lucretian Renaissance*, 4). In one chapter of her book on early modern worldmaking, Ayesha Ramachandran identifies an early modern epic tradition derived from Lucretius rather than from Virgil, arguing that we most clearly see early modern epic poets like Spenser and Camões tapping into a (non-Virgilian) Lucretian didactic and cosmological strain of epic in those spaces within their poems that are marked as feminine (*The Worldmakers*, 106–46).

29. Unlike the rest of *DRN*, the end of Book 4 is indebted more to lyric than to epic or didactic conventions. In Book 4, Lucretius draws extensively upon Greek and Latin love lyric traditions. Although such influences are difficult to track, there is a growing consensus that Lucretius was familiar with the poetry of young contemporaries such as Catullus, as well as with the Hellenistic poetry that inspired them (Kenney, "Doctvs Lvcretivs"). In Book 4, Lucretius draws on these lyric traditions to satirize both Roman culture and the lyric poetry that celebrates it. As Aya Betensky puts it, "it makes more sense to see, first of all, the traditions of diatribe and satire at work here [in Book 4 of *DRN*], pointing to the evils of a sick society" ("Lucretius and Love," 295). E. J. Kenney writes that "the device of attacking an adversary with weapons stolen from his own armoury is not the property of any school; it is one of the oldest tricks in the book. Nowhere does Lucretius use it with more effect than in his great diatribe on Love in Book IV" ("Doctvs Lucretius," 380). Kenney suggests that Lucretius is parodying Catullus directly when he writes of a lover who is poisoned by bitter thoughts even in the midst of his pleasures, at *DRN* 4.1135–38.

Such satire marks the gulf between Epicureanism's moral and social goals—mental calm and the retirement from public affairs—and the worldly orientation of Roman culture, particularly its obsessional and greedy approach to love and sex. Among Lucretius's contemporaries, Book 4 would undoubtedly have been read as an attack on Roman mores, and maybe even on the Roman lyric that celebrated them. While this may have been legible to early modern readers, Book 4's aggressive satirical orientation did nothing in early modernity to dissociate the poem from what it satirizes—love and lyric. That is, Book 4's attack on Roman cultural mores around love and Roman and Greek love lyric did not dissuade early moderns from reading these passages as inherently lyrical, or from integrating them into lyric verse. It is likely that speaking in a lyric idiom—whether earnestly or mockingly—made Book 4 easy to reabsorb into the lyric tradition in early modernity.

30. Diogenes Laertius writes that Epicurus's opinion on verse was that "only the wise man will be able to converse correctly about music and poetry, without however actually writing poems himself" (*Lives of Eminent Philosophers*, 10.121).

31. Lucretius repeatedly entreats his patron, Memmius, to pay attention and heed his argument. He fears that Memmius will be easily seduced from Epicurean teachings by the superstitions of priests: "Tutemet a nobis iam quovis tempore vatum / terriloquis victus dictis desciscere quares" (*DRN* 1.102–3).

32. On Lucretian analogy, see Schrijvers, "Le regard sur l'invisible"; Garani, *Empedocles Redivivus*.

33. In Greek, too, the word for alphabetical letters, *stoicheia*, is also the word for elemental particles such as atoms. Laurence de Looze discusses the analogy at some length in the first chapter of *The Letter and the Cosmos*. Duncan Kennedy suggests that "the word elementum may be an abecedarian coinage. . . . Strikingly, of course, this is not a random sequence of letters" (*Rethinking Reality*, 86).

34. The analogy between atoms and alphabetical letters occurs five times in *DRN*, at 1.196–98, 1.823–29, 1.912–14, 2.688–90, and 2.1013–14.

35. The phrase *moenia mundi* (walls of the world) appears at *DRN* 1.1102, 2.1045, 2.1144, 3.16, 5.119, 5.371, 5.454, 5.1213, and 6.123.

36. For a discussion of this moment, see Lezra, *Unspeakable Subjects*, 21–22.

37. The comment comes in Book 10 of the *Republic* (607b; Plato, *Complete Works*).

38. Aristotle also belittles natural philosophical poetry, but in a different way from Plato. In the *Poetics*, he judges that didactic verse is not properly mimetic, and thus not poetry: "Homer and Empedocles, however, have really nothing in common apart from their metre; so that, if the one is to be called a poet, the other should be termed a physicist rather than a poet" (1447b17–19; Aristotle, *The Complete Works*, vol. 2).

39. Horace wrote: "Aut prodesse volunt aut delectare poetae / aut simul et iucunda et idonea dicere vitae" (*Ars Poetica* lines 333–34 in Horace, *Satires, Epistles and Ars Poetica*). The lines are frequently misrepresented as reading "prodesse *et* delectare."

40. "rerum simulacra vagari / multa modis multis in cunctas undique partis / tenvia, quae facile inter se iunguntur in auris, / obvia cum veniunt, ut aranea bratteaque auri. / quippe etenim multo magis haec sunt tenvia textu / quam quae percipiunt oculos visumque lacessunt, / corporis haec quoniam penetrant per rara cientque / tenvem animi naturam intus sensumque lacessunt. / Centauros itaque et Scyllarum membra videmus / Cerbereasque canum facies simulacraque eorum / quorum morte obita tellus amplectitur ossa; / omne genus quoniam passim simulacra feruntur, / partim sponte sua quae fiunt aere in ipso, / partim quae variis ab rebus cumque recedunt / et quae confiunt ex horum facta figuris" (many images of objects stray / To and fro in every quarter and in many a way, / So delicate, they easily stick together when they meet, / As spider webs are wont, or gold to airy thinness beat. / Indeed, the texture of these images is yet more slight / Than that of images which fill the eyes and strike the sight, / Because they penetrate the body through its pores, and quicken / The mind's subtle stuff and strike the senses from within. / This is why monsters with their hodgepodge limbs appear to us, / Such as Centaurs and Scyllas, hounds with heads like Cerberus— / And phantoms of the dead, whose bones lie in the Earth's embrace— / Because all kinds of images are floating every place. / Some of them spontaneously arise out of thin air, / And some are shed from sundry different objects, and a share / Are formed of combinations of these figures; *DRN* 4.724–38).

41. Robert D. Brown argues that the insatiable lover's "flawed enjoyment of the sex act thus derives from a false idea of what constitutes sexual fulfillment. For unlike hunger and thirst, the sexual appetite is aroused not by depletion but accumulation [of semen] and it is satisfied by the expulsion, not the ingestion, of substance. The 'food of love' (*pabula amoris*, 1063)—*simulacra*, that is—feeds only the lover's passion, not his being" (*Lucretius on Love and Sex*, 75–76).

42. The "Suave, mari magno" passage, for example, was extremely controversial because it could easily be misinterpreted as counseling readers to take pleasure in the pain of others, but not a single early modern translator declined to render it into the vernacular.

43. As David Norbrook explains in the introduction to his and Reid Barbour's recent edition of Lucy Hutchinson's *DRN* translation, "the end of the fourth book violently divided readers in the early modern period. Lambinus, followed by Montaigne, lauded it as offering practical advice for the male reader seeking freedom from unruly desire. Pareus' commentary takes this line. . . . Many readers, however, were disturbed by the anti-romantic violence of the fourth book's conclusion, while others were affronted by its discussion of sexual practices and positions" (Hutchinson, *The Works of Lucy Hutchinson*, vol. 1, Part 1, lxii).

44. Dryden, *Sylvæ*, a3.

45. Quoted in Gillespie and Hardie, *The Cambridge Companion to Lucretius*, 12.

46. Foucault, "Theatrum Philosophicum," 169. On Foucault's interpretation of Deleuze's Lucretianism, see Goldberg, *The Seeds of Things*, 31–42.

47. Goldberg, 34.

48. On Ovid's rendition of the Narcissus myth as a mythologization of these lines, see Chapter 1.

49. In "The Early Stuart Epicure," Reid Barbour discusses the ways that the atom is eroticized in Stuart England. Here I am suggesting that *DRN* also sets readers up to desire the atom.

50. The word Lucretius uses for semen here is "seed" (*semine*, *DRN* 4.1034), one of his favorite names for atoms, which he frequently calls the "seeds of things" (*semina rerum*, first at *DRN* 1.59 and repeated many times thereafter).

51. On Renaissance seduction poetry's debt to Lucretian materialism, see Hyman, *Impossible Desire*, 27–52.

52. Like Gerard Passannante, who eloquently argues that for Renaissance readers "the experience of materialism did not involve the deliberate adoption of a philosophical paradigm or an intellectual commitment" (*Catastrophizing*, 3), I advocate a nondogmatic approach to Lucretian reception history. Early modern poets who disagreed fundamentally with Epicurean doctrine drew deeply from Lucretian thinking that links poetry, matter, and fantasy.

53. Twentieth-century theorists like Foucault, Deleuze, and Serres highlight these different aspects of Lucretian materialism that were also available to early modern readers. Serres's book on Lucretius maintains that Lucretian atomism is not a solid state physics but rather a physics of liquidity and chaos (*The Birth of Physics*, 3–5). Deleuze is fascinated by the *simulacrum*. As he argues in "The Simulacrum and Ancient Philosophy," an early essay appended to *The Logic of Sense*, the Lucretian *simulacrum* subverts the Platonic representational schema that valorizes the originary forms over all representations. It is this idea that so excites Foucault, who writes, optimistically, that "the philosophy of representation—of the original, the first time, resemblance, imitation, faithfulness—is dissolving; and the arrow of the simulacrum released by the Epicureans is headed in our direction" ("Theatrum Philosophicum," 172). It is because of Deleuze's work on the Epicurean concept of the *simulacrum* that Foucault believes that "perhaps one day, this century will be known as Deleuzian" (Foucault, 165). It is with the *simulacrum* that Deleuze may be able to fulfill his Nietzschean project of overturning Platonism: "What does it mean to 'reverse Platonism'? This is how Nietzsche defined the task of his philosophy, or, more generally, the task of the philosophy of the future" (*The Logic of Sense*, 253).

54. As Jonathan Goldberg has argued, "mechanical philosophy . . . is not the main contribution of Lucretius to atomist thought" (*The Seeds of Things*, 2).

55. Ferguson, "Saint Augustine's Region of Unlikeness," 843.

56. Ferguson, 844.

57. This argument, in relation to early modern poetry, is powerfully presented in the chapter on George Herbert in Stanley Fish's influential *Self-Consuming Artifacts*. Fish argues that Herbert's devotional lyrics stage the dissolution of reality (and syntax) in order to affirm the subsumption of human speech into divine speech, the "I" of the poet and the reader into the "all" of God: "Christ is discovered to be not only the substance of all things, but the performer of all actions . . . the moment of recognizing and entering into this wider, sacramental vision is also a moment when the 'I' surrenders its pretense to any independent motion and even to an independent existence" (*Self-Consuming Artifacts*, 173).

58. Important scholarship has shown that imagination, fiction, and fable remained important to the early modern scientific enterprise, despite early modern protestations to the contrary. See, for example, the work of Frédérique Aït-Touati, who cautions against relying on later divisions between the literary and the scientific to understand early modernity: "Understood as such a one-way transfer, the relation between what is literary and what is scientific postulates a fixed definition of each of the two domains. . . . Science as such did not yet have its own place, and its discourse had no fixed form; it made its appearance across a heterogeneous range of texts and domains" (*Fictions of the Cosmos*, 5).

59. Bacon, *The Advancement of Learning*, 23. In Bacon's time, this division was not as outsized as the rhetoric suggests, and does not really take on full force until midway through the seventeenth century.

60. Sprat writes that the members of the Royal Society have "been most rigorous" in showing "a constant Resolution, to reject all the amplifications, digressions, and swellings of style: to return back to the primitive purity, and shortness, when men deliver'd so many *things*, almost in an equal number of *words*. They have exacted from all their members, a close, naked, natural way of speaking; positive expressions, clear senses; a native easiness: bringing all things as near the Mathematical plainness, as they can" (Sprat, *The History of the Royal Society*, 113).

61. Bacon, *The Advancement of Learning*, 23.

62. This increasingly common perspective is echoed by major thinkers after him, such as Thomas Hobbes, who in his *Leviathan* (1651) writes: "To conclude, The Light of humane minds is Perspicuous Words, but by exact definitions first snuffed, and purged from ambiguity; *Reason* is the *pace*; Encrease of *Science*, the way; and the Benefit of man-kind, the *end*. And on the contrary, Metaphors, and senselesse and ambiguous words, are like *ignes fatui*; and reasoning upon them, is wandering amongst innumerable absurdities; and their end, contention, and sedition, or contempt" (I.v.36). Years later, John Locke would echo the sentiment: "I confess, in Discourses, where we seek rather Pleasure and Delight, than Information and Improvement, such Ornaments as are borrowed from them, can scarce pass for Faults. But yet, if we would speak of Things as they are, we must allow, that all the Art of Rhetorick, besides Order and Clearness, all the artificial and figurative application of Words Eloquence hath invented, are for nothing else but to insinuate wrong *Ideas*, move the Passions, and thereby mislead the Judgment; and so indeed are perfect cheat: And therefore however laudable or allowable Oratory may render them in Harangues and popular Addresses, they are certainly, in all Discourses that pretend to inform or instruct, wholly to be avoided" (*An Essay Concerning Human Understanding*, 452).

63. I discuss Ovid's debts to Lucretius and the interconnected early modern reception of the two Roman poets in Chapter 1.

64. The paradigmatic Renaissance example of poetic language that takes itself as its own reference is Petrarch's *Rime sparse*, in which the beloved's name, Laura, is a near homophone for the symbol of poetic glory, the *laurel* wreath. On this, see Freccero, "The Fig Tree and the Laurel." Freccero contrasts the specific self-referentiality of Petrarchan poetics to the structure of Augustinian language, which always ultimately refers to God.

65. "The same Lucretian themes appear in many Renaissance poems, and the response is the same in every case: the poet often echoes Lucretius's sentiment and reproduces Lucretius's descriptions, but he always rejects Lucretius's philosophy and replaces it with a Christian statement" (Goddard, "Epicureanism and the Poetry of Lucretius in the Renaissance," 243).

66. Quoted in Palmer, *Reading Lucretius in the Renaissance*, 182.

67. Quoted in Palmer, 182.

68. Palmer, 37.

69. The notion of poetry as a "toy" was widespread in the Renaissance. Poetry was associated with youth, and many poets describe their poetic endeavors as youthful follies to be set aside as they mature. Philip Sidney, who died at the age of thirty-two before he could grow out of his poetry phase, refers to his *Arcadia* as "this ink-wasting toy of mine" (Sidney, *The Major Works*, 249). On this, see Duncan-Jones, *Philip Sidney's Toys.*

70. Scève, *Œuvres complètes*, vol. 5.

71. The title of chapter 7 of volume 1 of Patin's *Études sur la poésie latine* is "Du poëme 'De la Nature.' L'Antilucrèce chez Lucrèce."

72. Gale, *Oxford Readings in Lucretius*, 3.

73. Blake, *The Complete Poetry and Prose*, 35.

74. In the mid-twentieth century, classical scholarship took a turn toward connecting Lucretian poetry to Epicurean philosophy. Paul Friedländer's influential and controversial 1941 article "Pattern of Sound and Atomistic Theory in Lucretius" connects the poem's verbal structures, such as alliteration, wordplay, and repetition, to the analogy between atoms and letters. Monica Gale explains that "since the 1960s . . . the idea that the *poetry* of the *DRN* is in itself a kind of rhetorical tactic—that is, that the poem's language is designed not just to *explain* the principles of Epicurean philosophy, but to *persuade* the reader of the validity of the system and, ultimately, to make a convert of him or her—has become widely accepted. . . . The notion that the *DRN* is to be read as a protreptic work, in which the poetry itself helps to draw the reader in and has a functional role to play in the process of conversion, has also been invoked by scholars addressing the problematic question of Epicurus' apparently negative attitude towards poetry" (Gale, *Oxford Readings in Lucretius*, 5). On *DRN*'s poetic format, see Gale, *Myth and Poetry in Lucretius*, 14–18, 129–55.

75. See Connat, "Mort et testament de Remy Belleau"; and Morrison, "Another Book from Ronsard's Library."

76. Goddard, "Epicureanism and the Poetry of Lucretius in the Renaissance," 244.

77. Hutchinson, *The Works of Lucy Hutchinson*, vol. 1, *Part 1*, 13.

78. Very recently there has been a wave of interest in and new editions of Cavendish's *Poems and Fancies*, signaling a shift in the collection's reception. See Cavendish, *Margaret Cavendish's "Poems and Fancies"*; Cavendish, *"Poems and Fancies" with "The Animal Parliament."*

79. In *The Death of Nature*, Carolyn Merchant influentially argued that the scientific revolution was grounded in the subjection by male scientists of a nature that was gendered female.

CHAPTER I

My sincere thanks go to Phillip John Usher, who read this chapter at a critical junction and offered enormously helpful comments.

1. Ronsard, *Les amours*. Ronsard revised his poems over the course of his career. Unless otherwise noted, citations of the first two books of *Les amours*, to Cassandre and Marie, refer to the GF-Flammarion edition, which reproduces the poems as they were first printed. When there are meaningful variations between early and late versions of the poems, I also supply the revised versions that were printed in the 1584 edition of Ronsard's *Œuvres*. Citations of the 1584 *Œuvres* and of all of Ronsard's later poetry, including the hymns and the *Sonnets pour*

Helene, refer to the Pléiade edition. Different editions of Ronsard's work use different indentation patterns, and to avoid visual inconsistency I have regularized them, preferring the streamlined formatting of the Pléiade edition. By the time the 1584 *Œuvres* came out, these lines read as follows: "Ces petits corps qui tombent de travers / Par leur descente en biais vagabonde, / Heurtez ensemble ont composé le monde / S'entr'acrochans de liens tous divers" (Ronsard, *Œuvres complètes*, vol. 1).

2. Unless otherwise noted, all translations from French are mine, though I have consulted English translations of Ronsard's poetry when available, including those in Ronsard, *Selected Poems*; Ronsard, *Cassandre*; and https://oeuvresderonsard.wordpress.com.

3. In the 1584 *Œuvres*, these lines are revised to "L'ennuy, le soing et les pensers couvers / Tombez espais en mon amour profonde, / Ont acroché d'une agrafe feconde / Dedans mon cœur l'amoureux univers" (Ronsard, *Œuvres complètes*, vol. 1).

4. Petrarca, *Petrarch's Lyric Poems*, sonnet 1, line 2.

5. On Lucretius and the Pléiade, see Castor, *Pléiade Poetics*; Fraisse, *L'influence de Lucrèce en France au seizième siècle*; Lestringant, *La renaissance de Lucrèce*; Pantin, *La poésie du ciel en France*; and Schmidt, *La poésie scientifique en France au XVIe siècle*.

6. Hardie, "Lucretius and the Delusions of Narcissus," 82.

7. Giorgio Agamben charts a "medieval phantasmology" that "was born from a convergence between the Aristotelian theory of the imagination and the Neoplatonic doctrine of the pneuma as a vehicle of the soul" (*Stanzas*, 23).

8. Agamben's account omits Lucretius, which allows Agamben to claim that "in all of the classical world there is nothing similar to the conception of love as a phantasmatic process" that he traces in his (Aristotelian and Platonic) account of the amorous image (Agamben, 82).

9. Plato outlines his theory of vision in *Timaeus* 45c (*Complete Works*).

10. Ford, in Gillespie and Hardie, *The Cambridge Companion to Lucretius*, 234.

11. In his exhaustive review of Ronsard's philosophical sources, which focuses mainly on the hymns, Isidore Silver points out that Ronsard's earlier poems tend to follow the *Timaeus*, whereas the later hew more closely to Genesis and move toward Aristotle's opinion that the universe is eternal ("Ronsard's Reflections on Cosmogony and Nature," 224–26). Malcolm Quainton makes a similar point in *Ronsard's Ordered Chaos*, 7.

12. In his annotations on *DRN*, Montaigne fantasized a work-around for this prohibition on immortality: "Ut sunt diuersi atomorum motus non incredibile est sic conuenisse olim atomos aut conuenturas ut alius nascatur montanus" (Since the movements of the atoms are so varied, it is not unbelievable that the atoms once came together, or will come together again in the future, so that another Montaigne be born; Screech, *Montaigne's Annotated Copy of Lucretius*, 11).

13. Ovid, *Metamorphoses* 15.871–72; Ovid, *The Metamorphoses of Ovid*, 15.876–77. Ironically, Ovid mentions Lucretius in his list of immortal poets, in a line that manages to simultaneously emphasize *DRN*'s immortality and the earth's mortality: "carmina sublimis tunc sunt peritura Lucreti, / exitio terras cum dabit una dies" (The verses of sublime Lucretius will perish only then when a single day shall give the earth to doom; Ovid, *Amores* 1.15.23–24).

14. Lynn Enterline writes of Ovid's monumentalizing that "when Ovid claims 'ore legar populi . . . uiuam,' he is echoing Ennius' famous epitaph, 'uolito uiuus per ora uirum' ('Living, I fly through the mouths of men'). Like his predecessor, this author claims to 'live' *per ora*. Similarly, commentators often note that beginning with *iamque opus exegi*, the narrator revisits a series of highly conventional topoi in his closing passage. Most obviously, he echoes Vergil and Horace (particularly Odes 3.30, 'exegi monumentum'). But he also draws on a host of

other texts known to us now only in fragments. In other words, Ovid's final lines may claim to represent something essential to the author—*parte . . . meliore mei*—and thus to constitute a culminating moment of authorial self-presentation. But the self depicted in these lines turns out to be a palimpsest of other voices, a complex fabric of quotations" (*The Rhetoric of the Body from Ovid to Shakespeare*, 56).

15. Shakespeare, *Shakespeare's Sonnets*, sonnet 15, lines 11–14.

16. Simone Fraisse comments that what she calls Ronsard's "sensualisme" is no passing phase, but persists from 1552 all the way through the 1570s: "Defying his contemporaries, Ronsard quarrels with Plato. When such a debate strikes his fancy, it is in Lucretius that Ronsard finds support" (*L'influence de Lucrèce en France au seizième siècle*, 107).

17. The Pléiade edition of Ronsard's works does not use accent marks on Helene's name. This is consistent with Ronsard's own spelling. I only use accent marks when referring to the historical woman, Hélène de Surgères, to whom the collection was addressed.

18. In a sonnet addressed to the Cardinal of Lorraine included in the collection of *Sonnets à diverses personnes* that Ronsard assembled in his 1584 *Œuvres*, he inverts the conceit of "Pardonne moy, Platon" to attack Epicureanism, albeit in a less lighthearted way. Ronsard flatters the cardinal by denying the possibility of Epicurean chance; he rules by art, not chance: "Le monde ne va pas, comme dit Epicure, / Par un cas fortuit, mais il va par raison: / Chacun le peut juger, voyant vostre maison, / Qui d'art regit la France, et non pas d'avanture. / D'une prudence jointe à la sage nature / Vous prevoyez des temps l'une et l'autre saison, / En si grande jeunesse ayant le chef grison, / Vous assemblez tout seul un Janus en Mercure" (The world does not run by chance, / Like Epicurus says, but rather by reason; / Everyone knows this who sees your house, / Which rules France with art and not with chance. / With wisdom combined with wise Nature, / You predict the weather from season to season / So young, yet with such grey hair, / You are Janus and Mercury in one person; sonnet 17, lines 1–8).

19. Judging from the will of Remy Belleau, Ronsard's good friend and the subject of Chapter 2, Ronsard, Belleau, and their fellow Pléiade poets probably read *DRN* in the 1514 Paris Navagero edition or the 1515 Venice Aldine edition, until the appearance of Denis Lambin's magisterial editions of Lucretius, the first of which was published in 1563 in Paris and Lyon, and then reprinted in 1564, 1565, and 1570. (On the presence of Lucretius in Ronsard's and Belleau's libraries, see Connat, "Mort et testament de Remy Belleau"; and Morrison, "Another Book from Ronsard's Library.") Lambin dedicated Book 2 of his magnificent 1563 edition of *DRN* to Ronsard. (On the dedications of Lambin's *DRN*, see Palmer, *Reading Lucretius in the Renaissance*, 176–91.) Lambin's is also the edition of *DRN* Montaigne owned and heavily annotated. In sixteenth-century France, readers would also have used the seven Sebastian Gryphius editions printed in Lyon from 1534 to 1576, based on the 1500 Aldine edition, but without commentary. The first French translation of *DRN*, by Michel de Marolles, did not appear until 1650.

20. Lucretius was associated above all with Virgil. In her study of annotations in fifteenth-century *DRN* manuscripts, Ada Palmer notes that "more than half of our manuscript annotators marked lines in the *De rerum natura* that Virgil imitated" (*Reading Lucretius in the Renaissance*, 120).

21. On Montaigne's annotations on *DRN*, see Screech, *Montaigne's Annotated Copy of Lucretius*.

22. Ronsard must have read Lucretius by this point, because he draws on him in his first book of *Amours*, published in 1552. On Ronsard's copies of *DRN*, see n. 19 above.

23. Wes Williams gives a beautiful account of how Montaigne read and absorbed *DRN* in "'Well said/well thought'" in Norbrook, Harrison, and Hardie, *Lucretius and the Early Modern*, 135–60).

24. Palmer, *Reading Lucretius in the Renaissance*, 57.

25. "Only 29 precent [of the manuscripts] have one or more notes on atomism or related fundamentals" (Palmer, *Reading Lucretius in the Renaissance*, 65). However, "questions of Epicurean moral philosophy are annotated in twenty-nine copies (56 percent), more than mark vocabulary, poetry, or notabilia, and more than twice as many as contain even a single note on atomism" (Palmer, 70).

26. Palmer, 5.

27. Palmer, 96.

28. In addition to "Que philosopher c'est apprendre à mourir" and the "Apologie," another key Lucretian essay of Montaigne's is "Sur des vers de Virgile" (III.5).

29. While Ronsard's early copy of *DRN* would be a magnificent find, I also heed Michael Screech's caution against believing that a reader's annotations tell the whole story of what they glean from a text: "The excitement of having Montaigne's copy to hand should not lead us to expect every quotation in the *Essais* nor every echo of the ideas of Lucretius to be duly docketed on the flyleaves or in the margins. Montaigne did not read, think or write in so mechanical a way. . . . Absence of comment on any particular page of the copy does not prove a lack of interest" (*Montaigne's Annotated Copy of Lucretius*, 41).

30. The subtitle of Stephen Greenblatt's field-establishing (though controversial) *The Swerve* is *How the World Became Modern*. Jacques Lezra and Liza Blake, editors of the recent *Lucretius and Modernity*, trouble the question of *DRN*'s modernity while still making it the frame for their analysis: "How do we account for the work's modernity, if that is indeed what it is?" (*Lucretius and Modernity*, 2). I appraise the scholarly orientation toward *DRN*'s modernity in my article "The Mind Is Its Own Place."

31. Screech writes: "In taking this *Lucretius* to heart, Montaigne was joining a club. He, like Lambinus and those great men who are cited in the volume, knew how to enjoy beautiful Latin verse without the slightest harm to their faith or morals. Or so they protested. In the case of a group which included Dorat and Ronsard we can largely take them at their word" (*Montaigne's Annotated Copy of Lucretius*, 18).

32. "Primum enim poëtarum Gallorum sine controuersia princeps" (Lucretius, *De rerum natura*, ed. Lambin, 99).

33. Lambin's dedications are as follows: Book 1 to Henri de Mesmes, Book 2 to Ronsard, Book 3 to Germain Vaillant de Guélis, Book 4 to Muret, Book 5 to Adrien Turnèbe, Book 6 to Jean Dorat.

34. The Pléiade poets were united by education: most of them studied with the great Hellenist Jean Dorat (1508–1588). Though membership shifted, notable members of the group include Pierre de Ronsard, Joachim du Bellay, Jacques Peletier du Mans, Remy Belleau, Jean-Antoine de Baïf, Pontus de Tyard, Étienne Jodelle, and sometimes Guillaume des Autels, Nicolas Denisot, and Marc-Antoine Muret.

35. On the practice of commenting on vernacular poetry in the Renaissance, and Muret's commentary in particular, see the introduction to Muret, *Commentaires au premier livre des "Amours" de Ronsard*, vii–lxiv.

36. Isidore Silver argues that Ronsard is the primary source of information for the commentary, and that he is the real author of the commentaries after 1553 ("Three Commentaries of the 'Amours' by Muret and Belleau").

37. The relationship was contentious. Palmer discusses their on-again, off-again friendship and the role Lucretius played in it, in *Reading Lucretius in the Renaissance*, 94–103.

38. Muret, *Commentaires au premier livre des "Amours" de Ronsard*, 21.

39. Muret, 30.

40. Muret, xv.

41. Muret, 45–46.

42. Muret, 46.

43. The differences between Muret's and Belleau's commentaries owe something to the differences between the two collections of *Amours*. The editors of the modern edition of Belleau's commentary write that his is "a second commentary, as vast as Muret's . . . but very different in its close agreement with Ronsard's new love poetry" (Belleau, *Commentaires au second livre des "Amours" de Ronsard*, vii). While the first collection of *Amours*, addressed to Cassandre, is written in a high style rich with allusions to the Greek myths evoked by Cassandre's name, the second, to a young Bourgeuil girl of modest birth named Marie, cultivates a simpler, low style. The collection opens with Ronsard complaining to Pontus de Tyard that he comes under fire from critics no matter what style he employs: "Thiard, chacun disoit à mon commencement, / Que j'estoi trop obscur au simple populaire: / Aujourd'hui, chacun dit que je suis au contraire, / Et que je me dements parlant trop bassement" (Tyard, when I began they accused me / Of being unintelligible to the general populace / But now they say the opposite, that I / Distort myself by speaking in too low a style; lines 1–4). Perhaps in response to the simple, plain style of the *Amours de Marie*, Belleau's commentary itself is restrained. In each entry, Belleau summarizes the argument of the poem under discussion, and then gives a series of remarks about the text. Gone are most of the *auctoritates* of Muret's commentaries. See Belleau, *Commentaires au second livre des "Amours" de Ronsard*, xxii.

44. See Michael Reeve's chapter, "Lucretius in the Middle Ages and Early Renaissance," in Gillespie and Hardie, *The Cambridge Companion to Lucretius*, 205–13.

45. Belleau, *Commentaires au second livre des "Amours" de Ronsard*, f. 22 r.

46. The best-known medical text that modeled itself on *DRN* is Girolamo Fracastoro's 1555 Neo-Latin scientific didactic work on syphilis.

47. Screech suggests that Montaigne used this cure for a different purpose: to distract himself from his grief over the death of his friend, Étienne de la Boëtie: "[Lucretius] helped Montaigne over his grief for the recent loss of la Boëtie by drowning his loving friendship in a series of sexual *affaires*. (So the notes may suggest)" (*Montaigne's Annotated Copy of Lucretius*, 18).

48. Ovid, *Remedia amoris* 441–45.

49. Belleau, *Commentaires au second livre des "Amours" de Ronsard*, f. 8 r.

50. Sandys, *Ovid's Metamorphoses Englished*, 159–60. For a discussion of Sandys's translations of Lucretius, see Gillespie in Gillespie and Hardie, *The Cambridge Companion to Lucretius*, 248–49.

51. Sandys, *Ovid's Metamorphoses Englished*, 159.

52. Sandys, 160.

53. Hardie, in Gillespie and Hardie, *The Cambridge Companion to Lucretius*, 120.

54. In a wonderful paper, Camilla Temple convincingly argues that Ovid's Pygmalion story is also a "version of the simulacrum narrative" ("The Erotic Encounter and the Love-Suicide," 6).

55. Ovid, *Metamorphoses* 3.415–17; Ovid, *The Metamorphoses of Ovid*, 3.415–17. R. J. Tarrant, the editor of the Oxford edition of the *Metamorphoses* that I use here, gives the crucial

"umbra" of the last line as "unda," but acknowledges that the Parisinus, Florentinus, and Laurentianus codices have "umbra." I have updated the text to "umbra."

56. Ovid, *Metamorphoses* 3.430–36; Ovid, *The Metamorphoses of Ovid*, 3.430–36.

57. Fraisse, *L'influence de Lucrèce en France au seizième siècle*, 24.

58. Marullus, *Poems*, lines 5–6, emphasis mine.

59. See especially the hymns to Jupiter, Venus, and the Sun.

60. Fraisse also demonstrates—not without some unease—that several of these Christian poets drew extensively on Lucretius's heretical reflections (from Book 3) on death and the mortality of the soul (*L'influence de Lucrèce en France au seizième siècle*, 109–25).

61. Ronsard's first collection of hymns, dedicated to the Cardinal de Chastillon, was published in 1555, and the second, to Marguerite de Navarre (Marguerite de France), sister to the king, in 1556.

62. The "Hynne du printemps" imitates Lucretius's hymn to Venus: "Alors d'un nouveau chef les bois furent couverts, / Les prez furent vestus d'habillements tous verts, / Les vignes de raisins: les campagnes porterent / Le froment qu'à foison les terres enfanterent, / Le doux miel distilla du haut des arbrisseaux, / Et le laict savoureux coula par les ruisseaux" (Then the woods were covered with a new canopy, the meadows were clothed in bright green raiment, the vines with grapes; the fields bore corn which the earth brought forth without travail, sweet honey dripped down from the shrubs, and delicious milk flowed in streams; lines 41–46). The translation is from Ford, *Ronsard's Hymns*, 253.

Both "L'Hynne de la Philosophie" and the "Hynne de l'Hyver" channel Lucretius's famous lines in praise of Epicurus. Lucretius writes: "primum Graius homo mortalis tollere contra / est oculos ausus primusque obsistere contra, / quem neque fama deum nec fulmina nec minitanti / murmure compressit caelum, sed eo magis acrem / irritat animi virtutem, effringere ut arta / naturae primus portarum claustra cupiret. / ergo vivida vis animi pervicit, et extra / processit longe flammantia moenia mundi" (the first among them who dared raise / His human eyes to her [Superstition] was Greek, the first man to withstand her. / Neither the myths of gods, nor lightning bolts, nor threatening thunder / Of heaven hindered him but, rather, all the more they fired / His mind's courage, so that he was the first man who desired / To break the close-barred gates of Nature down. The vital force / Of his intelligence prevailed, and he advanced his course / Far past the blazing bulwarks of the world, and roamed the whole / Immeasurable Cosmos in his mind and in his soul; *DRN* 1.66–73). By imitating these lines, Ronsard implies that in his natural philosophical hymns, he, like Lucretius and Epicurus before him, will look into the depths of nature.

63. In "L'Hynne de l'Esté," Ronsard writes: "l'un fut Hermafrodite, / (Le Printemps est son nom) de puissance petite, / Entre masle et femelle, inconstant, incertain, / Variable en effet du soir au lendemain. / L'Esté fut masle entier, ardant, roux, et colere, / Estincelant et chaud, ressemblant à son pere, / Guerrier, prompt et hardi, toujours en action, / Vigoureux, genereux, plein de perfection, / Ennemi de repos: l'Autonne fut femelle, / Qui n'eut rien de vertu ny de puissance en elle. / L'Hyver fut masle entier, monstrueux et hideux, / Negeux, tourbillonneux, pluvieux et venteux, / Perruqué de glaçons, herissé de froidure, / Qui fist peur en naissant à sa mere Nature" (One was hermaphrodite [Spring is his name], of little strength, halfway between male and female, inconstant, uncertain, variable in his effect from one day to the next; Summer was entirely male, hot, red-headed and irritable, sparkling and warm, like his father, warriorlike, nimble and bold, always active, vigorous, noble, full of perfection, the enemy of repose. Autumn was female and contained nothing courageous or powerful. Winter was also male, monstrous and ugly, snowcovered, tornado-like, rainy and windy, with icicles on his hair,

bristling with cold, who terrified Nature his mother at his birth; lines 109–22). The translation is from Ford, *Ronsard's Hymns*, 256–57.

64. Ronsard's palace of Nature must also be read in connection with the medieval Neo-platonic allegories of nature such as Alain de Lille's *De planctu naturae* and Bernard Silvestris's *Cosmographia*. The "Hynne de l'Autonne" thus seems to be mediating medieval visions of nature with the naturalism of *DRN*.

65. The translation is from Ford, *Ronsard's Hymns*, 264.

66. Ford argues that Autumn nevertheless has a part to play in this cycle: "The sacred union which results between Bacchus and Autonne marks . . . not a sterile end but a new beginning" (*Ronsard's Hymns*, 266).

67. When Autumn encounters her future husband, Bacchus, she proves herself up to the task: "Si tost que Bacchus vit Autonne la pucelle, / Venus luy fist descendre au cœur une etincelle / Par les yeux envoyée, et tout soudainement / Il devint amoureux, et si ne sceut comment. / Il sent dedans ses os une peste qui erre / De mouelle en mouelle, et luy fait telle guerre, / Qu'avec un grand souspir gemissant est contraint / De confesser qu'Amour l'a vive-ment attaint" (As soon as Bacchus saw the maiden Autumn, / Venus sent a spark through his eyes / And into his heart, and all of a sudden / He fell in love, and did not know how. / He feels a plague coursing through his bones / From marrow to marrow, and causing him such strife, / That with a great wailing sigh he is forced / To admit that Love has violently conquered him; lines 393–400).

68. Near the end of the book Lucretius warns that the frenzied lovemaking he has described earlier has no place in the marriage bed because it impedes conception: "nec molles opu' sunt motus uxoribus hilum. / nam mulier prohibet se concipere atque repugnat, / clunibus ipsa viri Venerem si laeta retractat / atque exossato ciet omni pectore fluctus; / eicit enim sulcum recta regione viaque / vomeris atque locis avertit seminis ictum. / idque sua causa consuerunt scorta moveri, / ne complerentur crebro gravidaeque iacerent / et simul ipsa viris Venus ut concinnior esset; / coniugibus quod nil nostris opus esse videtur" (Wanton wiggling's of no use for wives—no, not one bit— / For a woman prevents pregnancy this way, resisting it, / When she grinds her buttocks against the man's member as it thrusts, / Gyrating, her whole body turned to jelly with her lust. / By doing this, she turns the furrow away from the straight and true / Path of the ploughshare, and the seed falls by the wayside too. / Whores thus have their own reasons for wriggling—so that they can / Spend less time pregnant, and to make it better for the man. / Clearly, though, our wives can have no use for such an art; *DRN* 4.1268–77).

69. The translation is from Ford, *Ronsard's Hymns*, 262.

70. Fraisse, *L'influence de Lucrèce en France au seizième siècle*, 93.

71. "The writers of the Pléiade took no more from the Invocation to Venus than what Jean Lemaire himself took" (Fraisse, 93).

72. Fraisse, 93.

73. Fraisse, 93.

CHAPTER 2

1. Simone Fraisse remarks upon this, attributing it to what she calls a "certain sensual constancy" in Ronsard (*L'influence de Lucrèce en France au seizième siècle*, 107).

2. The traditional dating is to the mid-50s BCE, but Gregory Hutchinson has argued for a composition date of 48 or 49 BCE, at the beginning of the civil war ("The Date of *De Rerum Natura*").

3. Most translators make this explicit. A. E. Stallings expands Lucretius's opening words, "Aeneadum genetrix," to a full line: "Life-stirring Venus, Mother of Aeneas and of Rome." When the prominent Pléiade poet Joachim du Bellay translated the first twenty-two lines of *DRN* into French (the first translation of Lucretius into French) for a collection of ancient sources to accompany Louis Le Roy's translation of Plato's *Symposium*, he renders the first line as "O la mere d'Enée, ancestre des Romains" (O, mother of Aeneas, ancestor of the Romans; Du Bellay, *Œuvres poétiques*, vol. 6, part 1, 403).

4. The full passage reads: "effice ut interea fera moenera militiai / per maria ac terras omnis sopita quiescant. / nam tu sola potes tranquilla pace iuvare / mortalis, quoniam belli fera moenera Mavors / armipotens regit, in gremium qui saepe tuum se / reicit aeterno devictus vulnere amoris, / atque ita suspiciens tereti cervice reposta / pascit amore avidos inhians in te, dea, visus, / eque tuo pendet resupini spiritus ore. / hunc tu, diva, tuo recubantem corpore sancto / circumfusa super, suavis ex ore loquelas / funde petens placidam Romanis, incluta, pacem" (Meanwhile, Holy One, both on dry land and on the deep, / Make the mad machinery of war drift off to sleep. / For only you can favour mortal men with peace, since Mars, / Mighty in Arms, who oversees the wicked work of war / Conquered by Love's everlasting wound, so often lies / Upon your lap, and gazing upwards, feasts his greedy eyes / On love, his mouth agape at you, Famed Goddess, as he tips / Back his shapely neck, his breath hovering at your lips. / And as he leans upon your holy body, and you reach / Your arms around him, Lady, sweet-talk him with honeyed speech, / Pleading for a quiet peace for Romans; *DRN* 1.29–40).

5. Belleau's reputation for learning was won at the expense of being a bit of a spoilsport. Du Bellay calls Belleau "[s]avant et vertueux" in his *Regrets* (sonnet 145, line 2), and in Ode 25 of his second book of odes, Ronsard calls Belleau "un trop sec biberon / Pour un tourneur d'Anacreon" (too dry a drinker / For a translator of Anacreon; Ronsard, *Œuvres*, vol. 1, lines 1–2).

6. These works are, in the order mentioned, the *Odes d'Anacréon* (1556), the *Bergerie* (1565 with an addition in 1572), *Commentaire au Second livre des amours de Ronsard* (1560), *Discours de la vanité, pris de l'Ecclesiaste. Églogues sacrées, prises du Cantique des Cantiques* (published with the *Pierres* in 1576), *Les petites inventions* (1556), and *Les amours et nouveaux eschanges des pierres precieuses: vertus & proprietez d'icelles* (1576).

7. On *ataraxia* in the Greek tradition from Democritus to Epicurus, see Warren, *Epicurus and Democritean Ethics*. On Epicurus's garden see Harrison, *Gardens*, 71–82; Wycherley, "The Garden of Epicurus."

8. The Ixion myth appears in the second of Pindar's *Pythian Odes* (21–48) as well as in the *Aeneid* (6.587) and Ovid's *Metamorphoses* (Book 12). In their notes to the poem, Guy Demerson and Maurice Verdier cite Diodorus of Sicily (*Bibliotheca historica* 5.69) and Aeschylus (*Eumenides* 719–20) as Belleau's likely sources (Belleau, *Œuvres poétiques*, vol. 4, 319 n. 2).

9. Lines 1–2. All poems from Belleau's *Seconde journée de la Bergerie* are cited by line number, and citations refer to Belleau, *Œuvres poétiques*, vol. 4. Henceforth citations will be provided in the text.

10. The focus on kisses also owes much to the *Basia* of Johannes Secundus, from which Belleau drew much material and inspiration. On Belleau's use of Secundus in the *Bergerie*, see Prévot, "Les emprunts de Rémy Belleau à Jean Second dans ses 'Baisers.'"

11. Lines 63–65. Belleau's *Pierres* are cited by line number, and citations refer to Belleau, *Les amours et nouveaux eschanges des pierres précieuses*. Henceforth citations will be provided in

the text. Belleau's prose dedication to the king and the 1576 and 1578 *Discours* that introduce the collection will also be cited by line numbers in the text.

12. Connat, "Mort et testament de Remy Belleau."

13. Belleau, *Œuvres poétiques*, vol. 5, lines 47–58.

14. The idea of poets as natural philosophers, or all-knowing, comes from Homer, and was popular with the Pléiade.

15. Belleau, *Œuvres poétiques*, vol. 3, lines 37–41.

16. For Belleau as a poet to the Guise family, see Rieu, "La *Bergerie* de Rémy Belleau."

17. Belleau, *Œuvres poétiques*, vol. 3, lines 1–3.

18. For more on the lapidary tradition, see Baisier, *The Lapidaire Chrétien*; Chayes, *L'éloquence des pierres précieuses*; Evans and Serjeantson, *English Mediaeval Lapidaries*; Meyer, *Les plus anciens lapidaires français*. Scholars have taken pains to document Belleau's sources: he was steeped in tradition, and had he only consulted Marbode (which seems unlikely), he would still have gleaned from the cardinal the collected wisdom of the ancients. Belleau is even aware of the preclassical, Egyptian origins of the lapidary tradition, mentioning the Chaldeans as the progenitors of the tradition.

19. La Taille, *La géomance abrégée*; Lemaire de Belges, *La couronne margaritique*.

20. "quippe ita formido mortalis continet omnis, / quod multa in terris fieri caeloque tuentur / quorum operum causas nulla ratione videre / possunt ac fieri divino numine rentur" (For certainly all men are in the clutches of a dread— / Beholding many things take place in heaven overhead / Or here on earth whose causes they can't fathom, they assign / The explanation for these happenings to powers divine; *DRN* 1.151–54). Or, as he says to Memmius, chiding him prematurely for abandoning Epicurean teachings, "[t]utemet a nobis iam quovis tempore vatum / terriloquis victus dictis desciscere quares" (Sooner or later, you will seek to break away from me, / Won over by doomsayer-prophets; *DRN* 1.102–3).

21. Belleau, *Œuvres poétiques*, vol. 2, lines 15–30.

22. Belleau, line 14.

23. "Hunc igitur terrorem animi tenebrasque necessest / non radii solis neque lucida tela diei / discutiant, sed naturae species ratioque" (This dread, these shadows of the mind, must thus be swept away / Not by rays of the sun nor by the brilliant beams of day, / But by observing Nature and her laws; *DRN* 1.146–48).

24. Erasmus's 1516 *Paraclesis* is exemplary of sixteenth-century text that draws a distinction between the complex, obfuscatory rhetoric and the plain persuasion of New Testament rhetoric. Erasmus's emphasis on pious curiosity and the transformative power of the text also resonate with Belleau's description of lapidary force.

25. Braybrook, "Science and Myth in the Poetry of Remy Belleau," 281.

26. Coogan, Brettler, and Newsom, *The New Oxford Annotated Bible*, 2 Corinthians 3:2–3.

27. There are other examples in ancient myth of women turning to stone: Niobe, for example. Medusa famously turns men to stone with her eyes. A counterpoint to the petrification theme is Pygmalion, who vivifies a stone statue.

28. At least some of them also seem to have understood the debt that the *Pierres* owed to Lucretius. Jean Dorat's prefatory verses to the *Pierres* paraphrase the hymn to Venus, making Venus the muse and guide for Belleau's poetry. Dorat combines the imagery of Lucretius's hymn with the maritime imagery of the "Suave, mari magno" passage that opens Book 2 in order to praise the exploratory and economic value of Belleau's stones. According to Dorat, Belleau's Venus is a modern mercantile rendition of Lucretius's Venus, who controls land and

sea. We know from Dorat's dedication of Lambin's edition of Lucretius that he not only knew *DRN* but was a savvy reader of Lucretius and a skilled mimic. On Dorat and Lambin, see Passannante, *The Lucretian Renaissance*, 87–88.

29. Although no printed record tells us which friends published the *Œuvres*, the editor's introduction to the 1578 edition says that they are "his closest friends, honorable and virtuous men, attentive to the reputation and memory of the deceased" (Belleau, *Œuvres poétiques*, vol. 1, 27). The version of the *Pierres* printed in the *Œuvres* is much expanded from the original 1576 publication: Belleau's friends add ten more stone-poems, the "Discours" in verse, and "Prométhée premier inventeur des anneaux & de l'enchasseure des pierres." Although much admired in the sixteenth century, the *Pierres* went relatively unappreciated until the late nineteenth and twentieth centuries.

30. The *Tumulus*, a collection of twenty-five poems written in Belleau's memory, was published in 1577; almost every poem contains a mention of the *Pierres*. Ronsard pens a lovely testament to the man who had been one of his closest friends: "Ne taillez, mains industrieuses, / Des pierres pour couvrir BELLEAU, / Luymesme a basti son tombeau / Dedans ses Pierres precieuses" (Busy hands, make / No stones to cover BELLEAU, / Who himself built his tomb / In his *Pierres précieuses*; Belleau, *Œuvres poétiques*, vol. 5, 310).

31. Belleau, *Œuvres poétiques*, vol. 1, 75–76. In later editions Belleau will change the dedicatees of the collection.

32. In "Elegie de P. de Ronsard, à Chretophle de Choiseul, Abbé de Mureaux," which follows Belleau's "Epistre" and functions as a liminary verse to the collection, Ronsard uses the same image of books buried and forgotten because of war: "Tant de livres perdus, miseres de la guerre, / Tant d' arts laborieux, et tant de gestes beaux / Qui sont ores sans nom, les hostes des tombeaux" (So many lost books, casualties of war / So many elaborate works, and so many great acts / Which today go unsung, denizens of tombs; Belleau, *Œuvres poétiques*, vol. 1, lines 102–4).

33. This is Belleau's "Au Seignevr Ivlles Gassot Secretaire du Roy" (Belleau, *Œuvres poétiques*, vol. 1, 76).

34. Belleau, *Œuvres poétiques*, vol. 2, lines 13–18.

35. Belleau, lines 21–24.

36. Belleau, *Œuvres poétiques*, vol. 1, lines 35–38, 41–42.

37. Belleau, line 46.

38. Chayes, *L'éloquence des pierres précieuses*, 211. The magnet was commonly included in classical, medieval, and Renaissance lapidaries as a precious stone. For a brief overview of lapidary lore about the magnet, see Lecouteux, *Dictionnaire des pierres magiques et médicinales*.

39. Braybrook, "Remy Belleau and the *Pierres precieuses*," 194.

40. The quoted passage continues: "Comme un ardant limier au plus espais du bois / Lance et poursuit le cerf pour le mettre aux abois, / Et de nez odoreux et d'haleine flairante / Choisist l'air échauffé de la beste courante" (Like a bloodhound in the thickest woods / Hunts and chases the deer to run it down / And with its sensitive nose and heavy breath / Tastes the air warmed by the running beast; 39–42). The image of beloved as hunted and lover as hunter is taken from Petrarch, and was extremely common in Renaissance love poetry.

41. Braybrook, "Remy Belleau and the *Pierres precieuses*," 197.

42. Belleau, *Œuvres poétiques*, vol. 5, 216.

43. Braybrook, "Science and Myth in the Poetry of Remy Belleau," 285. For more on the Christian overtones of the ruby in Belleau's work, see Chayes, "'Tromper les plus clair-voyans,'" 201. Christian lapidaries tend to refer back to passages in Exodus, Isaiah, Jeremiah,

Ezekiel, and Revelations that mention stones. Aaron is said to have worn a breastplate adorned with twelve stones, and Jerusalem is built on a foundation of the same stones. A number of critics have pointed out the fact that almost all of the stones Belleau includes in his collection (excluding the magnet) are among those mentioned in the Bible. See Braybrook, "Remy Belleau et les pierres précieuses de l'Apocalypse."

44. Faisant, "Gemmologie et imaginaire," 104.

45. "ces bèrgeres y travaillent sans cesse, l'une apres le labeur industrieux de quelque gentil ouvrage de broderie, l'autre apres un lassis de fil retors, ou de fil de soye de couleur, à grosses mailles & mailles menues, & croy pour servir de ret & de pantiere à surprendre & empestrer les yeux, ou le cueur de quelque langoureux berger" (These shepherdesses work ceaselessly, one industriously at the task of some pleasant piece of embroidery, using twisted yarn or colored silk threads, with big and little stitches, to entrap or surprise and enchant the eyes or the heart of some languorous shepherd; Belleau, *Œuvres poétiques*, vol. 2, 57).

46. "cette ville est riche de toutes les commoditez que les bergers, chevriers, bouviers, laboureurs pourroient souhaitter, fust pour trouver panetieres ouvrees & taillees au poinçon avec leurs écharpes, colliers herissez de clous pour les mâtins, houlettes tournees, pollies & bien ferrees, fust de pince, fust de crochet, musettes au ventre de cerf à grand bourdon, embouchees de cornes de Dain, ou de laton, fleutes, flageollets de canne de sureau" (This town is rich in all the goods that shepherds, goatherds, cowherds, and laborers could want, whether they seek breadbaskets that are open and trimmed to the bodkin with their scarves, collars studded with nails for mastiffs, or turned, polished, and nicely tightened crooks. Or pliers, bobbins, great bags made from the bellies of deer, stoppered with deer horns, or brass, or foil; Belleau, 106–7).

47. For Belleau on art and the artist in the *Bergerie*, see Braybrook, "Remy Belleau and the Figure of the Artist"; Rieu, "La *Bergerie* de Remy Belleau." See also Demerson's preface to the second volume of his edition of Belleau's *Œuvres* for his reading of the *Bergerie*. For Belleau's contribution to the pastoral, see Joukovsky's chapter on Belleau in Niderst, *La pastorale française*. A general work on mannerism is Dubois, *Le maniérisme*.

48. Belleau, *Œuvres poétiques*, vol. 2, xxxv.

49. For this influential argument, see Jeanneret, "Les œuvres d'art dans 'La bergerie' de Belleau."

50. Dubois, *L'invention au XVIe siècle*, 19. For the ways in which invention is related to both art and science as a process of making, see also Spiller, *Science, Reading, and Renaissance Literature*; Aït-Touati, *Fictions of the Cosmos*.

51. Belleau, *Œuvres poétiques*, vol. 1, lines 54–56.

52. Faisant, "Gemmologie et imaginaire," 88.

53. Ronsard's 1555 "Hymne à Henri II de ce nom" is another poem that links the king's majesty to the abundant energies of his people and the riches of his dominions.

54. The pastoral was the patronage genre par excellence for poets like Belleau. "In sum, the bucolic genre, far from being a recent invention, had become the conventional frame for official lyricism," writes Demerson (Belleau, *Œuvres poétiques*, vol. 2, xii).

CHAPTER 3

Elizabeth Harvey gave me penetrating and transformative comments on several different versions of this chapter. Her thinking and words are on every page, and for that I am enormously grateful. Timothy Harrison was also an indispensable interlocutor and guide at a crucial moment of revision.

1. Lines 5–8. Donne's poems are cited by line number, and citations refer to *The Complete Poems of John Donne*. Henceforth citations will be provided in the text.

2. In a brilliant reading of the end of "A Valediction Forbidding Mourning" John Freccero presents the compasses also as tools for charting celestial motion ("Donne's 'Valediction: Forbidding Mourning'").

3. Stallings confirmed in private correspondence that the echo is "quite deliberate," writing that "it is a favorite line, and I could not hear the Lucretius without hearing the Donne."

4. Hutchinson, *The Works of Lucy Hutchinson*, vol. 1, Part 2, 265; Creech, *T. Lucretius Carus, the Epicurean Philosopher*, 123; Evelyn, *John Evelyn's Translation of Titus Lucretius Carus, De rerum natura*, 115.

5. Donne was well acquainted with classical atomist ideas and Lucretius's *DRN*. Records of his private library show many texts that deal explicitly with atomism, and he had personal connections with Henry Percy, the ninth Earl of Northumberland, whose so-called Northumberland circle, active at the beginning of the seventeenth century, included atomist luminaries such as Thomas Hariot, Walter Warner, Sir Walter Ralegh, Christopher Marlowe, and Nicholas Hill.

6. Harvey and Harrison, "Embodied Resonances," 984.

7. While Copernicus published his *De revolutionibus orbium coelestium* in 1543, Donne is responding to a revival of interest in that work from the 1590s onward, as well as to seventeenth-century works like Kepler's *Astronomia nova* (1609), which fanned the Copernican flames by proposing that the planets orbited elliptically, further upsetting the simplicity of the earth-centered medieval and Renaissance model of the cosmos.

8. Hirsch, "Donne's Atomies and Anatomies," 69.

9. Harvey and Harrison, "Embodied Resonances," 984.

10. While Donne laments the changes ushered in by the new philosophies, he is also endlessly attracted to and inquisitive about the new science. This is what Herbert Grierson and T. S. Eliot (who in the 1920s fought to bring Donne back into the canon of early modern literature) found so appealing about Donne's poetry, and what Dr. Johnson had earlier found so appalling. Grierson paid particular attention to what he construed as the similarities between Donne's poetry and Lucretius's, claiming that "metaphysical poetry, in the full sense of the term, is a poetry which, like that of . . . the *De Natura Rerum* . . . has been inspired by a philosophical conception of the universe and the rôle assigned to the human spirit in the great drama of existence" (Grierson, *Metaphysical Lyrics & Poems*, xiii). Eliot agreed, arguing that it was characteristic of both the seventeenth and the twentieth centuries that their poets must be "interested in philosophy . . . [that they] must be *difficult*" (Eliot, "The Metaphysical Poets," in *Selected Essays*, 289). For decades after Grierson and Eliot's influential pronouncements, critics debated how like or unlike *DRN* Donne's poetry is—that is, whether his poetry is properly philosophical, a "difficult" poetry that scrutinizes the place of humans in the universe.

11. I am indebted to Elizabeth Harvey for this point.

12. H. M. Richmond argues that many of the conceits in Donne's poetry that are characterized as being distinctively "metaphysical" are adapted from Ronsard's poetry ("Ronsard and the English Renaissance"). On Donne and Ronsard, see also Fuzier, "Donne sonnetiste"; Prescott, *French Poets and the English Renaissance*, 115.

13. Ramie Targoff terms Tertullian "Donne's favorite church father" and discusses Donne's use of Tertullian in "A Valediction Forbidding Mourning" in *John Donne, Body and Soul*, 73.

14. As Targoff puts it, discussing Donne's tendency to blur the lines between the material and the immaterial when he describes the soul, what is dogmatically impossible for a philosopher or theologian "can be imaginatively suggestive for a poet" (Targoff, 99). While Donne was, of course, a Christian, it was quite common for early modern poets who disagreed fundamentally with Epicurean doctrine to draw deeply from Lucretian thinking that links poetry, matter, and fantasy—every poet (all Christians) in this book does so. As Gerard Passannante has eloquently argued, for many Renaissance readers, "the experience of materialism did not involve the deliberate adoption of a philosophical paradigm or an intellectual commitment" (*Catastrophizing*, 3). Scholars of Donne have long recognized the poet's nondogmatic bent. In his essay on Satire III, Richard Strier calls this Donne's "radicalism," his desire to always hold open the possibility of new thought and lean away from dogmatism and conservatism ("Radical Donne").

15. On Tertullian and Lucretius, see Palmer, *Reading Lucretius in the Renaissance*, 131; Butterfield, *The Early Textual History of Lucretius' "De rerum natura,"* 56–57.

16. Donne's materialistic talk of the "soul" is also indebted to the young field of psychology (or study of the soul). Following Aristotle, early moderns believed that the soul had several degrees, and the study of certain "souls" (the nutritive or animal soul, for example) was understood to be a study of the body. Timothy Harrison alerted me to the importance of early modern psychology to Donne's thinking on the soul.

17. Like "The Dream," the elegy "To his Mistress Going to Bed" uses "angel" in an explicitly erotic context. Exhorting a woman to join him in bed, the speaker compares her to an angel, but the comparison quickly turns crude. "In such white robes Heaven's angels used to be / Received by men: thou, angel, bring'st with thee / A Heav'n like M'homet's Paradise; and though / Ill spirits walk in white, we eas'ly know / By this these angels from an evil sprite: / They set our hairs, but these the flesh upright" (lines 19–24).

18. Some date the poem earlier. Donne would have known the Countess of Huntingdon for some time because her mother married Sir Thomas Egerton and brought the three Stanley sisters into the household where Donne was a secretary. Thus, the poem could have been written after her marriage in 1603. There are also debates as to the poem's authorship. In manuscript the poem is headed "Sir Walter Ashton to the Countess of Huntingdon," but it was printed in 1635 as Donne's. The Longman edition (used here) includes it in the Dubia; Grierson did not believe the poem was Donne's, though Milgate is sure it is, and the editors of the Variorum edition include it as Donne's. I am quite convinced it is Donne's, largely because its thematic concerns fit seamlessly with poems like the "Obsequies to the Lord Harington," *FA*, "The Second Anniversary: Of the Progress of the Soul," and others.

19. "Suave, mari magno turbantibus aequora ventis, / e terra magnum alterius spectare laborem; / non quia vexari quemquamst iucunda voluptas, / sed quibus ipse malis careas quia cernere suave est. / suave etiam belli certamina magna tueri / per campos instructa tua sine parte pericli" (How sweet it is to watch from dry land when the storm-winds roil / A mighty ocean's waters, and see another's bitter toil— / Not because [anyone's troubles are a pleasing joy]— / Rather, it's sweet to know from what misfortunes you are free. / Pleasant it is even to behold contests of war / Drawn up on the battlefield, when you are in no danger; *DRN* 2.1–6, translation modified). On the Lucretian motif of shipwreck, see Blumenberg, *Shipwreck with Spectator*; Lestringant, "Lucrèce, la Renaissance et ses naufrages," in *La renaissance de Lucrèce*.

20. Donne reworks images of perspective and clear sight over and over, including satirically. In "Satyre Three," he writes of how "On a huge hill, / Craggèd and steep, Truth stands, and he that will / Reach her, about must, and about go, / And what the hill's suddenness

resists, win so" (lines 79–82). A spectacular example is the parody of the clear sight in *Ignatius his Conclave*, where from the vantage point of a high hill the poet sees not just heaven, or earth, but hell: "When I had surveid al the Heavens, then . . . In the twinckling of an eye, I saw all the roomes in Hell open to my sight" (Donne, *Ignatius his Conclave*, 7). "And by the benefit of certaine spectacles, I know not of what making, but, I thinke, of the same, by which Gregory the great, and Beda did discerne so distinctly the soules of their friends, when they were discharged from their bodies, and sometimes the soules of such men as they knew not by sight, and of some that were never in the world, and yet they could distinguish them flying into Heaven, or conversing with living men, I saw all the channels in the bowels of the Earth; and all the inhabitants of all nations, and of all ages were suddenly made familiar to me. I thinke truely, Robert Aquinas when he tooke Christs long Oration, as he hung upon the Crosse, did use some such instrument as this, but applied to the eare: And so I thinke did he, which dedicated to Adrian 6, that Sermon which Christ made in prayse of his father Joseph: for else how did they heare that, which none but they ever heard?" (Donne, 8–9).

21. On the watchtower trope in Donne's poetry, particularly in *The Second Anniversary*, see Harvey and Harrison, "Embodied Resonances."

22. Petrarca, *Petrarch's Lyric Poems*, lines 1–2.

23. Although Donne is invested in the idea that he can write relationships into being in his personal epistles, the link between writing and the formation of relationships comes under the most pressure in his patronage poems. Donne's struggles to establish himself professionally underline the importance of his patronage poems: as a young man, Donne ruined his career by secretly wedding his employer's young niece, then spent much of his professional life—until he entered the church in 1615—scrambling to get back into the good graces of the nobility and repair his prospects. Donne contracted a secret marriage to Anne More in 1601. Donne was secretary to Lord Egerton, the Keeper of the Great Seal, and Anne was Lady Egerton's niece. When the marriage was discovered, Donne was briefly thrown into prison, and the bride's father, Sir George More, refused to reconcile with the couple until 1609. Donne was disappointed at the change in his prospects, and oppressed by the knowledge that he had sentenced his wife to a small, impoverished life. As the contemporary pun went, "John Donne, Anne Donne, Undone."

24. Hill's volume, the only one he ever published, was the subject of mockery from the time of its publication in 1601. Ben Jonson's epigram 133 derides its "atomi ridiculous." On the reception of Hill's work, see Gillespie and Hardie, *The Cambridge Companion to Lucretius*, 244. On Gassendi and the seventeenth-century revival of atomism, see LoLordo, *Pierre Gassendi and the Birth of Early Modern Philosophy*.

25. The November 19, 1627 marriage sermon for the Earl of Bridgewater's daughter, in John Donne, *The Sermons of John Donne*, 5. All citations of Donne's sermons refer to this electronic text archive.

26. This is a favorite theme of Donne's. On disintegration, see, for example, the 1627 sermon on Matthew 22:30, or the 1629 Christmas sermon on John 10:10. A similar anxiety is expressed in the Holy Sonnet 1, "Thou hast made me."

27. Stephen Clucas records several instances of Donne's contemporaries analogizing atoms to the souls of sinners: "More's atoms were not 'merely passive', but 'rouse up themselves on high.' Thomas Traherne's atoms, too, rouse themselves up, and become analogous with the regenerated soul of the sinner" ("Poetic Atomism in Seventeenth-Century England," 338).

28. Shrijvers, "Seeing the Invisible: A Study of Lucretius' Analogy in the *De rerum natura*," in *Oxford Readings in Lucretius*, 262–63. Taken too far, the analogy could begin to

look something like "the conception of the literary work as microcosm," an analogy that "found its most elaborate and extensive expression in Neoplatonism, [which] also springs in the last analysis from the vision of the world as the creation of a divine artist" (Schrijvers, 264).

29. Donne, *The Sermons of John Donne*, 4. On the nothing trope in English Renaissance literature, see Archdeacon, "The 'Nothing' Trope."

30. Donne, *The Sermons of John Donne*, 16.

31. Quoted in Barbour, "The Early Stuart Epicure," 175.

32. Donne, *Letters to Severall Persons of Honour*, 63–64.

33. Nicholas Hardy reads the passage differently, arguing that Donne's letter to Wotten misunderstands or parodies atomism by representing it as chaotic and casual: "Donne's contrast between order and atomic disorder fails to acknowledge that Lucretius is a poet of the former as well as the latter" ("Natural Reason and the Laws of Nature in Early Modern Versions of Lucretius," in Norbrook, Harrison, and Hardie, *Lucretius and the Early Modern*, 209). I see Donne's selective engagement with Lucretian ideas not as hostile or uncomprehending but rather as a strong adaptation; Donne was not pious in his use of Lucretius but adapted *DRN* to his own uses, even when that meant leaving some things out or altering others.

34. Although forms and derivations of the verb *inclinare* (to lean, bend, or incline) from which Lucretius derives the noun *clinamen* occur several times in *DRN*, *clinamen* occurs only once, at *DRN* 2.292.

35. Smith, *The Critical Heritage*, 69.

36. Smith, 69. No small quantity of ink has been spilled over which "Idea" Drury represented. Arguing that we need to "lighten the heavy burden that has been placed on Donne's 'Idea of a woman,'" Anthony Russell lists the many options: "Elizabeth has been designated as a symbol of Christ the Logos, the World Soul ('Anima Mundi'), 'Sapientia Creata,' the restored image of God in man, the Paracelsian 'Anatomia Mundi,' Astraea, and even, predictably, the Virgin Mary herself" ("'Thou Seest Mee Striue for Life,'" 375). For the same idea, see also Donne's poem "The Primrose." "I walk to find a true-love, and I see / That 'tis not a mere woman that is she, / But must or more or less than woman be. / Yet know I not which flower / I wish, a six or four: / For should my true love less than woman be, / She were scarce anything; and then, should she / Be more than woman, she would get above / All thought of sex, and think to move / My heart to study her, not to love; / Both these were monsters. Since there must reside / Falsehood in woman, I could more abide / She were by art than nature falsified" (lines 8–20).

37. John Carey astutely remarks that "Donne's argument is a reversible coating, but the imaginative kernel remains constant." Donne will often express "new opinion[s] . . . us[ing] the image he had used to express its contrary." Carey advises Donne's readers to "watch the shaping imagination instead of the transient opinions" (*John Donne: Life, Mind, and Art*, 11).

38. See the end of Chapter 1 for a discussion of prevailing scholarly consensus on the Lucretian influence in sixteenth-century French lyric.

CHAPTER 4

1. An anonymous prose translation, a manuscript copy of which now resides in the Bodleian Library, may have been completed around the same time. On this, see Barbour, "Anonymous Lucretius"; Hutchinson, *The Works of Lucy Hutchinson*, vol. 1, *Part 1*, xxxii.

2. Reid Barbour and Stephen Clucas both show that the atomist influence in England appeared earlier in the seventeenth century than previously thought, particularly in poetry (Barbour, *English Epicures and Stoics*; Clucas, "Poetic Atomism in Seventeenth-Century England"). Barbour discusses Hutchinson's translation in the context of the Epicurean revival in "Between Atoms and the Spirit."

3. Evelyn, *An Essay on the First Book of T. Lucretius Carus De Rerum Natura*, 3.

4. On Cavendish's *Poems and Fancies*, see Chapter 5. On comparisons between Cavendish and Hutchinson, see Norbrook, "Margaret Cavendish and Lucy Hutchinson."

5. Evelyn, *An Essay on the First Book of T. Lucretius Carus De Rerum Natura*. Though he completed a translation of the full *DRN*, Evelyn published only the first book. The full translation was published for the first time in 2000 (Evelyn, *John Evelyn's Translation of Titus Lucretius Carus, "De rerum natura"*). In Evelyn's first manuscript comment on the unpublished third book of *DRN*, he writes that he hopes to offer "som Antidote against the Poyson of the Errors, which our Author, here striues to convey vnder all the gildings of Poetry, and Arte" (Evelyn, xl–xli). However, as David Hopkins explains, "by 1657–8 he had abandoned any attempt to publish the full version, later telling Meric Casaubon that the manuscript now lay 'in the dust of [his] study, where 'tis likely to be for ever buried'" (in Gillespie and Hardie, *The Cambridge Companion to Lucretius*, 256).

6. In 1658, Sir Aston Cokain writes to his friend Alexander Brome about his plans to translate *DRN*: "I know a Lady that hath been about / The same designe, but she must needes give out: / Your Poet strikes too boldly home sometimes, / In geniall things, t'appear in womens rhimes, / The task is masculine, and he that can / Translate *Lucretius*, is an able man" (Cokain, "To my ingenuous Friend Mr. *Alexander Brome*," in *Small Poems of Divers Sorts*, 204).

7. Hutchinson, *The Works of Lucy Hutchinson*, vol. 1, *Part 1*, 13. Hutchinson's "wanton" anticipates the importance the word would come to have in Creech's translation of Lucretius. Norbrook explains: "If the wantonness of the Epicureans was 'notorious', it was Creech who was helping to make it so: 'wanton' occurs thirty-four times in his translation for five in Hutchinson's. Throughout his translation Creech interspersed passages from contemporary poets which heightened the erotic associations of Epicureanism, notably the lyrics of Abraham Cowley" (Hutchinson, lx).

8. Hutchinson, *Order and Disorder*, 3. Norbrook suggests that Hutchinson may have finished her translation of Book 6 and recopied Book 4—or perhaps rewritten it—in 1675 when she composed the dedicatory letter (Hutchinson, cxvii, cxxxii).

9. Hutchinson, 3.

10. Jonathan Goldberg rightly chastises critics who quote from and parse the *DRN* translation's dedicatory letter more than they do the text: "It almost seems as if the letter *is* the Lucretius" (*The Seeds of Things*, 157). I must admit to being guilty of this sin: because I am interested in *DRN*'s reception, I focus on the places readers, translators, and editors discuss their involvement with Lucretius—frequently in prefaces and other liminal texts.

11. Hutchinson, *The Works of Lucy Hutchinson*, vol. 1, *Part 1*, 7.

12. Hutchinson, *Order and Disorder*, 4.

13. Hutchinson, *The Works of Lucy Hutchinson*, vol. 1, *Part 1*, 15.

14. The Countess of Rochester's mother, Anne Wilmot, was Lucy Hutchinson's cousin.

15. British Library, Add. MS 19333 (n.d.). Barbour and Norbrook notice the same thing: "The line numbers inserted into the margin—either by Hutchinson or by another reader with access to an earlier draft—indicate that she had in fact translated these lines fully" (Hutchinson, *The Works of Lucy Hutchinson*, vol. 1, *Part 1*, lxii–iii).

16. Norbrook singles out Hutchinson's translation of Book 4 as particularly interesting as "a highly independent-minded response to Lucretius, and in its focus on this part of the poem as the only one Hutchinson considered to need such a critical re-writing" (Hutchinson, lxiv). Indeed, he argues that it is the only section of the translation where Hutchinson diverges from the original in a significant way: "There is only one case, however, where she considers it necessary to deviate from Lucretius on a large scale. At the end of the fourth book, she does systematically cut and rewrite Lucretius, but not, like Creech, to heighten and then condemn his wantonness, but on the contrary to find in the Epicurean poet a pattern for Puritan companionate marriage" (Hutchinson, lxi).

17. Hutchinson, 281. Like Hutchinson, John Evelyn also omits the end of *DRN* Book 4, declaring in a 1657 letter to Sir Richard Browne that "I had rather much that all the poems in the world should perish, then that anything of mine should contribute & minister to vice" (Evelyn, *John Evelyn's Translation of Titus Lucretius Carus, "De rerum natura,"* 125). While Thomas Creech translates more of the end of Book 4 than Hutchinson, he also omits sections. It was John Dryden who published a full translation of the end of Book 4 in his 1685 *Sylvae*, along with four other fragments of *DRN*. Of his decision to translate the end of Book 4, Dryden writes the following in his Preface: "'Tis true, there is something, and that of some moment, to be objected against my *Englishing* the Nature of Love, from the Fourth Book of *Lucretius*: And I can less easily answer why I Translated it, than why I thus Translated it. The Objection arises from the Obscenity of the Subject; which is aggravated by the too lively, and alluring delicacy of the Verses. In the first place, without the least Formality of an excuse, I own it pleas'd me: and let my Enemies make the worst they can of this Confession; I am not yt so secure from that passion, but tha I want my Authors Antidotes against it. He has given the truest and most Philosophical account both of the Disease and Remedy, which I ever found in any Author: For which reasons I Translated him. But it will be ask'd why I turn'd him into this luscious *English,* (for I will not give it a worse word:) instead of an answer, I wou'd ask again of my Supercilious Adversaries, whether I am not bound when I Translate an Author, to do him all the right I can, and to Translate him to the best advantage? If to mince his meaning, which I am satisfi'd was honest and instructive, I had either omitted some part of what he said, or taken from the strength of his expression, I certainly had wrong'd him; and that freeness of thought and words, being thus cashier'd in my hands, he had no longer been *Lucretius*" (Dryden, *Sylvæ,* a3r).

18. Hutchinson, *The Works of Lucy Hutchinson*, vol. 1, *Part 1*, 13.

19. Hutchinson, vol. 1, *Part 1*, 5.

20. Gerard Passannante reassesses the role Lucretius may have played in Ficino's philosophical and literary development, while also giving an overview of the field, in "Burning Lucretius."

21. The first early modern Latin poet really to lock horns with Lucretius on the subject of religion was Antonio della Paglia (1503–1570). His *De animorum immortalitate* (1535) is the first of several early modern anti-Lucretian poems, culminating in Cardinal de Polignac's *Anti-Lucretius* of 1747.

22. This has been called contrast-imitation—a useful way of describing particularly the fifteenth- and sixteenth-century Italian reception of DRN, where Latin didactic poets like Bonincontri and Pontano write Epicurean poems and then renounce them to strengthen their own Christian positions.

23. For an excellent account of the history and interpretation of poetic repudiations through the prism of Spenser's repudiation of Lucretius, see Ramachandran, "Edmund Spenser, Lucretian Neoplatonist."

24. Greenblatt, *The Swerve*, 1.

25. Greenblatt, 1. "I bought it," Greenblatt admits, "as much for the cover as for the classical account of the material universe" (Greenblatt, 1).

26. Greenblatt, 1.

27. Hutchinson, *The Works of Lucy Hutchinson*, vol. 1, *Part 1*, 79.

28. Gillespie and Hardie, *The Cambridge Companion to Lucretius*, 114 n. 13.

29. *The Cambridge Companion to Lucretius*, 112. The ode reads: "Paucus deorum cultor et infrequens / insanientis dum sapientiae / consultus erro, nunc retrorsum / vela dare atque iterare cursus / cogor relectos: namque Diespiter, / igni corusco nubila dividens / plerumque, per purum tonantis / egit equos volucremque currum, / quo bruta tellus et vaga flumina, / quo Styx et invisi horrida Taenari / sedes Atlanteusque finis / concutitur" (I was a stingy and infrequent worshipper of the gods all the time that I went astray, expert that I was in a mad philosophy. Now I am forced to sail back and repeat my course in the reverse direction. For Jupiter, who normally splits the clouds with his flashing fire, drove his thundering horses and flying chariot across a clear sky. At the heavy earth and wandering rivers, at that the Styx, and the dreaded abode of hated Taenarus, and the boundaries marked by Mount Atlas, were shaken; 1.34, lines 1–12, in Horace, *Odes*). Hardie reads the first lines as a description of Epicureanism, and the later lines as a return to the gods and repudiation of the atheism of Epicureanism. Virgil's *Georgics* 2.490–94 enact a similar motion.

30. Gillespie and Hardie, *The Cambridge Companion to Lucretius*, 117.

31. Philip Hardie notes that it is possible that Lucretius himself was partially responsible for the "conspiracy of silence," the refusal of his Augustan successors to name him in their writing. Lucretius "largely sets the parameters for the response to the *DRN* through his own statements about his relationship to his literary and philosophical predecessors" (*The Cambridge Companion to Lucretius*, 112).

32. Ramachandran, "Edmund Spenser, Lucretian Neoplatonist," 375.

33. Norbrook notes this, writing that "Hutchinson situates herself in the long Christian tradition in which poets apologize for earlier, sinful works—a tradition that always had the effect of reminding readers of how powerful those earlier writings must have been for their ill effects to occasion such penitence" (Hutchinson, *Order and Disorder*, xviii). On recantation in Renaissance poetry, see Phillippy, *Love's Remedies*.

34. In a 1492 letter to Martinus Preminger, Ficino claimed that he had burnt a *commentariola*—"commentariolis in Lucretium meis"—written when he was a youth (a *puer*) in what Michael Reeve guesses was probably around 1457–1458 (*The Cambridge Companion to Lucretius*, 210). On Ficino and Lucretius, see Brown, *The Return of Lucretius to Renaissance Florence*, 16–41; Passannante, *The Lucretian Renaissance*, 69; Palmer, *Reading Lucretius in the Renaissance*, 38 n.109.

35. See Snyder, "Marsilio Ficino's Critique of the Lucretian Alternative." This is true also of Aristotle, whose works preserved Epicureanism through the Middle Ages by vigorously and repeatedly attempting to refute Epicurean arguments.

36. Hutchinson, *The Works of Lucy Hutchinson*, vol. 1, *Part 1*, 7.

37. I am indebted to Mary Trull for this point, made in her generous comments on a paper I wrote on Hutchinson and Lucretius for the 2013 Shakespeare Association of America conference.

38. Generally, critics see Hutchinson's description of domestic translation as a way of trivializing the work, but she could also be salvaging the work of translation (though not its "wanton" subject, Lucretius) by separating it from pleasure.

39. Hutchinson, *The Works of Lucy Hutchinson*, vol. 1, Part 1, 9, 11.

40. Du Bartas's depiction of pleasure-seeking matter in his *La sepmaine* (1578, with *La seconde semaine* in 1584), either in the original French or in Joshua Sylvester's English translations, may have influenced later English readers of Lucretius and colored their perception of atomist philosophy. Du Bartas's descriptions of matter as a *laïs* (which Sylvester explains in his "Index of the hardest Words" as "a beutifull & costly Harlot of Corynth, frequented by many gallants of Greece") is very similar to later English rhetoric on atomism (Du Bartas, *Du Bartas His Deuine Weekes and Workes*, lii6r).

41. Lucretius considered *DRN* itself a translation of sorts, of Greek ideas into Latin.

42. Another time: "quo magis inceptum pergam pertexere dictis" (Thus all the more / Reason to take the thread up where I had left off before; *DRN* 6.42).

43. Hutchinson, *The Works of Lucy Hutchinson*, vol. 1, Part 1, xx.

44. Cited by Barbour and Norbrook in Hutchinson, xxxvii. Barbour and Norbrook agree with the commentator's judgment, asserting that Creech makes Lucretius more erotic than he already is (Hutchinson, lviii, lx).

45. Behn, "To the Unknown DAPHNIS on his Excellent Translation of *Lucretius*," in Creech, *T. Lucretius Carus, the Epicurean Philosopher*, C2r.

46. Behn, "To the Unknown DAPHNIS on his Excellent Translation of *Lucretius*," in Creech, C2r.

47. Cokain, "To my ingenuous Friend Mr. *Alexander Brome*," in *Small Poems of Divers Sorts*, 204.

48. Similar accusations were leveled at Mary Wroth, whom Edward Denny, in his poem "To Pamphilia from the father-in-law of Seralius" called a "Hermophradite in show, in deed a monster." The much-quoted poetic exchange between Wroth and Denny is preserved in the Nottingham University Library, MSS CL LM 85/1–5.

49. Mary Evelyn, Johns Evelyn's wife, did the woodcut.

50. Hutchinson, *The Works of Lucy Hutchinson*, vol. 1, Part 1, 5.

51. The poem is attached as an appendix to Norbrook, "Lucy Hutchinson Versus Edmund Waller."

52. Norbrook, 73, lines 1–6.

53. Norbrook, 64.

54. Waller, "To his Worthy Friend Master Evelyn Upon His Translation of Lucretius" in Evelyn, *John Evelyn's Translation of Titus Lucretius Carus, "De rerum natura,"* 16.

55. The way Hutchinson uses gender as a category might profitably be compared to the work the Quakers Priscilla Cotton and Mary Cole do on the word "woman" in their pamphlet defending the rights of women to preach, "To the Priests and People of England" (1655). Cotton and Cole argue that although scripture does indeed forbid women preaching, the word "woman" in that context must be understood as a term for weakness—on the part of either gender—not for actual women: "But it's weakness that is the woman by the Scriptures forbidden" (Salzman, *Early Modern Women's Writing*, 147). In Cotton and Cole's hands, "woman" becomes a term for the weakness of fallen humanity in general: "the woman, or weakness, that is man" (Salzman, 147). While such an argument makes no claims for the equality of men and women, it makes the weakness of women (as it is described in the Bible, from Eve onward) a figure for the weakness of all fallen humanity.

56. Lucretius's influence on Hutchinson's *OD* has long been recognized. See, for example, Goldberg *The Seeds of Things*, 122–78.

57. See Miller, "Maternity, Marriage, and Contract."

58. Hutchinson, *Order and Disorder*, 3.

59. Milton, *Paradise Lost*, 1.26. On *Paradise Lost* and *OD*, see Wilcher, "'Adventurous Song' or 'Presumptuous Folly.'"

60. Hutchinson, *Order and Disorder*, 3.

61. Hutchinson, *Order and Disorder*, 5.372, 374–77. Henceforth quotations from the body of *Order and Disorder* will be cited in text.

62. Elegy 2A, lines 5–6, 13–14, in Norbrook, "Lucy Hutchinson's 'Elegies,'" 490.

63. It is surprising that early commentators could possible take *OD* to be the work of a man given the text's astonishing perspective, unmatched anywhere in early modern English literature, on childbirth and motherhood. The only competition might be Milton's allegory of Sin and Death in *Paradise Lost.*

64. Elegy 12, lines 26–32, in Norbrook, "Lucy Hutchinson's 'Elegies,'" 509.

65. Hutchinson, *Order and Disorder*, 174 n. 324.

66. Elegy 1, lines 53–56, in Norbrook "Lucy Hutchinson's 'Elegies,'" 488.

67. The way Hutchinson uses the "Suave, mari magno" passage stands in interesting contrast to Milton's, on which see Hock, "The Mind Is Its Own Place."

CHAPTER 5

I owe Julie Crawford an immense debt of gratitude for the precise and generative comments she gave me on an early version of this chapter.

1. After its initial publication in 1653, *P&F* was revised, rearranged, and reprinted in 1664, and again in 1668.

2. Though Cavendish's claim that she could not read Latin has complicated accounts of her response to Lucretius, the broad similarities between *P&F* and *DRN* are indisputable. Cavendish would have had access to Lucretian ideas and poetry not only from conversations in her salon, frequented in Paris by the leading lights of mechanical philosophy, but also from literary traditions, from conversations with her husband, brothers, and later brother-in-law, and from those excerpts of *DRN* that were available in English translation. While in the 1650s, major discussions of atomism centered primarily on philosophical attempts to incorporate Epicurean thought into a Christian worldview or to develop a materialist and mechanical philosophy, Lucretian ideas about the relationship of poetry and nature were also available to Cavendish in English poetry. Scholarship has documented the Lucretian influence on English poets as important as Chaucer, Spenser, and Donne. The *Cambridge Companion to Lucretius*, particularly the articles by Valentina Prosper, Philip Ford, and Stuart Gillespie on *DRN*'s Renaissance reception, provides a good overview. Many English works contained translated passages from *DRN*. In her work on probable sources for Cavendish's Lucretian references, Emma Rees writes that "several versions and critiques of parts of Lucretius's doctrine were available to Cavendish," including Robert Greville's *Nature of Truth* (1640), Kenelm Digby's *Two Treatises* (1644), Guillaume de Salluste Du Bartas's *Holy Days and Weeks* (1605), George Sandys's *A Relation of a Journey Begun Anno Domini 1610* (1615), George Hakewill's *Apologie* (1635), John Evelyn's partial translation of *De rerum natura* (1656), and Walter Charleton's *Epicurus's Morals* (1654) (Rees, *Margaret Cavendish* 56–57). In addition, Florio's translation of Montaigne (1603) contained many passages from Lucretius. On Cavendish's sources, see also Clucas, "Poetic Atomism in Seventeenth-Century England."

3. Many critics have commented on Cavendish's poetics of variety. Among those, Sylvia Bowerbank, Hero Chalmers, Line Cottegnies and Nancy Weitz, and Emma Rees link her verse to Lucretius in particular (Bowerbank, "The Spider's Delight"; Chalmers, "'Flattering Division,'" in *Authorial Conquests*, ed. Cottegnies and Weitz; Cottegnies and Weitz, in the introduction to *Authorial Conquests*; and Rees, *Margaret Cavendish*, 54–79).

4. About thirty-five years ago, Sylvia Bowerbank, an important scholar of *P&F*, wrote that "even those of us who are attracted to [Cavendish's] personality and ideas cannot help but wish she had been a more disciplined writer. It is also useful, then, to see Cavendish's place in literary history as a cautionary tale for those of us who would suggest that craftsmanship and order are masculine, and artlessness and chaos are feminine. Do we really want to create a literary ghetto called the 'female imagination' and claim as its characteristic style of expression, anarchic formlessness?" ("The Spider's Delight," 407).

Although a very small proportion of Cavendish scholarship focuses on her poetry, the work that does is excellent, including Bowerbank, "The Spider's Delight"; Chalmers, "'Flattering Division'"; Dodds, *The Literary Invention of Margaret Cavendish*; and Dodds, "Bawds and Housewives." Brandie Siegfried and Liza Blake's recent editions of *P&F* will undoubtedly lead to an increase of work on the collection (Cavendish, *"Poems and Fancies" with "The Animal Parliament"*; Cavendish, *Margaret Cavendish's "Poems and Fancies"*).

5. For an account of *P&F* as bad poetry, as well as the history of such judgments, see Dodds, "Bawds and Housewives." Many critics argue that atomism was ultimately unimportant to Cavendish's natural philosophical thought: Anna Battigelli, for example, argues that "Cavendish was finally less interested in atomism as a theory of matter than as an explanatory discourse for the political and emotional turmoil that surrounded her" (*Margaret Cavendish and the Exiles of the Mind*, 39).

6. The first chapter of Cavendish's *Philosophicall Fancies*, "Of Matter and Motion," argues that there is only one matter, containing infinite degrees (not, as atomists like Lucretius claim, an infinite quantity of stand-alone particles). This is the account of matter that Cavendish will continue to develop over the course of her career.

7. Classical atomist physics is often credited with inspiring the investment of what is commonly called the Epicurean revival (in the 1650s) in mechanical philosophy. On the Epicurean "revival" in England, Robert Kargon's is the classic account (*Atomism in England from Hariot to Newton*). See also Kroll, *The Material Word*. Stephen Clucas has analyzed the presentation of fire atoms in the works of several English thinkers in order to contest Kargon's assertion that the revival of atomist thought in England drew inspiration primarily from Pierre Gassendi's atomism ("The Atomism of the Cavendish Circle").

However, atomism was far more flexible and widespread than it has often been made out to be. As Reid Barbour has shown, atomism was a significant presence in the Stuart court far before the 1650s, expressing itself largely in poetry ("The Early Stuart Epicure"; *English Epicures and Stoics*). See also Clucas, "Poetic Atomism in Seventeenth-Century England." Barbour and Clucas have also demonstrated that atomism in general, and *DRN* in particular, was as appealing to royalists as it was to parliamentarians and Puritans (Barbour, "The Early Stuart Epicure"; Clucas, "Poetic Atomism in Seventeenth-Century England"). On atomism and political identity, see Norbrook, "Margaret Cavendish and Lucy Hutchinson."

Critics who read atomism as an expression of Cavendish's politics include Battigelli, Rees, and Chalmers. Battigelli argues that Cavendish uses atomism as a metaphor for "the body politic and for the mind" (*Margaret Cavendish and the Exiles of the Mind*, 40). Cavendish is not interested in atomism as "a theory of matter" but rather as an "explanatory discourse for the political and emotional turmoil that surrounded" her, mainly to account for the number of tragic events in her personal life, such as the consecutive deaths of her family members and the uncertainty she experienced during the years of exile (Battigelli, 39–40). Rees's chapter on *DRN* and *P&F* argues that "a specifically Lucretian approach to poetry is fundamentally political, in that it grants unpopular or subversive ideas the possibility of a public platform" (*Margaret Cavendish*, 55). Despite Rees's attention to the formative role of *DRN* in Cavendish's poetics, like Battigelli, she maintains that Cavendish's atomism is "dependent on politico-religious sympathies" (Rees, 73 n. 20). Chalmers argues that the "delight in disorder" trope, exemplified in Robert Herrick's work but also present in Cavendish's poetry, has royalist overtones (" 'Flattering Division' ").

8. My argument is structurally similar to Reid Barbour's claim that Francis Bacon adopted atomism not for its physical content but as a habit of thought or approach to knowing (Barbour, "Bacon, Atomism, and Imposture"). It also resonates with Gerard Passannante's questions about Marsilio Ficino: "What if Ficino was interested not only in the philosophy of *De rerum natura* (which he would later vehemently condemn, as Snyder and Hankins have done much to help us understand) but also in the poem itself? Could the great Renaissance reviver of Platonism have also been reading *De rerum natura* as a model for his own philosophical revival [of philosophical poetry]?" ("Burning Lucretius," 274).

9. Cavendish, "Another Epistle to the Reader," *Philosophical and Physical Opinions,* C2v. Cavendish published *The Philosophical and Physical Opinions* in 1655, and published a revised and expanded version (under the slightly altered title, *Philosophical and Physical Opinions*) in 1663. In the later edition she writes that "in this Work of mine you will find, not only my Former Philosophical Opinions Enlarged, but much Reformed and Corrected" (Cavendish, "An Epistle to the Reader," br). However, in her *Observations upon Experimental Philosophy*, Cavendish does not hesitate to approvingly cite one of the early atomist poems ("The Reason Why Thoughts Are Made in the Head") she claims to have waived: "I have declared my opinion thereof twelve years since, in my work of *Poetical Fancies*, which then came out the first time; and I thought it not unfit to insert here, out of the same book, these following lines, both that my meaning may be the better understood, and that they may witness I have been of that opinion so many years ago" (*Observations upon Experimental Philosophy*, 212–13).

10. As Jonathan Goldberg puts it, when Cavendish turns from atomism toward vitalist monism after the publication of *P&F*, that rejection "is mainly a refusal of a kind of mechanical philosophy that is not the main contribution of Lucretius to atomist thought" (*The Seeds of Things*, 2). Goldberg argues that Cavendish could renounce atomism in name while still retaining some of its principles, perhaps in order to reconceive of and revise atomism altogether. As Goldberg explains, Cavendish's "vitalist monism . . . is akin at the most significant level of analysis to Lucretian problematics and formulations" (Goldberg, 149).

11. Cavendish, *Poems, and Fancies*, A4r, A6r. Cavendish uses italics with great frequency in her printed works, but to avoid visual distraction, I do not reproduce them. Both poems and prose from *P&F* are cited from the 1653 edition, and poems will be cited by line number in the text. While I have opted to use the first edition (1653) of Cavendish's text here, Brandie Siegfried's print edition (using the 1668 edition) and Liza Blake's online edition (a "best-text" or "conflated" edition) are both excellent.

12. Cavendish, "To Naturall Philosophers," *Poems, and Fancies*, A6r.

13. In the 1655 version of *The Philosophical and Physical Opinions*, she clarifies her earlier comments about her lack of learning: "And when I said I never convarst an hour with professed Philosophers . . . I did not think my readers would have been so rigid as to think I excluded

my husband, brothers, and the rest of my family, neither are they profest Philosophers nor Scholers, although they are learned therein" (Cavendish, "To the Reader," *The Philosophical and Physical Opinions*, A4v).

14. Cavendish, "To Naturall Philosophers," *Poems, and Fancies*, A6r.

15. Cavendish, "To all Noble, and Worthy Ladies," *Poems, and Fancies*, A3v.

16. Cavendish, "To Naturall Philosophers, " *Poems, and Fancies*, A6v.

17. Emma Rees calls this a "a good-natured nod to the eulogistic opening of *De Rerum Natura*" (*Margaret Cavendish*, 73 n. 23).

18. I thus disagree with Stephen Hequembourg, who has recently argued that Cavendish's allegorical Nature is at odds with her materialist philosophy: "In this sense, the content of the poem makes its form impossible; or, we might say, its philosophy is at odds with its fiction. Cavendish imposes an allegorical structure onto a work that explicitly rejects the kind of dualist ontology that makes allegory conceivable in the first place. It is a problem that Cavendish might have learned from Lucretius, who invokes the old gods to inspire a poem that proves they do not exist" ("The Poetics of Materialism in Cavendish and Milton," 176).

19. The classic account of figurality in classical literature in general, including *DRN*, is Erich Auerbach's essay on "Figura" (*Scenes from the Drama of European Literature*). More recently, Amanda Jo Goldstein argues convincingly that "*De rerum natura* presents figuration as the basic action and passion of matter" (*Sweet Science*, 25).

20. The poem is substantially revised in the 1664 and 1668 editions. For a comparison of all three versions, see Blake's digital edition of *P&F* (http://poemsandfancies.rblake.net/).

21. Dodds, "Bawds and Housewives," n.p.

22. Dodds, n.p.

23. Cavendish, "Epistle Dedicatory," *Poems, and Fancies*, A2r.

24. There are many ways in which Epicurean philosophy has been gendered female as opposed to a male Platonism (or Stoicism): Epicureanism's perceived hedonism and sensuality, its emphasis on matter instead of (Platonic or Aristotelian) form, and, in early modernity, *DRN*'s frequent translation into vernacular languages, which made it accessible to women. On the gendering of Epicureanism in the ancient world, see Gordon, *The Invention and Gendering of Epicurus*. Several critics have commented upon the sympathy of early modern women for Epicurean thought. See, for example, Barbour, "The Early Stuart Epicure," 194. For a sensitive reading of the place of gender in the interactions between Lucretius and Plato in the context of Renaissance epic, see Chapter 3 of Ramachandran, *The Worldmakers*.

25. The Cavendish library contained several editions of Diogenes's *Lives*: 1524, 1546, and 1570 Latin translations, as well as a 1692 English translation, which would have been acquired after Cavendish's death in 1673 (Noel, *Bibliotheca Nobilissimi Principis Johannis Ducis de Novo-Castro*, 15, 17).

26. There were some notable seventeenth-century women whose learning and connections put them in conversation with the foremost male thinkers of their day. Lucy Hutchinson (1620–1681), the subject of Chapter 4 and likely the first English translator of the complete *DRN* and the author of numerous theological and poetic works, was well known to Cavendish. Anne Conway (1614–1679) developed a Platonist metaphysics that was published posthumously in 1692, *The Principles of the Most Ancient and Modern Philosophy* (a translation from the original anonymous Latin publication in 1690).

27. Although in her early work, Cavendish persistently represents herself as an outsider to both the literary and the natural philosophical establishments, her later works engage explicitly with both ancient and modern philosophy. Furthermore, letters show that even in the 1650s

she maintained correspondence with major intellectual figures, such as Constantijn Huygens. See Akkerman and Corporaal, "Mad Science Beyond Flattery." On Cavendish's early philosophical engagements, see also Semler, "Margaret Cavendish's Early Engagement with Descartes and Hobbes" and "The Magnetic Attraction of Margaret Cavendish and Walter Charleton."

28. In *Against the Logicians* 8.9, Sextus Empiricus ascribes the principle of truth in sense perception to Epicurus, but no Epicurean articulation of the principle survives in the letters that have come down to us. On both Sextus and the Epicurean principle more generally, see Vogt, "All Sense-Perceptions Are True," in Lezra and Blake, *Lucretius and Modernity.* Lucretius discusses this principle in Book 4: "invenies primis ab sensibus esse creatam / notitiem veri neque sensus posse refelli. / nam maiore fide debet reperirier illud, / sponte sua veris quod possit vincere falsa. / quid maiore fide porro quam sensus haberi / debet? an ab sensu falso ratio orta valebit / dicere eos contra, quae tota ab sensibus orta est? / qui nisi sunt veri, ratio quoque falsa fit omnis" (You'll find the concept of the true is formed and has its root / In the senses, their testimony such that no one can refute. / For there must be a higher court to which you can appeal / That on its own can disprove what is false by what is real. / Besides, on what except the senses can you more rely? / Shall reason, based on the senses' false witness, testify / Against those very senses out of which it's wholly sprung? / For if the senses are untrue, all reasoning is wrong; *DRN* 4.478–85).

29. Hutchinson, *The Works of Lucy Hutchinson,* vol. 1, *Part 2,* 489. The quote is from the great Lucretius editor Cyril Bailey.

30. On Lucretian analogy, see Schrijvers, "Le regard sur l'invisible"; Garani, *Empedocles Redivivus.*

31. As Philip Hardie puts it, "The *De Rerum Natura* is a poem of confident certainties. . . . but to this is added a didactic voice that projects what might be called a rhetoric of uncertainty" (*Lucretian Receptions,* 231).

32. Cavendish, "An Epistle to Mistris Toppe," *Poems, and Fancies,* A4r.

33. As such, Cavendish's skeptical fancy would stand in sharp contrast to the typical caricature of those sectarian groups emerging in the 1650s such as the Quakers, as mistaking fancy or wild imagination for the Holy Spirit producing zeal.

34. Liza Blake and Bronwen Price both discuss the infrequency with which Cavendish uses "I" (Blake, "Reading Poems [and Fancies]," n.p; Price, "Feminine Modes of Knowing and Scientific Enquiry," 133).

35. Two of the most recent scholars to argue that error and carelessness were fundamental to the scientific method include Werlin, "Francis Bacon and the Art of Misinterpretation," and Simon, "Andrew Marvell and the Epistemology of Carelessness."

36. In 1667, Cavendish became the first woman to visit the Royal Society. "The experiments which the Society had arranged for that day included the weighing of air, the dissolution of mutton in sulfuric acid, the demonstration of the power of a sixty-pound magnet, Robert Boyle illustrating his theory of colors, and Robert Hooke demonstrating his microscope" (Mendelson, *Margaret Cavendish,* 47). Three hundred years passed before the Society invited another woman.

37. Price argues that in the seventeenth century poetic fancy begins to be gendered female, in contrast to "emerging discourses of rationalism and empiricism" ("Feminine Modes of Knowing and Scientific Enquiry," 124). Gabrielle Starr argues that for Cavendish, "fancy is an epistemic tool, because the frontiers of knowledge are subject to imaginative vision alone" ("Cavendish, Aesthetics, and the Anti-Platonic Line," 298).

38. In *Observations upon Experimental Philosophy*, in the section titled "Of Art, and Experimental Philosophy," Cavendish attacks Hooke, whom she quotes as having written in the Preface to his *Micrographia* that "remedies [for human reason] can only proceed from the real, the mechanical, the experimental philosophy" (Cavendish, *Observations upon Experimental Philosophy*, 49). Cavendish takes umbrage at this because hers is precisely what Hooke denigrates as a "philosophy of discourse and disputation." The body of the *Observations*, for example, opens with "An Argumental Discourse" "between the rational parts of [Cavendish's] mind concerning some chief points and principles in natural philosophy" and "some new thoughts," which "to oppose and call in question the truth of [her] former conceptions, caused a war in [her] mind" (Cavendish, 23). The discourse between these two sets of thoughts is laid out so as to be judged by the "arbitration of the impartial reader" (Cavendish, 43). Cavendish avers later that discourse "shall sooner find or trace nature's corporeal figurative motions, than deluding arts can inform the senses. . . . And hence I conclude, that experimental and mechanic philosophy cannot be above the speculative part" (Cavendish, 49).

39. Cavendish, 9.

40. Again, Anne Conway and Lucy Hutchinson are two notable exceptions. Although nothing is known of Conway's early education, her correspondence course with Henry More, the noted Cambridge Platonist, gave her an extraordinary philosophical training later in life. As Hutchinson tells it, because her mother dreamed before giving birth that her daughter would be in some way extraordinary, no expense was spared in her classical education.

41. Cavendish, "To the Reader," *Observations upon Experimental Philosophy*, 11. This is not to say that Cavendish was not interested in joining scholarly conversations with those "bred up" to learning. From her earliest forays into print, Cavendish was concerned that her books be read by scholars and included in university libraries. *Observations upon Experimental Philosophy* includes a prefatory epistle, "To the Most Famous University of Cambridge," requesting their consideration of the work.

42. Cavendish, 214.

43. On the *ignis* in *lignum*, see Lezra, *Unspeakable Subjects*, 20–23.

44. Cavendish will claim that her later philosophical opinions are derived from the 1653 *Philosophicall Fancies*, which was published alongside *P&F*. The 1663 *Philosophical and Physical Opinions* are "not only my Former Philosophical Opinions Enlarged, but much Reformed and Corrected" (Cavendish, *The Philosophical and Physical Opinions*, b1r). The 1664 *Philosophical Letters*, too, find their origin in the 1653 *Philosophicall Fancies*: "The Principles, Heads and Grounds of my Opinions are my own . . . and the first time I divulged them, was in the year 1653. since which time I have reviewed, reformed and reprinted them twice" (Cavendish, *Philosophical Letters*, c1).

45. Liza Blake's online edition of the *P&F* is a welcome antidote to this long-standing critical habit: Blake presents the atomist poems as constituting a structure that shifts meaningfully between editions of the *P&F* ("Reading Poems [and Fancies]," in *Margaret Cavendish's "Poems and Fancies"*).

46. Known as both the Newcastle and the Cavendish circle, the salon—including Hobbes, Descartes, Mersenne, and Gassendi—convened in Paris in the 1640s. On the group, see Clucas, "The Atomism of the Cavendish Circle"; Sarasohn, "Thomas Hobbes and the Duke of Newcastle." On Cavendish's debt to the mechanical philosophy of her guests, see Hutton, "In Dialogue with Thomas Hobbes." On the English context of mechanical philosophy more generally, see Kargon, "Walter Charleton, Robert Boyle, and the Acceptance of Epicurean Atomism in England."

47. Sarasohn, "A Science Turned Upside Down," 297. Sarasohn discusses Cavendish's skepticism, but sees it as purely expedient: "Cavendish had no choice but to advocate a full-scale skepticism; the path to conventional knowledge was closed to her" (Sarasohn, 292). Reduced to strategy, Cavendish's skeptical thought is less interesting than its goals; Cavendish "used the skeptical methodology of the new science not only to attack traditional natural philosophy, but also as a weapon in her battle for the recognition of female intellectual equality" (Sarasohn, 289). Sarasohn's more recent book on Cavendish contains an updated assessment of Cavendish's atomism (*The Natural Philosophy of Margaret Cavendish*).

48. Battigelli, *Margaret Cavendish and the Exiles of the Mind*, 9.

49. Cavendish, *"The Blazing World" and Other Writings*, 187.

50. Cavendish, 188.

51. Cavendish, "An Epistle to Mistris Toppe," *Poems, and Fancies*, A5r.

52. An earlier generation of aristocratic male poets frequently framed their literary works as the products of idle time. Sir Philip Sidney, for example, frequently referred to his literary works as toys. On this, see Newcomb, *Reading Popular Romance in Early Modern England*, 37–41; Duncan-Jones, *Philip Sidney's Toys*. Among Cavendish's contemporaries of both genders, "idle time" was shorthand of sorts for royalists who had gone into exile or been otherwise expelled from their homes, duties, and habits. In his dedicatory epistle to the reader, Laudian apologist Peter Heylyn writes that his massive *Cosmographie* was the work of leisure time: "For being by the unhappiness of my Destinie, or the inficility of the times, deprived of my Prefer-ments, and devested of my Ministeriall Function (as to the ordinary and publique exercise thereof) I cannot choose but say I have leisure enough; the opportunity of spending more idle hours (if I were so minded) than I ever expected or desired" (Heylyn, *Cosmographie in Four Bookes*, A2r).

53. See Mendelson, "Women and Work."

54. Cavendish cites these lines in a dedicatory epistle to her *Sociable Letters*, 4.

55. Cavendish, 4.

56. Cavendish, "Epistle to the Reader," *Poems, and Fancies*, A7r.

57. In "A True Relation of my Birth, Breeding, and Life" (1656) Cavendish extols her mother for her skills in estate management (*Paper Bodies*, 49).

58. Cavendish, "Epistle to the Reader," *Poems, and Fancies*, A7r.

59. Chalmers argues that Cavendish's poetry is "a sublimation of the energies that she would otherwise use in managing her husband's household" ("'Flattering Division,'" 130). Likewise, Dodds argues that "traditionally feminine pursuits of the domestic arts are trans-formed into the metaphorical basis for and justification of Cavendish's poetics" (*The Literary Invention of Margaret Cavendish*, 10).

60. Wendy Wall discusses the affinity between kitchen and laboratory work in chapter 5 of her *Recipes for Thought*.

61. Cavendish, "Epistle Dedicatory," *Poems, and Fancies*, A2r.

62. On spinning as an image tying poetry to women's work, see Rees, "A Well-Spun Yarn: Margaret Cavendish and Homer's Penelope," in Clucas, *A Princely Brave Woman*. On spinning as an image for feminine mental activity, see Bowerbank, "The Spider's Delight."

63. Cavendish, "To all Noble, and Worthy Ladies," *Poems, and Fancies*, A3r.

64. Cavendish's tone in this passage on color and ornament may be tongue-in-cheek, given that Boyle and other experimentalists were also deeply concerned with questions of color. Chapter 20 of part 1 of Cavendish's *Observations upon Experimental Philosophy* attacks Boyle and others for their views on color.

65. In his diary, Samuel Pepys dwells on Cavendish's clothing and person when describing first meeting the duchess: "[Met] My Lady Newcastle, going with her coachmen and footmen all in velvet; herself (whom I never saw before), as I have heard her often described (for all the town-talk is nowadays of her extravagancies), with her velvet-cap, her hairs about her ears, many black patches because of pimples about her mouth, naked necked without anything about it, and a black just-au-corps; she seemed to me a very comely woman—but I hope to see more of her on May-day" (April 26, 1667, *The Diary of Samuel Pepys*, 8:186).

66. Cavendish, "To all Noble, and Worthy Ladies," *Poems, and Fancies*, A3r.

67. Cavendish, "An Epistle to Mistris Toppe," *Poems, and Fancies*, A4r.

68. On pastime in seventeenth-century politics and poetry, see Marcus, *The Politics of Mirth*.

69. Picciotto, *Labors of Innocence in Early Modern England*, 169–70. Picciotto is quoting from *The Early Essays and Ethics of Robert Boyle*, 244.

70. Cavendish writes in a dedicatory epistle to her husband that "your Grace is not only a lover of virtuosos, but a virtuoso yourself, and have as good, and as many sorts of optic glasses as anyone else" (*Observations upon Experimental Philosophy*, 4).

71. Cavendish, "An Epistle to Mistris Toppe," *Poems, and Fancies*, A4r.

72. On the role ignorance plays in Cavendish's natural philosophy, see Price, "Feminine Modes of Knowing and Scientific Enquiry."

73. Cavendish, "To Naturall Philosophers," *Poems, and Fancies*, A6r.

74. Deborah Boyle maintains that both editions of *The Philosophical and Physical Opinions* (one published two years after *P&F* in 1655, with a second edition in 1663) argue for a form of "local knowledge"; Boyle claims that "although no part of nature can know the whole truth about nature, there are what we might dub 'local knowledges,' the different knowledges possessed by different parts of nature due to their different motions" ("Margaret Cavendish's Nonfeminist Natural Philosophy," 204).

75. Cavendish attributes her mature ability to piece together the world's language to her husband. When she was younger, she "found the World too difficult to be understood by my tender yeers, and weak capacity, that till the time I was married, I could onely read the letters, and joyn the words, but understood nothing of the sense of the World, until my Lord, who was learned by experience, as my Master, instructed me" (Cavendish, *The World's Olio*, 47).

76. Cavendish, "Of Languages," in *The World's Olio*, 13–14. In chapter 11 of the *Defense*, Joachim du Bellay makes much the same argument (*Les regrets*).

77. James Fitzmaurice troubles the picture of Cavendish as a solitary genius by examining how family attachments influenced her writing ("Fancy and the Family").

78. Cavendish, *The Life of the Thrice Noble, High, and Puissant Prince William Cavendish*, (a)1v–(a)2v.

79. Cavendish, *Sociable Letters*, 140.

80. Cavendish, *Sociable Letters*, 222.

81. Lucy Hutchinson, who translated Lucretius, depicts her translation as similarly solitary: she writes that she toiled over her translation of Lucretius in the seclusion of her children's nursery: "I did not employ any serious studie in [translating Lucretius], for I turnd it into English in a roome where my children practizd the severall qualities they were taught, with their Tutors, & I numbred the sillables of my translation by the threds of the canvas I wrought in, & sett them downe with a pen & inke that stood by me" (Hutchinson, *The Works of Lucy Hutchinson*, vol. 1, *Part 1*, 7).

82. Cavendish, *Sociable Letters*, 157.

83. Cavendish, 157.
84. Cavendish, 157.
85. Cavendish, 157–58.
86. Cavendish, 156.
87. Cavendish, 157–58.
88. Cavendish, *Paper Bodies*, 56.
89. Bowerbank, *Speaking for Nature*, 5. Bowerbank writes that Lucretius's analogy of atoms and letters troubles the status of language and law, divine or otherwise. Kroll, on the other hand, situates Cavendish's interest in the atom-letter analogy in the context of early modern scientific developments (*The Material Word*).
90. Cavendish, "Of Speech," *The World's Olio*, 23–24. The same motif reappears throughout Cavendish's work, as in this poem about echoes: "As severall Letters do a word up-joyne, / So severall Figures through the Aire combine. / The Aire is waxe, words Seale, and give the Print, / Those words an Eccho in the Aire do mint" (Cavendish, "What Makes Eccho," *Poems, and Fancies*, lines 3–6).
91. Goldberg also emphasizes the Lucretian valences of Cavendish's professions of illiteracy, arguing that her claims to have illegible handwriting is a form of difference predicated on a common material basis, which "points to the material trace as a basic analytic unit." For Goldberg, the difference between elements in Lucretius and the illegible letterforms in Cavendish "can be related to the ways in which Cavendish rewrites atomism as vitalism" (*The Seeds of Things*, 132).
92. Cavendish, *Sociable Letters*, 147.
93. Cavendish, "To Naturall Philosophers," *Poems, and Fancies*, A6r. Cavendish will assert this more powerfully in later works: "[T]he opinion of atoms, is fitter for poetical fancy, than for serious philosophy; and this is the reason I have waived it in my philosophical works" (Cavendish, *Observations upon Experimental Philosophy*, 129).
94. Gabrielle Starr explains the necessity of Cavendish's paired defense of women and poetry: "Cavendish constantly defended her capacity as a woman to write and the worth of her writing; inevitably this meant she engaged in the defense of poesy. Her sensitivity to the precarious position of women's writing made her all the more aware of the state of imaginative literature in general, whether in light of Platonic injunctions against poets, the new empirical values of natural philosophy, or Puritan denunciations of fancy" ("Cavendish, Aesthetics, and the Anti-Platonic Line," 296).
95. Sidney, *The Major Works*, 235.
96. Cavendish, *Observations upon Experimental Philosophy*, 272.
97. Cavendish, *"The Blazing World" and Other Writings*, 123–24.
98. Walters, *Margaret Cavendish*, 19.

EPILOGUE

1. Rochester's poems are cited by line number, and citations refer to Wilmot, *The Poems*. Henceforth citations will be provided in the text.
2. Not all, of course. Rochester's "The Imperfect Enjoyment" is part of a long tradition of impotence poems stretching back to Ovid's *Amores* 3.7.
3. "Aeneadum genetrix, hominum divumque voluptas, / alma Venus, caeli subter labentia signa / quae mare navigerum, quae terras frugiferentis / concelebras, per te quoniam genus

omne animantum / concipitur" (Life-stirring Venus, Mother of Aeneas and of Rome, / Pleasure of men and gods, you make all things beneath the dome / Of sliding constellations teem, you throng the fruited earth / And the ship-freighted sea—for every species comes to birth / Conceived through you; *DRN* 1.1–5).

4. Meeker, "Libertine Lucretius," 226–27. On libertine Lucretians in France, see also Meeker, *Voluptuous Philosophy*.

5. Meeker, "Libertine Lucretius," 227.

6. Eric Baker writes that "to characterise Lucretius' impact on the age of the Enlightenment is a daunting task. Virtually every major figure of the period was in some way influenced by Lucretius" (in Gillespie and Hardie, *The Cambridge Companion to Lucretius*, 274).

7. Palmer writes that "the first author to use atomism while specifically retaining the title 'Epicureanism' was Pierre Gassendi, who in the seventeenth century attempted to hybridize Epicureanism, skepticism, and Christianity. This slow and relatively limited penetration of Epicurean atomism and mechanical theory into scientific circles before Gassendi cannot be attributed to a lack of access to Epicurean sources; by 1600 publishers had printed thousands of copies of Lucretius. Although Lucretius had thousands of readers before the seventeenth century, however, 'Epicurean' remained less an intellectual label than a term of abuse, synonymous in public discourse with heresy, atheism, and, often, sodomy" (*Reading Lucretius in the Renaissance*, 5). Though there had been earlier groupings of interest in atomism—the group around Henry Percy, ninth Earl of Northumberland, in the early years of the seventeenth century, and later the Cavendish circle in Paris in the 1640s—Gassendi's *Commentary on the Tenth Book of Diogenes Laertius* (1649), *Treatise on Epicurean Philosophy* (1649), and posthumous *Syntagma philosophicum* (1658) were pivotal in solidifying the influence of classical atomism on modern science.

8. Palmer, *Reading Lucretius in the Renaissance*, 5.

9. Palmer, 6.

10. Palmer, 6.

BIBLIOGRAPHY

Agamben, Giorgio. *Stanzas: Word and Phantasm in Western Culture*. Translated by Ronald L. Martinez. Minneapolis: University of Minnesota Press, 1993.

Aït-Touati, Frédérique. *Fictions of the Cosmos: Science and Literature in the Seventeenth Century.* Chicago: University of Chicago Press, 2011.

Akkerman, Nadine, and Marguérite Corporaal. "Mad Science Beyond Flattery: The Correspondence of Margaret Cavendish and Constantijn Huygens." In "Essays from the Fifth Biennial International Margaret Cavendish Conference," *Early Modern Literary Studies*, Special Issue 14 (May 2004): 2.1–21.

Althusser, Louis. *Philosophy of the Encounter: Later Writings, 1978–87*. London: Verso, 2006.

Archdeacon, Anthony. "The 'Nothing' Trope: Self-Worth in Renaissance Poetry." *Literature Compass* 11, no. 8 (2014): 549–59.

Aristotle. *The Complete Works of Aristotle*. Edited by Jonathan Barnes. 2 vols. Princeton: Princeton University Press, 1984.

Auerbach, Erich. *Scenes from the Drama of European Literature*. Minneapolis: University of Minnesota Press, 1984.

Bacon, Francis. *The Advancement of Learning*. Edited by Michael Kiernan. Vol. 4. Oxford Francis Bacon. Oxford: Clarendon Press, 2000.

Baisier, Léon. *The Lapidaire chrétien*. New York: AMS Press, 1969.

Barbour, Reid. "Anonymous Lucretius." *Bodleian Library Record* 23, no. 1 (2010): 105–11.

———. "Bacon, Atomism, and Imposture: The True and the Useful in History, Myth, and Theory." In *Francis Bacon and the Refiguring of Early Modern Thought: Essays to Commemorate the Advancement of Learning (1605–2005)*, edited by Julie Robin Solomon and Catherine Gimelli Martin, 17–44. Aldershot: Ashgate, 2005.

———. "Between Atoms and the Spirit: Lucy Hutchinson's Translation of Lucretius." *Renaissance Papers* (1994): 1–16.

———. "The Early Stuart Epicure." *English Literary Renaissance* 23, no. 1 (1993): 170–200.

———. *English Epicures and Stoics: Ancient Legacies in Early Stuart Culture*. Amherst: University of Massachusetts Press, 1998.

Battigelli, Anna. *Margaret Cavendish and the Exiles of the Mind*. Lexington: University Press of Kentucky, 1998.

Belleau, Remy. *Commentaires au second livre des "Amours" de Ronsard*. Edited by Marie Madeleine Fontaine and François Lecercle. Travaux d'Humanisme et Renaissance 214. Geneva: Droz, 1986.

———. *Les amours et nouveaux eschanges des pierres précieuses*. Edited by Maurice Verdier. Geneva: Droz, 1973.

———. *Œuvres poétiques*. Edited by Guy Demerson. 5 vols. Paris: H. Champion, 1995–2003.

Betensky, Aya. "Lucretius and Love." *Classical World* 73, no. 5 (1980): 291–99.

Blake, Liza. "Reading Poems (and Fancies): An Introduction to Margaret Cavendish's *Poems and Fancies*." In *Margaret Cavendish's "Poems and Fancies": A Digital Critical Edition*, edited by Liza Blake. Website published May 2019. http://library2.utm.utoronto.ca/poemsand fancies/.

Blake, William. *The Complete Poetry and Prose of William Blake*. Edited by David V. Erdman. New York: Anchor Books, 1988.

Bloom, Harold. *The Anxiety of Influence: A Theory of Poetry*. Oxford: Oxford University Press, 1973.

Blumenberg, Hans. *Shipwreck with Spectator: Paradigm of a Metaphor for Existence*. Cambridge: MIT Press, 1997.

Bowerbank, Sylvia. *Speaking for Nature: Women and Ecologies of Early Modern England*. Baltimore: Johns Hopkins University Press, 2004.

———. "The Spider's Delight: Margaret Cavendish and the 'Female' Imagination." *English Literary Renaissance* 14, no. 3 (1984): 392–408.

Boyle, Deborah. "Margaret Cavendish's Nonfeminist Natural Philosophy." *Configurations* 12, no. 2 (2004): 195–227.

Boyle, Robert. *The Early Essays and Ethics of Robert Boyle*. Carbondale: SIU Press, 1991.

Braybrook, Jean. "Remy Belleau and the Figure of the Artist." *French Studies* 37, no. 1 (1983): 1–16.

———. "Remy Belleau and the *Pierres precieuses*." *Renaissance Studies* 3, no. 2 (1989): 193–201.

———. "Science and Myth in the Poetry of Remy Belleau." *Renaissance Studies* 5, no. 3 (1991): 277–87.

British Library, Add. MS 19333.

Brown, Alison. *The Return of Lucretius to Renaissance Florence*. Cambridge, Mass.: Harvard University Press, 2010.

Brown, Robert D. *Lucretius on Love and Sex: A Commentary on "De Rerum Natura" IV, 1030–1287, with Prolegomena, Text, and Translation*. Columbia Studies in the Classical Tradition 16. Leiden: Brill, 1988.

Butterfield, David. *The Early Textual History of Lucretius' "De rerum natura."* Cambridge: Cambridge University Press, 2013.

Carey, John. *John Donne: Life, Mind and Art*. London: Faber and Faber, 1981.

Castor, Grahame. *Pléiade Poetics: A Study in Sixteenth-Century Thought and Terminology*. Cambridge: Cambridge University Press, 1964.

Cavendish, Margaret. *"The Blazing World" and Other Writings*. London: Penguin, 1994.

———. *The Life of the Thrice Noble, High, and Puissant Prince William Cavendish*. London: Printed by A. Maxwell, 1675.

———. *Margaret Cavendish's "Poems and Fancies": A Digital Critical Edition*. Edited by Liza Blake. Website published May 2019. http://library2.utm.utoronto.ca/poemsandfancies/.

———. *Natures Pictures Drawn by Fancies Pencil to the Life*. London: Printed for J. Martin and J. Allestrye at the Bell in Saint Paul's Church-yard, 1656.

———. *Observations upon Experimental Philosophy*. Edited by Eileen O'Neill. Cambridge: Cambridge University Press, 2001.

———. *Paper Bodies: A Margaret Cavendish Reader*. Edited by Sara Mendelson and Sylvia Bowerbank. Peterborough: Broadview Press, 2000.

————. *Philosophical Letters, or: Modest Reflections upon Some Opinions in Natural Philosophy, Maintained by Several Famous and Learned Authors of This Age*. London, 1664.

————. *Philosophicall Fancies. Written by the Right Honourable, the Lady Newcastle*. London: Printed by Tho: Roycroft, for J. Martin, and J. Allestrye, at the Bell in St. Pauls Churchyard, 1653.

————. *The Philosophical and Physical Opinions, Written by Her Excellency the Lady Marchioness of Newcastle*. London: For J. Martin & J. Allestrye, 1655.

————. *Philosophical and Physical Opinions, Written By the Thrice Noble, Illustrious, and Excellent Princess, the Lady Marchioness of Newcastle*. London: Printed by William Wilson, 1663.

————. *Poems, and Fancies: Written by the Right Honourable, the Lady Margaret Countesse of Newcastle*. London: printed by T. R[oycroft]. for J. Martin and J. Allestrye at the Bell in Saint Pauls Church Yard, 1653.

————. *"Poems and Fancies" with "The Animal Parliament."* Edited by Brandie R. Siegfried. Toronto: University of Toronto Press, 2018.

————. *Sociable Letters*. New York: Garland, 1997.

————. *The World's Olio*. London: Printed for J. Martin and J. Allestrye, 1655.

Chayes, Evelien. *L'éloquence des pierres précieuses: De Marbode de Rennes à Alard d'Amsterdam et Remy Belleau; Sur quelques lapidaires du XVIe siècle*. Paris: Champion, 2010.

————. "'Tromper les plus clair-voyans': The Counterfeit of Precious Stones in the Work of Rémy Belleau." In *On the Edge of Truth and Honesty: Principles and Strategies of Fraud and Deceit in the Early Modern Period*, edited by Toon Houdt, 183–222. Leiden: Brill, 2002.

Clucas, Stephen. "The Atomism of the Cavendish Circle: A Reappraisal." *The Seventeenth Century* 9, no. 2 (1994): 247–73.

————. "Poetic Atomism in Seventeenth-Century England: Henry More, Thomas Traherne, and Scientific Imagination." *Renaissance Studies* 5, no. 3 (2008): 327–40.

————, ed. *A Princely Brave Woman: Essays on Margaret Cavendish, Duchess of Newcastle*. Farnham: Ashgate, 2003.

Cokain, Sir Aston. *Small Poems of Divers Sorts*. London: Printed by Wil. Godbid, 1658.

Connat, M. "Mort et testament de Remy Belleau." *Bibliothèque d'Humanisme et Renaissance* 6 (1945): 328–56.

Coogan, Michael D., Marc Z. Brettler, and Carol A. Newsom, eds. *The New Oxford Annotated Bible with the Apocrypha: New Revised Standard Version*. 4th ed. New York: Oxford University Press, 2010.

Cottegnies, Line, and Nancy Weitz, eds. *Authorial Conquests: Essays on Genre in the Writings of Margaret Cavendish*. London: Associated University Presses, 2003.

Creech, Thomas, trans. *T. Lucretius Carus, the Epicurean Philosopher, His Six Books De Rerum Natura Done into English Verse, with Notes*. Oxford, 1682.

Deleuze, Gilles. *Difference and Repetition*. Translated by Paul Patton. New York: Columbia University Press, 1995.

————. *The Logic of Sense*. New York: Columbia University Press, 1990.

Diogenes Laertius. *Lives of Eminent Philosophers*. Vol. 2, *Books 6–10*. Translated by R. D. Hicks. Loeb Classical Library. Cambridge, Mass.: Harvard University Press, 1925.

Dodds, Lara. "Bawds and Housewives: Margaret Cavendish and the Work of 'Bad Writing.'" *Early Modern Studies Journal* 6 (2014): 29–65.

————. *The Literary Invention of Margaret Cavendish*. Pittsburgh: Duquesne University Press, 2013.

————. "'Poore Donne Was Out': Reading and Writing Donne in the Works of Margaret Cavendish." *John Donne Journal* 29 (2010): 133–74.

Donne, John. *The Complete Poems of John Donne*. Edited by Robin Robbins. Harlow: Pearson, 2010.

————. *Ignatius his Conclave: An Edition of the Latin and English Texts with Introduction and Commentary*. Edited by T. S. Healey. Oxford: Oxford University Press, 1969.

————. *Letters to Severall Persons of Honour*. Edited by Charles Edmund Merrill, Jr. New York: Sturgis & Walton, 1910.

————. *The Sermons of John Donne*. Edited by Kimberley Johnson. Provo: Brigham Young University Press, 2012. https://lib.byu.edu/collections/john-donne-sermons/.

Dryden, John. *Sylvæ, or, The Second Part of Poetical Miscellanies*. London: Jacob Tonson, 1685.

Du Bartas, Guillaume de Salluste. *Du Bartas His Deuine Weekes and Workes*. Translated by Joshua Sylvester. London: Humfrey Lownes, 1613.

Du Bellay, Joachim. *Les regrets, précédé de Les antiquités de Rome et suivi de La défense et illustration de la langue française*. Paris: Gallimard, 1975.

————. *Œuvres poétiques*. Edited by Henri Chamard. Vol. 6, part 2, *Discours et traductions*. Paris: M. Didier, 1970.

Dubois, Claude-Gilbert. *Le maniérisme*. Paris: P.U.F., 1979.

————, ed. *L'invention au XVIe siècle*. Bordeaux: Presses Universitaires de Bordeaux, 1987.

Duncan-Jones, Katherine. *Philip Sidney's Toys*. London: British Academy, 1980.

Eliot, T. S. *Selected Essays*. London: Faber and Faber, 1934.

Enterline, Lynn. *The Rhetoric of the Body from Ovid to Shakespeare*. Cambridge: Cambridge University Press, 2004.

Evans, J., and M. S. Serjeantson. *English Mediaeval Lapidaries*. London: Early English Text Society, 1933.

Evelyn, John. *An Essay on the First Book of T. Lucretius Carus De Rerum Natura*. London: Printed for Gabriel Bedle, and Thomas Collins, 1656.

————. *John Evelyn's Translation of Titus Lucretius Carus, "De rerum natura": An Old-Spelling Critical Edition*. Edited by Michael M. Repetzki. Frankfurt am Main: Peter Lang, 2000.

Faisant, Claude. "Gemmologie et imaginaire: Les pierres précieuses de Remy Belleau." In *L'invention au XVIe siècle*, edited by Claude-Gilbert Dubois, 83–106. Bordeaux: Presses Universitaires de Bordeaux, 1987.

Ferguson, Margaret W. "Saint Augustine's Region of Unlikeness: The Crossing of Exile and Language." *Georgia Review* 29, no. 4 (1975): 842–64.

Fish, Stanley Eugene. *Self-Consuming Artifacts: The Experience of Seventeenth-Century Literature*. Berkeley: University of California Press, 1972.

Fitzmaurice, James. "Fancy and the Family: Self-Characterizations of Margaret Cavendish." *Huntington Library Quarterly* 53, no. 3 (1990): 199–209.

Ford, Philip. *Ronsard's Hymns: A Literary and Iconographical Study*. Tempe, Ariz.: Medieval and Renaissance Texts and Studies, 1997.

Foucault, Michel. "Theatrum Philosophicum." In *Language, Counter-memory, Practice: Selected Essays and Interviews*, edited by Donald F. Bouchard, 165–98. Oxford: Blackwell, 1977.

Fraisse, Simone. *L'influence de Lucrèce en France au seizième siècle: Une conquête du rationalisme*. Paris: A.G. Nizet, 1962.

Freccero, John. "The Fig Tree and the Laurel: Petrarch's Poetics." *Diacritics* 5, no. 1 (1975): 34–40.

———. "Donne's 'Valediction: Forbidding Mourning.'" *ELH* 30, no. 4 (1963): 335–76.

Friedländer, Paul. "Pattern of Sound and Atomistic Theory in Lucretius." *American Journal of Philology* 62, no. 1 (1941): 16–34.

Fuzier, Jean. "Donne sonnetiste: Les Holy Sonnets et la tradition européenne." In *De Shakespeare à T. S. Eliot: Mélanges offerts à Henri Fluchère*, edited by Marie-Jeanne Durry et al., 153–71. Paris: Didier, 1976.

Gale, Monica, ed. *Myth and Poetry in Lucretius*. Cambridge: Cambridge University Press, 1994.

———, ed. *Oxford Readings in Lucretius*. Oxford: Oxford University Press, 2007.

Garani, Myrto. *Empedocles Redivivus: Poetry and Analogy in Lucretius*. London: Routledge, 2007.

Gillespie, Stuart, and Philip Hardie, eds. *The Cambridge Companion to Lucretius*. Cambridge: Cambridge University Press, 2007.

Goddard, Charlotte Polly. "Epicureanism and the Poetry of Lucretius in the Renaissance." PhD diss., University of Cambridge, 1991.

Goldberg, Jonathan. *The Seeds of Things: Theorizing Sexuality and Materiality in Renaissance Representations*. New York: Fordham University Press, 2009.

Goldstein, Amanda Jo. *Sweet Science: Romantic Materialism and the New Logics of Life*. Chicago: University of Chicago Press, 2017.

Gordan, Phyllis Walter Goodhart. *Two Renaissance Book Hunters: The Letters of Poggius Bracciolini to Nicolaus De Niccolis*. New York: Columbia University Press, 1991.

Gordon, Cosmo. *A Bibliography of Lucretius*. London: Hart-Davis, 1962.

Gordon, Pamela. *The Invention and Gendering of Epicurus*. Ann Arbor: University of Michigan Press, 2012.

Greenblatt, Stephen. *The Swerve: How the World Became Modern*. New York: W.W. Norton, 2011.

Grierson, Herbert J. C., ed. *Metaphysical Lyrics & Poems of the Seventeenth Century, Donne to Butler*. Oxford: Clarendon Press, 1921.

Hardie, Philip. *Lucretian Receptions: History, the Sublime, Knowledge*. Cambridge: Cambridge University Press, 2009.

———. "Lucretius and the Delusions of Narcissus." *Materiali e discussioni per l'analisi dei testi classici* 20/21 (1988): 71–89.

———. *Virgil's Aeneid: Cosmos and Imperium*. Oxford: Oxford University Press, 1986.

Harrison, Robert Pogue. *Gardens: An Essay on the Human Condition*. Chicago: University of Chicago Press, 2009.

Harvey, Elizabeth D., and Timothy M. Harrison. "Embodied Resonances: Early Modern Science and Tropologies of Connection in Donne's *Anniversaries*." *ELH* 80, no. 4 (2013): 981–1008.

Hequembourg, Stephen. "The Poetics of Materialism in Cavendish and Milton." *Studies in English Literature 1500–1900* 54, no. 1 (2014): 173–92.

Heylyn, Peter. *Cosmographie in Four Bookes: Containing the Chorographie and Historie of the Whole World, and All the Principall Kingdomes, Provinces, Seas and Isles Thereof.* London: Printed for Henry Seile, 1657.

Hirsch, David. "Donne's Atomies and Anatomies: Deconstructed Bodies and the Resurrection of Atomic Theory." *Studies in English Literature, 1500–1900* 31, no. 1 (1991): 69.

Hobbes, Thomas. *Leviathan*. Cambridge: Cambridge University Press, 1996.

Hock, Jessie. "A Broken Line: Lucretian Lineage in *The Logic of Sense*." In *Speculation, Heresy, and Gnosis in Contemporary Philosophy of Religion: The Enigmatic Absolute*, edited by Joshua Ramey and Matthew Farris, 61–72. London: Rowman and Littlefield, 2016.

———. "The Mind Is Its Own Place: Lucretian Moral Philosophy in *Paradise Lost*." In *Milton's Modernities: Essays on the Poet and His Influence*, edited by Feisal Mohamed and Patrick Fadeley, 67–84. Rethinking the Early Modern. Chicago: Northwestern University Press, 2017.

Horace. *Odes and Epodes*. Translated by Niall Rudd. Cambridge, Mass.: Harvard University Press, 2004.

———. *Satires, Epistles, and Ars Poetica*. Translated by H. Rushton Fairclough. Cambridge, Mass.: Harvard University Press, 1926.

Hutchinson, Gregory. "The Date of *De Rerum Natura*." *Classical Quarterly* 51 (2001): 150–62.

Hutchinson, Lucy. *Lucy Hutchinson's Translation of Lucretius: De Rerum Natura*. Edited by Hugh de Quehen. London: Duckworth, 1996.

———. *Order and Disorder*. Edited by David Norbrook. Oxford: Wiley-Blackwell, 2001.

———. *The Works of Lucy Hutchinson*. Vol. 1, *The Translation of Lucretius: Part 1, Introduction and Text*. Edited by Reid Barbour and David Norbrook. Oxford: Oxford University Press, 2012.

———. *The Works of Lucy Hutchinson*. Vol. 1, *The Translation of Lucretius: Part 2, Commentary, Bibliography, and Index*. Edited by Reid Barbour and David Norbrook. Oxford: Oxford University Press, 2012.

Hutton, Sarah. "In Dialogue with Thomas Hobbes: Margaret Cavendish's Natural Philosophy." *Women's Writing* 4, no. 3 (1997): 421–32.

Hyman, Wendy Beth. *Impossible Desire and the Limits of Knowledge in Renaissance Poetry*. Oxford: Oxford University Press, 2019.

Jeanneret, Michel. "Les œuvres d'art dans 'La bergerie' de Belleau." *Revue d'histoire littéraire de la France* 1 (1970): 1–13.

Kargon, Robert. *Atomism in England from Hariot to Newton*. Oxford: Clarendon Press, 1966.

———. "Walter Charleton, Robert Boyle, and the Acceptance of Epicurean Atomism in England." *Isis* 55, no. 2 (1964): 184–92.

Kennedy, Duncan F. *Rethinking Reality: Lucretius and the Textualization of Nature*. Ann Arbor: University of Michigan Press, 2002.

Kenney, E. J. "Doctvs Lvcretivs." *Mnemosyne* 23, no. 4 (1970): 366–92.

Kroll, Richard W. F. *The Material Word: Literate Culture in the Restoration and Early Eighteenth Century*. Baltimore: Johns Hopkins University Press, 1991.

La Taille, Jean de. *La géomance abrégée de Jean de La Taille de Bondaroyz, . . . pour sçavoir les choses passées, présentes et futures. Ensemble le Blason des pierres précieuses, contenant leurs vertus et propriété*. Paris: L. Breyer, 1574.

Lecouteux, Claude. *Dictionnaire des pierres magiques et médicinales*. Paris: Imago, 2011.

Lemaire de Belges, Jean. *La couronne margaritique*. Lyon, 1549.

Lestringant, Frank, ed. *La renaissance de Lucrèce*. Cahiers Centre V. L. Saulnier. Paris: PUPS, 2010.

Lezra, Jacques. *Unspeakable Subjects: The Genealogy of the Event in Early Modern Europe*. Stanford: Stanford University Press, 1997.

Lezra, Jacques, and Liza Blake. *Lucretius and Modernity: Epicurean Encounters Across Time and Disciplines*. New York: Palgrave Macmillan, 2016.

Locke, John. *An Essay Concerning Human Understanding*. London: Penguin, 1997.

Lokaj, Rodney. "Strepitumque Acherontis avari: Petrarchan Descent to the Hades of Lucretius." *Rivista di cultura classica e medioevale* 48, no. 2 (2006): 339–85.

LoLordo, Antonia. *Pierre Gassendi and the Birth of Early Modern Philosophy.* Cambridge: Cambridge University Press, 2006.

Looze, Laurence de. *The Letter and the Cosmos: How the Alphabet Has Shaped the Western View of the World.* Toronto: University of Toronto Press, 2016.

Lucretius Carus, Titus. *Extraits de Lucrèce avec un commentaire, des notes et une étude sur al poésie, la philosophie, la physique, le texte et la langue de Lucrèce.* Edited by Henri Bergson. Paris: C. Delagrave, 1884.

———. *The Nature of Things.* Translated by A. E. Stallings. London: Penguin, 2007.

———. *Titi Lucreti Cari De rerum natura libri sex.* Edited by Cyril Bailey. Oxford: Clarendon Press, 1947.

Marcus, Leah S. *The Politics of Mirth: Jonson, Herrick, Milton, Marvell, and the Defense of Old Holiday Pastimes.* Chicago: University of Chicago Press, 1989.

Marullus, Michael. *Poems.* Translated by Charles Fantazzi. Cambridge, Mass.: Harvard University Press, 2012.

Meeker, Natania. "Libertine Lucretius." *Rivista di storia della filosofia* 67, no. 2 (2012): 226–27.

———. *Voluptuous Philosophy: Literary Materialism in the French Enlightenment.* New York: Fordham University Press, 2006.

Mendelson, Sara Heller. *Margaret Cavendish.* Farnham: Ashgate, 2009.

———. "Women and Work." In *A Companion to Early Modern Women's Writing*, edited by Anita Pacheco, 58–76. New York: Wiley-Blackwell, 2002.

Merchant, Carolyn. *The Death of Nature: Women, Ecology, and the Scientific Revolution.* San Francisco: Harper & Row, 1980.

Meyer, Paul. *Les plus anciens lapidaires français.* Paris: Franck, 1909.

Miller, Shannon. "Maternity, Marriage, and Contract: Lucy Hutchinson's Response to Patriarchal Theory in Order and Disorder." *Studies in Philology* 102, no. 3 (2005): 340–77.

Milton, John. *Paradise Lost.* Edited by Barbara K. Lewalski. Oxford: Blackwell, 2007.

Morrison, Mary. "Another Book from Ronsard's Library: A Presentation Copy of Lambin's Lucretius." *BHR* 25 (1963): 561–66.

Muret, Marc-Antoine. *Commentaires au premier livre des "Amours" de Ronsard.* Edited by Aldo Castellani, Jacques Chomarat, Marie-Madeleine Fragonard. Travaux d'Humanisme et Renaissance 207. Geneva: Droz, 1985.

Newcomb, Lori Humphrey. *Reading Popular Romance in Early Modern England.* New York: Columbia University Press, 2013.

Niderst, Alain, ed. *La pastorale française: De Rémi Belleau à Victor Hugo.* Paris: Centre d'Étude et de Recherche d'Histoire des Idées de la sensibilité, 1991.

Noel, Nathaniel. *Bibliotheca Nobilissimi Principis Johannis Ducis de Novo-Castro &c. Being a Large Collection of Books . . . Which Will Be Sold by Nath. Noel, . . . The Books May Be View'd from the 2d of March 1718–19, till the Day of Delivery, the 17th Instant.* London, 1719.

Norbrook, David. "Lucy Hutchinson's 'Elegies' and the Situation of the Republican Woman Writer (with Text)." *English Literary Renaissance* 27, no. 3 (1997): 468–521.

———. "Lucy Hutchinson Versus Edmund Waller: An Unpublished Reply to Waller's a Panegyrick to My Lord Protector." *The Seventeenth Century* 11, no. 1 (1996): 61–86.

———. "Margaret Cavendish and Lucy Hutchinson: Identity, Ideology, and Politics." *In-Between: Essays and Studies in Literary Criticism* 9, nos. 1–2 (2000): 179–203.

———. "Milton, Lucy Hutchinson, and the Lucretian Sublime: The Sublime Object." *Tate Papers* 13 (Spring 2010): 1–23. https://www.tate.org.uk/research/publications/tate-papers/13/milton-lucy-hutchinson-and-the-lucretian-sublime.

Norbrook, David, Stephen Harrison, and Philip Hardie, eds. *Lucretius and the Early Modern.* Oxford: Oxford University Press, 2015.

Nottingham University Library, MSS CL LM 85/1–5.

Nussbaum, Martha. *The Therapy of Desire: Hellenistic Ethics in Its Rhetorical and Literary Context.* Princeton: Princeton University Press, 1994.

Ovid. *The Art of Love and Other Poems.* Edited and translated by J. H. Mozley, revised by G. P. Goold. 2nd ed. Cambridge, Mass.: Harvard University Press, 1979.

———. *Heroides, Amores.* Translated by Grant Showerman, revised by G. P. Goold. 2nd ed. Cambridge, Mass.: Harvard University Press, 1977.

———. *The Metamorphoses of Ovid.* Translated by Allen Mandelbaum. New York: Harcourt Brace, 1993.

———. *P. Ovidi Nasonis Metamorphoses.* Edited by R. J. Tarrant. Oxford: Oxford University Press, 2004.

Palmer, Ada. *Reading Lucretius in the Renaissance.* Cambridge, Mass.: Harvard University Press, 2014.

Pantin, Isabelle. *La poésie du ciel en France dans la seconde moitié du seizième siècle.* Geneva: Droz, 1995.

Passannante, Gerard. "Burning Lucretius: On Ficino's Lost Commentary." *Studies in Philology* 115, no. 2 (2018): 267–85.

———. *Catastrophizing: Materialism and the Making of Disaster.* Chicago: University of Chicago Press, 2019.

———. *The Lucretian Renaissance: Philology and the Afterlife of Tradition.* Chicago: University of Chicago Press, 2011.

Patin, Henri. *Études sur la poésie latine.* 2 vols. Paris: Librairie de L. Hachette et Cie, 1868.

Pepys, Samuel. *The Diary of Samuel Pepys.* Edited by Robert Latham and William Matthews. 11 vols. London: Bell & Hyman, 1970–84.

Petrarca, Francesco. *Petrarch's Lyric Poems: The "Rime Sparse" and Other Lyrics.* Translated by Robert M. Durling. Cambridge, Mass.: Harvard University Press, 1976.

Phillippy, Patricia. *Love's Remedies: Recantation and Renaissance Lyric Poetry.* Lewisburg: Bucknell University Press, 1995.

Picciotto, Joanna. *Labors of Innocence in Early Modern England.* Cambridge, Mass.: Harvard University Press, 2010.

Plato. *Complete Works.* Edited by John M. Cooper and D. S. Hutchinson. Indianapolis: Hackett, 1997.

Polignac, Melchior de. *Anti-Lucretius, sive De Deo et natura.* Paris, 1747.

Prescott, Anne Lake. *French Poets and the English Renaissance: Studies in Fame and Transformation.* New Haven: Yale University Press, 1978.

Prévot, Georges. "Les emprunts de Rémy Belleau à Jean Second dans ses 'Baisers' (2e journée de la Bergerie)." *Revue d'histoire littéraire de la France* 3 (1921): 321–39.

Price, Bronwen. "Feminine Modes of Knowing and Scientific Enquiry: Margaret Cavendish's Poetry as Case Study." In *Women and Literature in Britain, 1500–1700,* edited by Helen Wilcox, 13–139. Cambridge: Cambridge University Press, 1996.

Prosperi, Valentina. *Di soavi licor gli orli del vaso: La fortuna di Lucrezio dall'Umanesimo alla Controriforma.* Turin: Aragno, 2004.

Quainton, Malcolm. *Ronsard's Ordered Chaos: Visions of Flux and Stability in the Poetry of Pierre de Ronsard.* Manchester: Manchester University Press, 1980.

Ramachandran, Ayesha. "Edmund Spenser, Lucretian Neoplatonist: Cosmology in the *Fowre Hymnes.*" *Spenser Studies* 24, no. 1 (2009): 373–411.

———. *The Worldmakers: Global Imagining in Early Modern Europe.* Chicago: University of Chicago Press, 2015.

Rees, Emma. *Margaret Cavendish: Gender, Genre, Exile.* Manchester: Manchester University Press, 2003.

Richmond, H. M. "Ronsard and the English Renaissance." *Comparative Literature Studies* 7, no. 2 (1970): 141–60.

Rieu, Josiane. "La *Bergerie* de Rémy Belleau: une 'fête' poétique à la gloire des Guises." In *Le mécénat et l'influence des Guises*, edited by Yvonne Bellenger, 251–78. Paris: Classiques Garnier, 1997.

Robertson, Lisa. *Nilling: Prose Essays on Noise, Pornography, the Codex, Melancholy, Lucretius, Folds, Cities, and Related Aporias.* Toronto: BookThug, 2012.

Ronsard, Pierre de. *Les amours (1552–1584).* Paris: GF-Flammarion, 1981.

———. *Cassandra.* Translated by Clive Lawrence. Manchester: Carcanet, 2015.

———. *Œuvres complètes.* Edited by Jean Ceard, Daniel Menager, and Michel Simonin. 2 vols. Paris: Gallimard, 1993.

———. *Selected Poems.* Translated by Malcolm Quainton and Elizabeth Vinestock. London: Penguin, 2002.

Russell, Anthony Presti. "'Thou Seest Mee Striue for Life': Magic, Virtue, and the Poetic Imagination in Donne's 'Anniversaries.'" *Studies in Philology* 95, no. 4 (1998): 374–410.

Salzman, Paul. *Early Modern Women's Writing: An Anthology, 1560–1700.* Oxford: Oxford University Press, 2000.

Sandys, George. *Ovid's Metamorphoses Englished, Mythologized, and Represented in Figures.* Oxford, 1632.

Sarasohn, Lisa. *The Natural Philosophy of Margaret Cavendish: Reason and Fancy During the Scientific Revolution.* Baltimore: Johns Hopkins University Press, 2010.

———. "A Science Turned Upside Down: Feminism and the Natural Philosophy of Margaret Cavendish." *Huntington Library Quarterly* 47, no. 4 (1984): 289–307.

———. "Thomas Hobbes and the Duke of Newcastle: A Study in the Mutuality of Patronage before the Establishment of the Royal Society." *Isis* 90, no. 4 (1999): 715–37.

Scève, Maurice. *Œuvres complètes.* Vol. 5, *Microcosme.* Edited by Michèle Clément. Paris: Classiques Garnier, 2013.

Schiesaro, Alessandro. *Simulacrum et imago: Gli argomenti analogici nel "De rerum natura."* Pisa: Giardini, 1990.

Schmidt, Albert-Marie. *La poésie scientifique en France au XVIe siècle.* Lausanne: Éditions Rencontre, 1970.

Schrijvers, P. H. "Le regard sur l'invisible: Étude sur l'emploi de l'analogie dans l'œuvre de Lucrèce." In *Lucrèce: Huit exposés suivis de discussions*, edited by David J. Furley, 79–114. Entretiens sur l'Antiquité Classique. Geneva: Fondation Hardt, 1978.

Screech, Michael A. *Montaigne's Annotated Copy of Lucretius: A Transcription and Study of the Manuscript Notes and Pen-Marks.* Geneva: Droz, 1998.

Semler, L. E. "The Magnetic Attraction of Margaret Cavendish and Walter Charleton." In *Early Modern Englishwomen Testing Ideas*, edited by Paul Salzman and Jo Wollwork, 55–74. London: Routledge, 2011.

———. "Margaret Cavendish's Early Engagement with Descartes and Hobbes: Philosophical Revisitation and Poetic Selection." *Intellectual History Review* 22, no. 3 (2012): 327–53.

Serres, Michel. *The Birth of Physics.* Manchester: Clinamen Press, 2000.

Shakespeare, William. *Shakespeare's Sonnets.* Edited by Stephen Booth. New Haven: Yale University Press, 2000.

Sidney, Sir Philip. *The Major Works.* New York: Oxford University Press, 2002.

Silver, Isidore. "Ronsard's Reflections on Cosmogony and Nature." *Publications of the Modern Language Association of America* 79, no. 3 (1964): 219–33.

———. "Three Commentaries of the 'Amours' by Muret and Belleau: A Significant Body of Prose Recovered for Ronsard." In *Three Ronsard Studies,* 109–67. Geneva: Droz, 1978.

Simon, David. "Andrew Marvell and the Epistemology of Carelessness." *ELH* 82, no. 2 (2015): 553–88.

Smith, A. J., ed. *John Donne: The Critical Heritage.* London: Routledge, 1975.

Snyder, James G. "Marsilio Ficino's Critique of the Lucretian Alternative." *Journal of the History of Ideas* 72, no. 2 (2011): 165–81.

Spiller, Elizabeth. *Science, Reading, and Renaissance Literature: The Art of Making Knowledge, 1580–1670.* Cambridge: Cambridge University Press, 2004.

Sprat, Thomas. *The History of the Royal Society.* Edited by Harold Whitmore Jones and Jackson I. Cope. St. Louis: Washington University Press, 1959.

Starr, Gabrielle. "Cavendish, Aesthetics, and the Anti-Platonic Line." *Eighteenth-Century Studies* 39, no. 3 (2006): 295–308.

Strier, Richard. "Radical Donne: 'Satire III.'" *ELH* 60, no. 2 (1993): 283–322.

Targoff, Ramie. *John Donne, Body and Soul.* Chicago: University of Chicago Press, 2009.

Temple, Camilla. "The Erotic Encounter and the Love-Suicide: The Ovidian Reception of Lucretius in Tasso's *Aminta.*" Paper presented at the Annual Meeting of the Shakespeare Association of America, Toronto, 2013.

Tiffany, Daniel. *Toy Medium: Materialism and Modern Lyric.* Berkeley: University of California Press, 2000.

Wall, Wendy. *Recipes for Thought: Knowledge and Taste in the Early Modern English Kitchen.* Philadelphia: University of Pennsylvania Press, 2015.

Walters, Lisa. *Margaret Cavendish: Gender, Science, Politics.* Cambridge: Cambridge University Press, 2014.

Warren, James. *Epicurus and Democritean Ethics: An Archaeology of Ataraxia.* Cambridge: Cambridge University Press, 2002.

Werlin, Julianne. "Francis Bacon and the Art of Misinterpretation." *PMLA* 130, no. 2 (2015): 236–51.

Wilcher, Robert. "'Adventurous Song' or 'Presumptuous Folly': The Problem of 'Utterance' in John Milton's *Paradise Lost* and Lucy Hutchinson's *Order and Disorder.*" *The Seventeenth Century* 21, no. 2 (2006): 304–14.

Wilmot, John, Earl of Rochester. *The Poems and "Lucinda's Rape."* Edited by Keith Walker and Nicholas Fisher. Chichester: Wiley-Blackwell, 2010.

Wycherley, R. E. "The Garden of Epicurus." *Phoenix* 13, no. 2 (1959): 73–77.

INDEX

adultery. *See* promiscuity

Agamben, Giorgio, 188

Althusser, Louis, 182

amethyst, 74, 80–81. *See also* lapidary tradition

analogy. *See* atoms

angels, 102–3, 105, 199. *See also* fantasy; *simulacra*

Anglesey, 1st Earl of (Arthur Annesley), 119–20, 122–23, 127–28, 144

animals, 1–2, 4, 50–51, 54, 63–64, 72, 88, 154, 177

Annesley, Arthur. *See* Anglesey, 1st Earl of

Aristotle, 44–45, 158, 170, 184, 188, 199

astronomy, 97, 198

atheism, 2–3, 43, 113, 121, 129, 176, 179, 204

atomism, 26, 36, 97, 99, 113–17, 153, 176, 190, 198, 201, 205, 208; Christianization of, 26, 30, 81, 111–15, 206, 215; classical, 16, 145, 158; early modern scientific, 24–25, 100, 117; Lucretian, 9, 16, 40, 42, 49–50, 107, 110, 154, 185; of Margaret Cavendish, 152, 157–58, 207–8, 212, 214; as materialism, 30; opponents of, 111, 114; and Petrarchism, 22, 100, 110; political valences of, 118, 132, 206–8. *See also* atoms; materialism

atoms, 2, 4, 13–14, 20, 23, 28–30, 66, 87, 97, 99, 123, 146, 148–49, 158, 170, 207, 214; analogy with alphabetical letters, 5, 9–12, 15–16, 28–29, 37, 113–16, 128, 145, 150, 155, 168, 180, 182–83, 187, 214; *clinamen* of, 16, 29, 45, 99, 113, 115–16, 123, 128, 148, 182; as dead, 145–46, 158; as emotions, 22, 29, 44, 110; desire for, 15, 185; figuration and, 6–7, 11, 15, 148–49; incorporeality of, 14, 16, 30; indestructibility of, 35, 37, 112, 188; invisibility of, 9, 11, 14, 107, 109, 114, 148, 152–53,

169–70; man as an atom, 112, 114, 128, 169; as metaphor for social relations, 99, 107, 109; physics of, 16, 22, 45, 125, 182, 185, 207; shape and size of, 30, 32–33, 96, 107, 164, 207; terms for, 10, 29, 155, 171, 183, 185; as wanton, 128, 134, 148–49, 152. *See also* atomism; Lucretius; *simulacra*

Auerbach, Erich, 209

Augustine, Saint, 17–19, 126

Autumn, 51–53, 77, 192–93

Bacchus, 53, 74, 80, 193

Bacon, Francis, 18–19, 186, 208

du Bartas, Guillaume de Salluste, 205–6

bawds, 148–49, 151–52

Behn, Aphra, 130

Bellay, Joachim du, 43, 190, 194, 213

Belleau, Remy, 17, 21, 23–25, 30, 56–58, 62–64, 100, 117, 189, 190, 194; *Bergerie*, 64–68, 83–84, 89–93, 194; career of, 81; commentary on Ronsard's *Amours*, 8, 23, 43–47, 62, 190–91; *Discours de la vanité*, 70–71; *Odes d'Anacréon*, 81–84; *Petites inventions*, 91–92; *Pierres précieuses*, 8, 62, 67–70, 72–81, 85–89, 92–93, 195–97

biography, 3, 8, 47, 120, 124–26, 180, 182

Blake, Liza, 190, 207, 210–11

Blumenberg, Hans, 199

the body, 17, 22, 27, 29–35, 37–39, 44, 48–49, 61, 66–67, 80, 150, 181, 184, 193–94; fragmentation of, 110, 112–13; of friendship, 115–16; indeterminacy of 12–14, 103, 136, 172–74; resurrection of, 97, 111–13; and soul, 95–6, 98–99, 101–5, 167, 199. *See also* corporeality

book-burning, 122–23, 126, 204, 208

Boyle, Robert, 162, 210, 212

ACKNOWLEDGMENTS

I have been grateful every day of writing this book for the support of my family, friends, mentors, and colleagues. The exemplary Timothy Hampton and Victoria Kahn were invaluable guides during the early stages of this project. They are, to this day, my models in writing as well as in teaching. Frank Bezner, Niklaus Largier, and Joanna Picciotto were also treasured interlocutors as the book found its footing. Early on, I met Catherine Talley and Daniel Hoffmann, my first (and best!) readers, and the best of friends. Cate thinks—and speaks—with greater rigor and clarity than anyone I know, and Daniel conjures and captures beauty at every moment. Their sensibilities shaped this book from the beginning. My heart and mind gained so much from so many during the years when this project first took form: I thank Sarah Chihaya, Joshua Craze, Sanders Creasy, Jessica Crewe, Jason Escalante, Rhiannon Graybill, Micha Lazarus, Ross Lerner, Danny Marcus, Ryan Perry, Jill Richards, and Tristram Wolff for their friendship, their conversation, and their intelligence.

At Vanderbilt University, I found an inspiring group of friends and colleagues. Leah Marcus, Lynn Enterline, Kathryn Schwarz, and Pavneet Aulakh were a formidable group of early modernists to join, and they could not have been friendlier, more supportive, or more inspiring. Lynn's conversation, kindness, and care are beyond compare; she is a mentor I will never deserve and a friend I will always treasure. Pav has become a dear friend and a generous reader and sharer of work. Other Vanderbilt friends and colleagues, especially Candice Amich, Piyali Bhattacharya, Matthew Congdon, Jennifer Fay, Lisa Guenther, Scott Juengel, Benjamin Legg, Ken MacLeish, Jesse Montgomery, Karen Ng, Rachel Pomerantz, Allison Schachter, Amaryah Shaye Armstrong, Hortense Spillers, Tariq Thachil, Ben Tran, and Rebecca Vandiver, have made Nashville my intellectual and emotional center. Allison Schachter and Ben Tran in particular have made Nashville feel like home.

For the past five years, I have split my time between Nashville and Berlin, and I also want to thank those dear friends, especially Joe Albernaz, Kirill Chepurin, Walter Johnston, Karen Minden, and Elena Vogman, who have made Berlin such a vibrant, thrilling place to spend my summers.

One of the great pleasures of growing in this profession has been getting to know so many brilliant, generous early modernists. I owe many of them debts of gratitude, and offer my particular thanks to Julie Crawford, Jane Newman, Richard Strier, and Jessica Wolfe.

Vanderbilt University has liberally supported the research and writing of this book. I am especially grateful to the Department of English, the Office of the Provost, and the Dean's Office of the College of Arts and Science. In 2018, I was lucky enough to be able to hold a book manuscript conference. Wendy Beth Hyman and Gerard Passannante graciously flew in to attend, and their penetrating and generous comments helped me bring the book's argument into its final form. Katherine Crawford, Lynn Enterline, Rick Hilles, Mark Jarman, Jonathan Lamb, Amanda Lehr, Mark Schoenfield, Kathryn Schwarz, and others also gave generously of their time and expertise during the workshop. At every step of the way, Dana Nelson, in her capacity as chair of Vanderbilt's Department of English, has gone above and beyond to support this project and my career. I cannot thank her enough.

Jerome Singerman and the rest of the staff at the University of Pennsylvania Press have been the perfect custodians for this book. I am eternally grateful for their acuity and professionalism. The anonymous reviewers for the press were incredibly helpful in refining my thoughts, especially Elizabeth Harvey, who was generous enough to reveal her identity and continue the conversation about the work in person and via email. She transformed this book.

I am deeply thankful to my oldest friends and to my family for their continuing love and support. Amanda Karanikolas and I began as college roommates, and it brings me great joy that she—now joined by Steve, Lucy, and Thomas—is still as close as family. I am so lucky to have so loving a clan as Sloan Fidler, Ruth Crowe, and Niko and Eli Crowe Fidler to call my own. Having Jim Quinn and Bob Deitchman in my life has made it fuller in so many ways. My parents, Nancy Tingley and Stanley Hock, have been endlessly loving, encouraging, and supportive, and I could not have written this book without them. Irina Gorokhovskaya and Vladimir Muzykantov have welcomed me into their lives with more love (and caviar) than I could ever have hoped for. I am so happy to be a part of their family.

Finally, words are insufficient to do justice either to the role Alex Dubilet has played in my life, and thus in the writing of this book, or to the magnitude of my gratitude for him. Alex loves with boundless generosity and thinks with passion and rigor. He is my constant companion and the source of my greatest joys. I cannot thank him enough for sharing his life with me, but I will never stop trying.

Earlier versions of two chapters appeared in the following publications and are reprinted here with permission: Chapter 5 as "Fanciful Poetics and Skeptical Epistemology in Margaret Cavendish's *Poems and Fancies*," in *Studies in Philology* 115, no. 4, Copyright @ 2018 by The University of North Carolina Press. Chapter 2 as "Waging Loving War: Lucretius and the Poetry of Remy Belleau," in *Romanic Review* 104, nos. 3–4 (May–November 2013): 275–93.

.

CPSIA information can be obtained
at www.ICGtesting.com
Printed in the USA
LVHW032010271120
672371LV00003B/3

9 780812 252729